The Old Chicago Neighborhood
Remembering Life in the 1940s

By Neal Samors and Michael Williams

Introduction by Edward M. Burke Essays by Fr. Andrew Greeley, Leon Despres, Jon Hahn, Bill Gleason, Bill Jauss and Sandra Pesmen

Published in the United States of America in 2003 by
Chicago's Neighborhoods, Inc.

First printing: April 2003.
Second printing: September 2003.

Edited by Neal Samors, Michael Williams, and Marcee Williams.

Produced by James B. Kirkpatrick of Kirk's Computer Service.

Book designed by Michael Williams.

Printed in Canada by Friesens Corporation.

ISBN: 0-9725456-0-3 (Softcover)
ISBN: 0-9725456-1-1 (Case)

Front Cover: *Irving Park and Seeley, 1944.* North Center   (Courtesy of the CTA.)

Back Cover: Top Left: *Tug-of-War, Roosevelt Road Beach, 1947.* Near South Side (Courtesy of the Chicago Park District.)
Top Right: *Mrs. Harry Riley and Children, ca. 1944.* Near North Side (Courtesy of the CTA.)
Bottom Left: *Children Cheer for the Cubs Victory over Harry "The Cat" Brecheen 3-1, 1948.* Lakeview (Courtesy of the Chicago Sun-Times.)
Bottom Right: *Service Guard, Marquette and Maryland, 1943.* Greater Grand Crossing (Courtesy of the Chicago Park District.)

Frontispieces:
Regal Theater, 47th and South Parkway, 1941. Grand Boulevard Photograph by Russell Lee. (Library of Congress)
Chicago Public Library, George M. Pullman Branch, 1944. Roseland (Courtesy of Special Collections and Preservation Division, Chicago Public Library.)
Jackson Park, ca. 1946. Woodlawn (Courtesy of the Chicago Park District.)
Service Guard, Marquette and Maryland, 1943. Greater Grand Crossing (Courtesy of the Chicago Park District.)

Page 8: Chicago Bungalow Neighborhood, Southwest Side, ca. 1940. (Private Collection)

For more information on this book as well as the authors' other works contact us at:

Neal Samors
E-mail: NSamors@aol.com
Website: www.chicagosneighborhoods.com

Michael Williams
E-mail: kkbmfw@earthlink.net

For my late parents, Joe and Bernette Samors, your love of Chicago and its neighborhoods motivates me to write about the city. The memory of both of you remains as my inspiration.

For my wife, Freddi, and my daughter, Jennifer, your support and encouragement keeps me going and has allowed me to pursue my "second career."

N.S.

For my mother, Sheila, a born storyteller...

M.W.

Table of Contents

Acknowledgments

The authors wish to gratefully acknowledge the support and contributions from many individuals who assisted in the completion of this book. More than 125 current and former residents of Chicago who lived in or near the city during the 1940s agreed to be interviewed for the project and their memories provide the basis for the book.

Among the many people who took time from their busy schedules to recall life in their Chicago neighborhoods during the '40s, some deserve special recognition because they wrote essays for the book, and others provided us with access to the photographs and memorabilia found in this publication

We deeply thank Chicago City Council Alderman Edward M. Burke, novelist and social scientist Fr. Andrew Greeley, former Alderman and attorney Leon Despres, sports writers Bill Gleason and Bill Jauss, and journalists Jon Hahn and Sandy Zuckerman Pesmen for providing stimulating and insightful essays about Chicago neighborhoods and parishes during the 1940s. Their essays capture the vibrancy and special nature of the decade in Chicago. Also special thanks to Dan Miller of the Chicago Sun-Times, Thomas O'Gorman, Phil Holdman, Cook County Circuit Court Judge Richard Elrod, Julia Bachrach and Robert Middaugh of the Chicago Park District, Jeff Stern of the Chicago Transit Authority, the staff of the Harold Washington Branch of the Chicago Public Library, Richard Bitterman, Deborah Mieko Burns of the Japanese American Service Committee, Bill Watson, Anthony Reibel, Mary Brace, Bill Swislow (for more information on Joe "40,000" Murphy go to interestingideas.com) and Keith Sadler for providing access to photographs and memorabilia that were used in the book.

A second group of individuals were both interviewees and referrals to the many other people interviewed in this book. They include: U.S. Magistrate Judge Ian Levin (who provided access to members of Chicago's legal community), Cook County Circuit Court Judges Richard Elrod and William Phelan, Illinois Appellate Court Judge Neil Hartigan, Playboy Magazine founder Hugh Hefner, Illinois Secretary of State Jesse White, former U.S. Congressman Morgan Murphy, Jr., former Superintendent Chicago Park District Edward Kelly, former Illinois State Senator Arthur Berman, attorneys Leonard Amari, James Casey, Joseph Lamendella, and Jerry Petacque, attorney and journalist Joel Weisman, businessmen Sam Carl, Frank Considine, Richard Jaffee, James McDonough, Andrew McKenna, Ron Michaels, Ron Newman, Jim O'Connor, Jack Sandner, and Lee Stern, sports agent Steve Zucker, journalists Ann Gerber, Rick Kogan, and Norman Mark, former Chicago Cardinal Donald Stonesifer, administrator Jim DeLisa, legal researcher Harriet Ellis, medical records administrator Nancy Bild Wolf, and jazz musicians Joe Levinson and Ted Saunders.

And, finally, our deepest thanks to all the other individuals who participated as interviewees, and whose recollections about Chicago neighborhood life in the 1940s made this book possible. They include, in alphabetical order: Dorothy Ash, U.S. District Judge Marvin Aspen, Jim Bachman, Bruce Bachmann, Dolores "Champ" Mueller Bajda, Sandy Bank, Estelle Gordon Baron, Irv Bemoras, Gerald Bender, Dr. Ira Bernstein, Charles Bidwill, Jr., Edward Brennan, Margaret Burroughs, Earl Calloway, Howard Carl, Dr. James P. Carter, David Cerda, Chuck Chapman, John Creighton, Bob Cunniff, Ron Davis, Raymond DeGroote, Anna Marie DiBuono, James Dowdle, Tom Doyle, George Dunne, Joesph Epstein, Alice Fink, Rick Fizdale, Johnny Frigo, and Truman Gibson.

Jack Hogan, Edie Phillips Horwitz, Dave Hussman, Tom Hynes, Bernie Judge, Penny Juhlan, Wayne Juhlan, Dorothy and Hiroshi Kaneko, Bob Kennedy, U.S. District Judge Charles Kocoras, Otho Kortz, Kay Kuwahara, Margaret Short Lamb, Marvin Levin, Ramsey Lewis, Hal Lichterman, Richard Lukin, Jack Mabley, Ed McElroy, Henry McGee, Jr., Blanche Majkowski, Ray Meyer, Hank Mitchell, George Mitsos, Joe Molitor, James Mowry, Bill Nellis, Ray Nordstrand, Mary McCarthy O'Donnell, Chiyoko Omachi, Andy Pafko, Mel Pearl, Mike Perlow, Billy Pierce, Lawrence Pucci, Frank Rago, Anthony Reibel, Lou Roskin, Howard Rosen, Sheldon Rosing, Dan Rostenkowski, Chuck Schaden, Arnold Scholl, Burt Sherman, Seymour Simon, Shirley Ochs Simon, Charles Simpson, Father Gene Smith, James Thommes, Dempsey Travis, Sheila Morris Williams, Adelaide Gredys Winston, Nancy Bild Wolf, and U.S. District Judge James Zagel.

Authors' Notes

This book is not meant to be a history of Chicago's neighborhoods in the 1940s. Instead, this book is a collection of memories about the experience of growing up and living in Chicago during that time. The stories are not told by us, but by the interviewees, in their own words. Our goal at the outset of this project was to find a diverse group of Chicagoans who could speak openly about their experiences in the '40s, be they positive or negative. The response was overwhelming. We are truly grateful to the interviewees for the rich body of experiences they related to us. Their honest and straightforward answers to our questions were, at times, nothing short of courageous.

Readers of this book may find neighborhood names that are unfamiliar to them. The issue of defining specific neighborhoods, parishes and community areas is a complex one. By the 1940s, the City of Chicago had already delineated 75 community areas, based on the work of the University of Chicago's Social Science Research Committee in cooperation with the United States Bureau of the Census. Community areas, unlike the 176 neighborhoods presently in Chicago, are based on census tracts and often have names that are, and were, unfamiliar to city residents. We have included neighborhood names that are cited by individual interviewees in their stories, but also refer to the larger community areas that match those on the map provided on page 15 in this book. The key issue is that neighborhood boundaries were more often psychological than specific.

Introduction

Edward M. Burke

Neighborhoods and parishes have been the essential building blocks of Chicago's growth and development from its earliest days. Chicago is first and foremost a city of neighborhoods. Its first neighborhood, the stockade-fenced Fort Dearborn, was probably America's western-most neighborhood when it was constructed in 1803. During the late 1820s, neighborhood life picked up at Wolf Point, a strategic small stretch of land at the juncture where the Chicago River forks to the north and south. This was home to one of the city's earliest settlements, the neighborhood containing the well-known Wolf Point Tavern, an important meeting place during fur-trapping days and the town's first genuine public house. Not far away, at Lake and Market Streets (now Wacker Drive), the true social center of Chicago was to be found, the Sauganash Tavern. Owned by the ubiquitous pioneer Mark Beaubien, no visitor or resident of this inn came away without being entertained by him on his fiddle. These proto-neighborhoods were places of refuge and shelter, community celebration and nourishment. This has remained Chicago's unique formula for neighborhood life for more than a century and three-quarters.

Since the beginning of Old St. Mary's, Chicago's first Roman Catholic parish in 1833, the same year Chicago incorporated as a town, all the ingredients for social and religious reinforcement were set in place. The establishment of St. Mary's school for girls and St. Joseph's school for boys by the Religious Sisters of Mercy provided the early population of Chicago with a primitive road map to heaven. Under the leadership of such devoted communities of religious men and women, the growing metropolis of Chicago would share with the burgeoning diocese of Chicago a remarkable capacity for helping to civilize the prairie. As the population of the city grew with teeming numbers of Irish immigrants, later followed by swelling numbers of Poles and Germans, the grid of ecclesiastical development expanded, forging a unique hybrid American urban religious institution, the city parish. Often, the boundaries of parish demarcation followed the characteristics of language, custom and culture. Within two decades of the city's incorporation in 1837, the grid of parishes across the flatland of urban Chicago kept pace with the arrival of each new ethnic resident. By 1848, Chicago had become its own diocese. And within little more than thirty years, by 1880, its exponential growth transformed it into one of the nation's fastest developing archdioceses. In the years before the American Civil War the skyline of Chicago was shaped by steeples, not skyscrapers. As the city was transformed into the capital of the American heartland by its marriage of commerce and industry, the masses fleeing European poverty and oppression found the landscape of Chicago far less forbidding and strange because of the softening touch and familiar signposts that the parishes of the city provided. Parishes would remain a tether of the old world, refreshed in the new.

The true significance of Chicago neighborhoods can be seen in their remarkable development in the decades that followed the Great Fire of 1871. With three-fifths of the central city in ruins, stretching from Roosevelt Road to Fullerton Avenue, the rebuilding of the urban grid and infrastructure became a singular priority. Out of the disaster came a host of new neighborhoods, and a flood of new residents to assist with the rebuilding. Many of the people coming to the city were Americans from New England who saw a singular opportunity for success in a fresh part of the country. Others came from across the length and breadth of Europe. This great mix of origins and cultures became an essential element in the expansion of Chicago neighborhoods and imbued them with their unique variety. Immigrants, too, were attracted to the expansive opportunities for employment here, especially in rough and tumble industries like the meat packing empires of the Chicago Stock Yards and the railroads that turned the city into the nation's rail hub.

In the decades that followed the fire, the population of the city doubled every ten years. From more than 250,000 residents in 1870, the dramatic waves of newcomers swelled the numbers to more than 500,000 by 1880. That number doubled once again to 1,000,000 by 1890 and 1,600,00 by 1900. The city was undergoing a tremendous boom as it began to lose the patina of its cow town identity. By the time the famed World's Colombian Exposition of 1893 took place in Chicago, the city was exhibiting a braggadocio and swagger that brimmed in its success and modernity. The city was awash in expanding neighborhoods, each developing its own peculiar character and identity. The city boasted more Poles than any other city in the world outside of Poland, more Germans than any city outside of Germany and more Irish than lived in Dublin. Customs and languages were carried to Chicago like treasure. They could be seen with bold variety and a peculiar confluence of traditions along the streets and roadways of neighborhood life.

Life in some immigrant neighborhoods could be exceedingly dangerous. Long before the Levee, a neighborhood of cheap rooming houses, brothels and thief dens, became famous for tourist muggings and wallet-liftings, one group of the early Chicago Irish settled along the Chicago River near Erie Street, in a placed called Kilglubbin. So serious were the grudge matches or faction fights there among the Irish from rival counties in Ireland that Chicago Police declared it a "no go zone" more than 150 years ago. Some neighborhoods took longer to civilize than others.

Nothing helped to civilize the variety of life across Chicago's neighborhoods than the Roman Catholic Church. Famous for its skills at organization and institution building, the growth of the Catholic Church in Chicago kept up a breakneck pace in meeting the needs and movements of its voluminous population of co-religionists in the city. Irish parishes were the first to ring out around the old parts of Chicago. The establishment of Old St. Patrick's in 1846 was quickly followed in 1848 by that of St. Bridget's on Archer Avenue, a parish established to meet the needs of the Irish who dug the Illinois and Michigan Canal. Back on Roosevelt Road, the Society of Jesus began Holy Family Parish in 1857, counting Mrs. O'Leary of fire fame among their members. The parish, miraculously, was spared by the flames due to ferocious winds blowing from the south. The pattern continued. As communities of Roman Catholics fanned out across the city, the trusted accouterments of Catholic life were quick to follow. This familiar pattern continued for other ethnic groups as well. With the arrival of large numbers of Polish and German immigrants in the post-fire decades, parishes meeting their special language and culture needs were also established by the Archdiocese of Chicago. Often, these parishes were staffed by fellow immigrant clergy who

became the guardians of both language and customs. Frequently, the churches erected by such immigrant communities resembled the great cathedrals found in their old countries. Today, their domes and spires still reach heavenward and display artistry and faith that is timeless.

The ever-growing network of parishes across the city became a powerful force for both the civilizing and educating of new immigrant groups. Schools were often more important to the newcomers than elaborate church buildings. The structure of parish life was not complete without a parish school in which young people were educated, often through the high school level. The bishops of the United States established the policy that every Catholic had the moral obligation of attending a parish school. Such parish schools also permitted the children of non-English speaking immigrants the opportunity to learn the language of American commerce and industry.

For many Chicagoans, neighborhoods and parishes were indistinguishable, identities that went beyond their secular and religious nature. For generations, if you asked a Chicagoan where they were from, they would most likely respond with the name of their parish. Parishes were shorthand identifications that quickly provided a host of social, cultural and economic statistics. Stories abound of Jewish and Protestant Chicagoans who found it saved them lots of time to just give the name of the local Catholic parish when asked where they lived. Parishes provided quick reference to location (South Side, West Side, North Side or suburb), or ethnic make-up (Irish from Visitation, Polish from St. Hedwig, German from St. Benedict, Bohemian from St. Paul or Italian from Our Lady of Pompeii). It also provided a ready reference for economic detail (working class folk at Nativity of Our Lord in Bridgeport, more advantaged, lace-curtain Irish at St. Mel on the West Side, or the well-to-do at St. Philip Neri in South Shore).

Parishes have been the true glue and identity of Chicago life for generations of Chicagoans. The most intricate and intimate of life's comings and goings took place amid the rigors, rules and regimes of parish life. The story of parishes is the story of schools, gymnasiums, religious pageants and countless weddings, funerals and Sunday Masses. But it is also more. Woven into the life cycle and heartbeat of parish life is the sustaining power of belonging and being home. In a less mobile age, when families lived in the same community for generations, parishes evoked a dominant sense of allegiance and loyalty transcending the realities and boundaries of common life. Experiences were shared and convoked a mutuality that lasted a lifetime. Parish ties were familiar and familial, providing a sense of turf and sacred space.

It is important to remember that Chicago was not just a city of Roman Catholic parishes. Many thousands of German and Scandinavian Lutherans, African-American Baptists, Scotch Presbyterians and many varieties of Eastern Orthodox Christians brought vigor, dignity and great success to the urban life of the city. Large numbers of Ukrainians and Russians populated the Near

Northwest Side. Andersonville, a community with a strong Swedish heritage, developed in the Edgewater community. The Greek Orthodox population, centered just west of the Loop in Greek Town along Halsted Street, became one of the city's oldest ethnic enclaves. Many residents of Greek Town were uprooted in the 1960s when the University of Illinois at Chicago campus was constructed on top of them. African-Americans settled in large numbers on Chicago's South Side, the Bronzeville neighborhood being a historic and cultural center for generations. Strong Jewish communities developed, first in the old Maxwell Street neighborhood, and then expanded west to Douglas Park, north to Humboldt Park, Albany Park, and Rogers Park, and south to South Shore. More affluent members of the Jewish community settled in Hyde Park along the lakefront environs near the University of Chicago. Each of these non-Catholic neighborhoods created rich and textured cultural communities that generated political and commercial leadership enriching Chicago.

The growth and development of Chicago neighborhoods and parishes reached a high point in the 1940s. Chicago was a vibrant, brawny survivor not only of the great Depression, but of the crime-filled era of Prohibition. The city's national political influence became significant and local residents took pride in the fact that Franklin Delano Roosevelt was nominated for his unprecedented third term as President in Chicago in 1940, and his fourth in 1944. Chicago's larger-than-life political leaders like Mayor Edward J. Kelly and his successor, Mayor Martin H. Kennelly, prided themselves on being "neighborhood" men. Each came from the city's Irish working class Bridgeport enclave that would go on to provide three more Chicago mayors in the 1950s, 1970s and 1990s. As World War II began, neighborhoods and parishes took on a particular role in supporting those tens of thousand of local GIs who were fighting half a world away. Neighborhoods and parishes took on deepened emotional significance as home and family, neighborhood and parish became symbols of American identity worth both fighting for and dying for.

However, in the decade that followed World War II, neighborhoods and parishes in Chicago underwent massive transition. Returning GIs found city housing a vanishing commodity and in the great population boom that ensued began a push out to perimeter suburbs. Also, the influx of new populations of African-Americans to older neighborhoods on the city's South Side, stimulated a further movement of families to outer city neighborhoods and the suburbs. This pattern continued through the 1960s and 1970s, which saw more than 500,000 white residents leave old neighborhoods and parishes and a growth of more than 300,000 African-American residents. Parishes underwent an equal change as the majority of African-Americans were not Roman Catholic. Parishes saw a drastic shift in their numbers of parishioners. Urban change was significant. Neighborhoods and parishes underwent massive transitions.

Chicago has always been a geography-focused city, due in no small part to its obsession with its own strategic location at the juncture of the prairie and Lake Michigan along the banks of the Chicago River. Location means everything. As Chicago's fortunes and geography expanded, neighborhoods and parishes became manageable everyday expressions of the local life of the big city, whether you are a newcomer or an old-timer in Chicago. This is where you learn to navigate the geographies and politics of local living. Chicagoans have always understood that the strength and stability of the city is dependent upon the quality of understanding and hope that exists within each local neighborhood. The vitality of any local community can never just be the result of urban government or municipal legislation. Rather, it is intricately dependent upon the goodwill and leadership that rises up among neighbors and local residents whose roots go deep into the prairie soil of Chicago.

Neighborhoods define our urban terrain and make livable the magnitude of our metropolis. The health of our city has always been measured by the fitness of our neighborhoods. Here, people are at home. People take charge. And the great challenges emerge within the rhythms and contours of daily life. Neighborhoods remain both a distinctive and enduring resource of everyday Chicago life. Bonded with the parishes of the past and present, they have helped the immigrant and newcomer fit in, and old-timers feel a sense of pride and ownership.

The true textures of Chicago life are to be discovered in the neat rows of bungalows, three-flats and six-flats that have been the timeless backbone of neighborhood life. They form a special expression of Chicago identity, together with the cottages, lakefront high-rises and apartments over countless shops, taverns, grocery stores and undertakers.

It is no accident that Chicago has become known as "The City of Neighborhoods." Neighborhoods have been our most vibrant resource and our most imaginative treasure. Gilded by the faith and history of religious loyalty, the parishes of the Archdiocese of Chicago brought an internal catalyst to Chicago's prairie success and human drama. Neighborhoods and parishes have been a winning combination in Chicago life, the twin pillars of allegiance and identity that have softened the harsh terrain of the nation's center and helped to make Chicago America's most American city.

Alderman Edward M. Burke is the Dean of the Chicago City Council. He has served as Alderman of Chicago's 14th Ward for more than three decades and he is a recognized expert on city budget matters. Alderman Burke is the Chairman of the City Council Committee on Finance. He entered politics in the footsteps of his father, Joseph, and became Democratic Committeeman of the 14th Ward in 1968 and alderman in 1969. Like his father, he was a Chicago Police Officer. Alderman Burke is also partner in the law firm of Klafter and Burke, as well as co-author of the book *Inside the Wigwam: Chicago Presidential Conventions, 1860-1996*. He lives with his wife on the city's Southwest Side.

Community Areas
City of Chicago
1940

Legend

1. Rogers Park
2. West Ridge
3. Uptown
4. Lincoln Square
5. North Center
6. Lakeview
7. Lincoln Park
8. Near North Side
9. Edison Park
10. Norwood Park
11. Jefferson Park
12. Forest Glen
13. North Park
14. Albany Park
15. Portage Park
16. Irving Park
17. Dunning
18. Montclare
19. Belmont Cragin
20. Hermosa
21. Avondale
22. Logan Square
23. Humboldt Park
24. West Town
25. Austin

26. West Garfield Park
27. East Garfield Park
28. Near West Side
29. North Lawndale
30. South Lawndale
31. Lower West Side
32. Loop
33. Near South Side
34. Armour Square
35. Douglas
36. Oakland
37. Fuller Park
38. Grand Boulevard
39. Kenwood
40. Washington Park
41. Hyde Park
42. Woodlawn
43. South Shore
44. Chatham
45. Avalon Park
46. South Chicago
47. Burnside
48. Calumet Heights
49. Roseland
50. Pullman

51. South Deering
52. East Side
53. West Pullman
54. Riverdale
55. Hegewisch
56. Garfield Ridge
57. Archer Heights
58. Brighton Park
59. McKinley Park
60. Bridgeport
61. New City
62. West Elsdon
63. Gage Park
64. Clearing
65. West Lawn
66. Chicago Lawn
67. West Englewood
68. Englewood
69. Greater Grand Cr.
70. Ashburn
71. Auburn Gresham
72. Beverly
73. Washington Heights
74. Mount Greenwood
75. Morgan Park

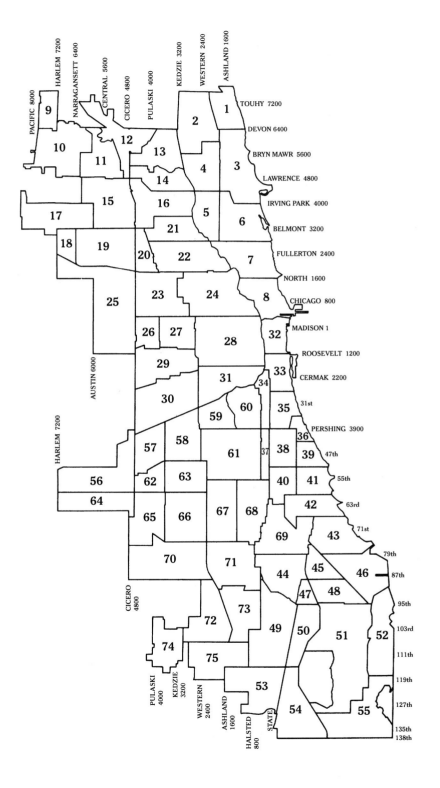

1947 — The Axial Year

Fr. Andrew Greeley

Much of the popular history of the last century and some of the serious history assumes that America changed dramatically in the 1960s. The assumption is made by those who matured in the 1960s and is despicably self-serving. The years before their advent, the time between the end of the Second World War — their parents' era — is dismissed as a time of rigidity, conformity, and "togetherness;" a time when women gave up the jobs they had during the war and settled for domesticity; a time of the emergence of suburban culture (still viciously attacked in such films as *American Beauty*).

In this assumption of moral and cultural superiority, the sixties generation ignores many obvious facts. All generations have their own form of conformity (such as the current political dogmas). A culture based on sex, drugs, and rock n' roll is not necessarily any less rigid in its demands. There is no evidence that this generation has produced any more great works of art and literature than its predecessors (where are their Fitzgeralds and Hemingways?) or more impressive political leadership. The proportion of women in the workforce increased since 1947. The goal of universal higher education meant that women and blacks had a chance to attend college, a necessary prerequisite for the development of the civil rights movement and feminism. Sexual liberation does not seem to have enhanced the levels of sexual satisfaction in society, nor is there any evidence on measures of happiness that there has been an increase in happiness. Nor, as far as we can tell, has mental health improved (though various chemicals such as Prozac may have made emotional stress easier to bear).

The real change in America came after the end of the war, especially in the late 1940s. This was the axial age of American history, the real turning point that shaped everything which has happened since. It was the time when permanent prosperity became a given in American life. The war was over indeed, but more was happening than just the end of the war. Slowly but surely Americans began to realize that the Great Depression was not coming back. Many of my family and friends were convinced that it would return. The Depression had always been with us. Eventually it would be with us again. Yet by the late 1940s, the young men with whom I had graduated from grammar school and who had not attended college were going back to school so that they could compete with the returning vets who were flooding onto college campuses. Slowly but surely it dawned on us that if the Depression did appear again, it would be a long way into the future. Now a half century later, it appears that, barring a catastrophe, we will never again have unemployment levels around 25%. The periodically recurring economic crises of the 19th and early 20th centuries had become a thing of the past.

Those TV commentators who compare any of the various recessions of the last 50 years with the Great Depression were either not around at the time or have read no economic history.

The reasons for the prosperity which has marked American history since 1940 and European history since 1960 are beyond the scope of this essay. My point is only that such prosperity, the "revolution of rising expectations," did not exist in our imagination in my neighborhood even as a remote possibility in 1945. By 1947, my generation of young people began to take the risk of betting on such a promise. By the time I was ordained and sent to a parish of successful professional-class Catholics, prosperity was taken for granted and everyone was eager to forget the memories of the Great Depression. Many of the people in this parish assumed that their success was a proof of their own worth (just as a somewhat older group my father's age thought that their failure and unemployment was proof of their own lack of worth). Both groups were caught up in the economic processes of their own era. My parishioners were not successful because they were men approved. They were successful because they were lucky. It would have been hard in that time and that place not to be a success. Only the drink could destroy you.

When my class graduated from high school in 1946, college choice was for the very few. Eight years later in my new parish, composed essentially of the same kind of people, it was assumed that everyone would go to college. The whole world had changed. All the other changes which would happen in the next half century, for weal or woe, were locked in by a flourishing economy which has never ceased to expand. Prosperity makes possible all kinds of other things — drugs, promiscuity, trophy wives, trips to Europe, postponement of work and marriage, voting Republican, movements, protests and all other luxuries which were not available on the West Side of Chicago in 1942. I rejoice in the expanded possibilities of life "beyond our dreams in 1942" and I accept the abuses that seem to be inherent in this expansion. I deplore and despise the failure of those who matured after 1960 to realize that it was not ever thus. Our generation didn't have senior trips. The next one went to Springfield, the one after that to DC, the one after that to Paris and on their junior trip! Good for them. Only don't think that these are inalienable rights that Americans have always had.

It may be that a half century is not enough time for people to learn how to live with prosperity. I'm not sure the rigid ideologies of the environmental movement point in that direction. But that argument is beyond the scope of this essay.

The standard of living has doubled three, perhaps four times since then. We were there when the first doubling was taking place. I have never seen any serious historiography that records what it was like, the excitement, the exhilaration, the hope of those very special times. I have tried in two of my novels, *A Midwinter's Tale* and *Younger Than Springtime*, to describe it narratively. Perhaps, however, it will take only a long time, a couple more decades for people to begin to understand what it was like to grow up in a depression and a war and then suddenly see the limits of our lives wiped away and the outer horizons of our hopes disappear. Now suddenly much was possible, not quite everything perhaps, but almost everything.

The men coming home from the service could go to college, obtain degrees (the visas to suburbia as David Riesman would later call them), marry and start families, purchase new cars, buy homes of their own, join country clubs and, God forgive them for it, vote Republican. To a generation which wants to start marriage with a home, like that in which they were raised, this may not seem like much. It did in 1935 and 1945 and indeed in the whole past history of the human condition.

It took our breath away in the bungalow belt around Division and Austin in those days. When I think about it, it still takes my breath away.

Returning Servicemen Usher in 1947, New Years Eve at the Keymen's Club, Madison and Cicero, 1946. Austin (Courtesy of Charles F. Simpson.)

Fr. Andrew M. Greeley is a priest, distinguished sociologist and best-selling author. He is a professor of social sciences and research associate at the National Opinion Research Center at the University of Chicago. He has written many books and articles on issues in sociology, education and religion and his column on political, church and social issues is carried by the New York Times News Service. Fr. Greeley is the author of more than 30 best-selling novels and the autobiography *Confessions of a Parish Priest*.

Hyde Park Politics in the 1940s
Leon Despres

The 1940s was an interesting decade in Hyde Park politics. Following the national trend, the Democratic Party grew to a majority and the Republican Party declined. The radical third parties, which found Hyde Park a hospitable resting place during the 1930s, withered. By the end of the decade there were definite signs of the independence in liberal politics which have characterized Hyde Park for decades afterwards.

Hyde Park had not always been predominantly Democratic but, on the contrary, had historically been Republican and the site of rivalries between branches of the Republican Party, between the grafters and the honest people, between the moderates and the extremists. It was a Republican battleground, and the winner of the Republican primary usually won the election. By the beginning of the 1940s, however, Roosevelt had become a great vote-getter in Hyde Park, as elsewhere.

During the early 1930s, when the nation was in economic turmoil, radical third parties found a welcome in Hyde Park. They never amassed huge votes but they gave promise of growing into a significant influence. In 1935, for example, the Socialist Party ran Maynard Krueger for alderman and garnered 600 votes. This was a small total but the Socialist Party members thought it was the beginning of a swelling influence. The Communist Party did not engage in open vote campaigns but it maintained a branch in Hyde Park and its adherents thought it would grow. By the beginning of the 1940s it was apparent that these parties were going nowhere.

At the beginning of the 1940s, Paul Douglas was in office as alderman of the 5th Ward. He was Professor of Economics at the University of Chicago and one of Hyde Park's most distinguished citizens. Before the 1940s he had engaged in genuinely independent and anti-Machine politics. In 1935 when Maynard Krueger was the Socialist candidate for alderman, Paul Douglas recruited Divinity Professor Joseph Artman to run, and substantially managed an energetic campaign which won several thousand votes. In 1939, to the astonishment of Hyde Parkers, Douglas became the Regular Democratic candidate for alderman. Hyde Park's peerless independent was running with the support of the Machine! This occurred for several reasons. The Machine was able to buy respectability by slating him. And, in addition, there was a contest inside the Democratic Machine between the Thomas Courtney wing and the Edward Kelly wing. Kelly, who was party Chairman and Mayor, knew that by supporting Douglas he would gain the margin he needed for victory.

Although elected by the Machine, Douglas was a splendid alderman. He dramatized the great social issues of the day. He was a star on issues of racial discrimination and relief of poverty. In 1942, however, he ran in the Democratic primary for Mayor against Kelly, lost, and resigned from the City Council to enter the Marines. Hyde Park was left without a strong Democratic candidate and without a functioning independent movement.

In 1943, the independent torch was grasped by University of Chicago History Professor Walter Johnson, who waged a praiseworthy anti-Machine campaign for alderman as a liberal Democrat, kept the movement alive, and gained a respectable total, but lost.

The last gasp of the radical movement occurred in 1948 when University of Chicago Economics Professor, and still Socialist, Maynard Krueger ran for Congress. To his supporters' enthusiasm, at a political rally for him, all 1,090 seats in the University of Chicago's Mandel Hall Auditorium were filled. Unfortunately the spectators were attracted less by Krueger than by the presence of Norman Thomas as speaker, and Krueger did poorly in the election. That was the end of radical third parties in Hyde Park, but not the end of independent liberal politics.

In 1947, Hyde Park was shaken to its political roots by an aldermanic campaign which was mixed independent and Machine. The 5th Ward Democratic Committeeman was Barnet Hodes, who relied on the money and the patronage army which the Machine furnished him. Without difficulty he elected his choice, Bertram Moss. In office, however, Moss realized he could win re-election on his own only if he showed signs of independence. He took a strong stand against the corruption of the Board of Education and the decline of the Chicago Public Schools. Refusing to kowtow to his Ward Committeeman who had elected him, Moss was marked for defeat. To win the election, however, Committeeman Barnet Hodes had to select a candidate who would attract the independent vote as Douglas had done in 1939. His choice was Robert Merriam, a University employee and the son of Charles E. Merriam, who had been one of Chicago's best aldermen years before. The name was magical. Charles Merriam was then Chairman of the University of Chicago Political Science Department. Robert Merriam was a war veteran and had written a book about the Battle of the Bulge. He was articulate, liberal, and intelligent. In the tightly contested 1947 election, he won. Just a few days before the election, Moss, fighting for his political life, flooded Hyde Park with an expensive, color-printed booklet filled with photographs and slogans intended to carry the day for him. It backfired. It was just too expensive. Merriam, the independent-Machine candidate, won in 1947 and won again for a second term.

The significance of these aldermanic elections was that they showed the stirrings and beginnings of an independent liberal Democratic movement in Hyde Park.

Other factors also foreshadowed a new political future for Hyde Park. After the war ended, Hyde Park was flooded with new residents, war veterans taking advantage of the GI Bill of Rights, and men and women who entered Hyde Park with a desire for a better world and a willingness to work for it.

In 1948 an event occurred, which, while not directly political, nevertheless greatly influenced the political texture of Hyde Park. The United States Supreme Court declared racially restrictive covenants illegal. This changed the quality of Hyde Park's population. It stimulated a flight of residents afraid of African-American penetration and also stimulated the determination of other residents to preserve and protect Hyde Park as "an inter-racial community of high standards." Thanks to leadership from the First Unitarian Society, the 57th Street Meeting of Friends, and Congregation KAM, the Hyde Park-Kenwood Community Conference was formed. It created an atmosphere of freedom and independence which contributed strongly to incubation of

independent liberal political movements. In 1949, the Independent Voters of Illinois was formed, with its strongest base in Hyde Park. By 1955, Hyde Park elected an independent alderman, and in 1956 a state representative. The die was cast.

Leon Despres has lived in the Hyde Park neighborhood for all except two years since he was born in 1908. He still practices as an attorney and was the Alderman from the 5th Ward for twenty years where he was known as "the conscience of the Chicago City Council." Leon was a key figure in civic improvements, education, ethics and good government. He and his wife still live in Hyde Park.

The "Nortwes" Side
Jon Hahn

I never knew I had a Chicago accent until we moved to Seattle, where there are no discernible accents, hardly any snow and ice storms, and absolutely no good Italian beef sandwiches.

My Chicago, in the 1940s, was pretty much bounded by Irving Park, Addison, Cicero and Central and latticed with elm-lined streets and alleys busy with junk men and fruit peddlers. This was the "new" neighborhood, where we lived on the just-above-ground floor in a red brick two-flat with our grandparents, great-aunt and uncle and great-grandparents. Downstairs we spoke Chicago; upstairs they spoke German. Sometimes we communicated by a series of code knocks on the radiator pipes. Or just plain yelling. People yelled a lot more then. And there was a wine cellar below the full concrete basement that smelled of homemade wine and sauerkraut.

No one in the neighborhood seemed to move away, even if only to those almost foreign suburbs with strange names like Arlington Heights or Mount Prospect. Places like Evanston and Winnetka seemed as distant and unattainable as, say, paradise, or New Jersey. Most people like us in the 1940s were living in the same bungalows or two-flats, or not far from, where their parents lived in the Depression. And we were the third generation ascendancy, inheriting all the prejudices and tastes and trappings that could be squeezed into an 800-square-foot-per-family lifestyle. Bowling leagues and occasional Cubs games at Wrigley Field were our Vegas. O'Hare Field was just a fenced-in, mostly military air strip that couldn't begin to match Midway Airport, but no one you knew actually flew anywhere.

Our neighborhood was referenced variously, sometimes as the Six Corners, where Irving Park, Cicero and Milwaukee came together. That configuration failed to impress our great-grandfather, who as family story goes once had a chance to buy part of that intersection for $1 per foot(!). Sometimes you said you lived in Portage Park, which was a quarter-mile-square park with indoor and outdoor swimming pools, athletic fields, playgrounds, tennis courts and horseshoe pits. And sometimes, even if you weren't Catholic, you told people you were from "St. Bart's" because St. Bartholomew Roman Catholic Church was an indirect but significant link to the Irish-Catholic political power structure downtown and through much of the city. Being Catholic *and* Democrat with a good voting record and a few connections was a big help in lining up one of the thousands of patronage jobs everyone seemed to want after World War II.

The 1940s were pre-Dutch Elm Disease, and cathedral elms created gothic corridors along the side streets. Old-style street lamp posts had open, screw-in bulbs that sent out little haloes of light as people sat on the front stoops or porches of their bungalows and two-flats. It was unthinkable to make a $.05 phone call when you could shout to, or walk to wherever or whomever you wanted to speak. There was plenty of room for kids to play red rover or spin tops in the street because not everyone had cars and those who did mostly parked them in one-car garages by the alley.

I was about twelve before I had met and mingled with enough South Siders – as foreign from our perspective as were the Polish aunts and uncles in Milwaukee – and discovered that *Dey talk diff'rent*. Even today,

I can hear *Sout'Side* on some tongues when we make the occasional pilgrimage back to the Old/New Neighborhood. We don't have any relatives left in the old, Old Neighborhood, where my Grosspa (actually, great-grandfather) Kuehner ran a blacksmith shop at about North Ave. and Larabee. Much of his business was shoeing horses for what then were about a dozen breweries.

Grandpa Hahn, who died before my twin sister and I were born in 1940, was a fireman in the small firehouse on Tripp, just north of Irving Park Rd. Our father recalled that if he or his brothers took too long in rushing the growler (covered tin beer pot) home from the tavern on Cicero Avenue, Grandpa Hahn would give them a thwacking with the razor strap that hung behind the bathroom door.

We didn't have a car – that had been sold when the war started and Dad went to work behind a punch press. So, we walked pretty much everywhere — to William P. Gray School, where our parents and older siblings had many of the same teachers we inherited; to the little three-checker Jewel Tea store with wooden floors, on Irving Park; to Schmidts' Bakery; Stanley's Drug Store; and to Tabor Evangelical & Reformed Church. And sometimes to Portage Park, although oftentimes Grandpa Kuhrt or Dad would stop the old wooden wagon behind Ole's Tavern at Irving Park and Laramie and take us into the long, dark establishment and take a little refreshment. "Now if Grandma or Mommy ask how was the park, you hafta tell them you had fun on the swings and playing in the sand, or we can't come back here again for free Coke and pretzels!"

We grew up knowing about the red-white-and-blue pennants hanging in front windows, signifying a son in the armed service. We also knew the significance of a Gold Star, memorializing a son who would never return from Europe or the Pacific. Europe seemed not so distant or foreign because every other house in the neighborhood had vestigial trappings of the old country, whether it was the kitchen table language or the music or the decor.

Probably because ethnicity and prejudices seemed as permanent then as the WPA sidewalks, there was a sort of cultural isolation from other neighborhoods. But it was all right to play with the Italian and Polish kids across the street or the Scotch-Irish ones next door. The only black we ever saw was the coal man, who was dropped off along with a couple tons of coal at the curb and spent most of a summer's day shoveling and pushing a wheelbarrow between the curb and our coal chute.

The more rigid line between people or neighborhoods was religion. Our family was very anti-Catholic – something about Grandma Hahn's having been sexually assaulted when she was a novitiate in the old country – and it was a big buzz if a Protestant family discovered one of their own

was dating a Catholic. I suppose the Catholics felt the same way in this Capulet and Montague thing. It came to rest on my head years later when I fell in love with a Polish-Catholic girl (Gasp!) in Schurz High and my mother went off the deep end. Ironically, she later converted to Catholicism, even though my big brother was an ordained Protestant minister.

We could play in the street or alleys together; we could swim at Portage Park or skitch behind cars in the winter together. But the Catholics, mostly Polish or Italian, held, or were held by, a doctrine that they were better-different. I remember my older sister coming home in tears because her best school and play friend down the block told my sister that she could never get to heaven because she wasn't Catholic. I knew that kids at St. Bart's School had some kind of lock on the good life because they got out of school for more religious holidays, and they were out of school and riding their bikes by William P. Gray Elementary, rattling sticks against the long iron fence while we languished in the June heat inside.

Summer vacation in the 1940s was a hot flash and a long simmer. Sometimes your mother would pack you off to a local Vacation Bible School. The YMCA on Irving Park and Kildare offered summer programs with field trips to the Borden Dairy, the Schwinn Bicycle plant, the Rosenwald (Sorry, Museum of Science & Industry) Museum, and, most memorable, the Stock Yards.

The Sears store at the Six Corners offered a wonderful year-round playground, where you could play Saturday morning hide-and-seek ("No fair going in bathrooms or dressing rooms") and filch hot cashews as you rode down the escalator. Or you could sneak over to ("Don't you kids ever go near there!") the "hobo jungle" alongside the railroad tracks east of Sears. The men who slept under pieces of Kenmore refrigerator boxes and built campfires there were always pleasant, and showed us how to catch "land crabs" with pieces of hot dog on a string. Like uncles, they warned us when we went onto the tracks to place pennies that would later be squashed by the Hiawatha as it made its 80 mph run to Milwaukee (most of those pennies vanished).

Further east, the Chicago & North Western Rwy. still was running steam engines, and you could lie in bed with the windows open on summer nights and visualize the locomotives as their laboring chug-chug-chugga-chugga-chugga blotted out the sound of the cicadas and locust.

That Sears store parking lot was not only the starting point for the annual Memorial Day and July 4th parades, but also the venue for a week-long summer carnival with special appearances by Roy Rogers and Trigger the Umpteenth.

Carnivals and Roy Rogers were tame, however, compared to Riverview Amusement Park. For years, our family went there for ethnic

Six Corners Shopping Area, Irving Park, Cicero, and Milwaukee, ca. 1938. Portage Park (Courtesy of the CTA.)

picnics, when whole pergola-centered picnic groves were reserved for German Day or Lithuanian Day. But the most special day was 5-Cent Day, when most – but not the very best – rides cost only a nickel. Admission cost about the same as a double-bill showing at the Portage Theatre, but it got you a whole day of high rides, sick-to-your-stomach thrills and a chance to maybe sneak around the side of a building to search for a peep of the bearded lady or the snake charmer. From atop some of the half-dozen or so roller coaster rides you could see the wood-hull mine-sweepers still being built for the Navy in the boatyard below on the North Branch of the Chicago River.

From the parachute ride tower – a feature transplanted from the original Colombian Exposition – you could see well out into Lake Michigan and far beyond the city boundaries to the north and west (the South Side seemed always hazy, perhaps from the steel mills near the south end of the lake). My older brother (remember, the minister?) once caused me to pee in my pants when our porch swing-type ride seat became stuck at the top of the parachute tower and stranded us for a small eternity. He gleefully swung the seat back and forth, side to side, telling me that I'd surely fall and make a big splat.

It was a time of innocence, when a 10-year-old boy was allowed to take the bus or streetcar and subway or "L" downtown. Although a certain percentage of weekly allowances went into Postal Savings or a Christmas Club account at the local S&L, spending money could be stretched farther by sneaking onto the streetcar behind a fat lady and transferring umpteen times, sometimes even the reverse direction. If you had lots of time, you could ride all the way to the south end of Western Avenue, back to the northern terminus, and then back to Irving Park and thence home. About the same cost and time could get you down to the Lincoln Park Zoo (Free Admission) on the Chicago Motor Coach double-decker bus.

The Irving Park streetcar went west only a bit past Narragansett, beyond which point was a string of cemeteries. Redoing the family graves there was occasion for a picnic that was schlepped out on the streetcar along with garden tools, stopping once we were afoot for some pansies, marigolds and other annuals. Redoing the graves was why the last weekend in May was then called Decoration Day. But the picnic lunch brought along made the cemeteries more like big rock gardens.

More ominous was the old Dunning Mental Hospital on the north side of Irving Park at the end of the streetcar line, with its foreboding brick dormitories and clinic buildings set back from the high brick-and-iron fence in a landscape of huge elms and wide lawns. Disheveled older people in pajamas and robes or overcoats stared blankly through the iron fence into a world of streetcars and parachute rides and Italian beef sandwiches and

Decoration Days they would never again enjoy. And insensitive adults would threaten youngsters: "That's where we're gonna put you if you don't behave!"

Not even the Catholics would say a thing like that.

Jon Hahn, currently a columnist for the *Seattle Post-Intelligencer*, was born and raised on Chicago's Northwest Side in the neighborhood that was called variably Portage Park, Six Corners or St. Bart's Parish. After graduating from Schurz High School, he attended several local colleges before receiving his B.A. in English from the University of Illinois at Urbana-Champaign. He worked as a reporter at the *Evanston Review* before going downtown to the *Chicago Daily News* as a labor and features writer. When the *Daily News* closed he moved to Seattle and lives there with his wife in Woodlinville, WA.

Let's All Go to the Park

Bill Gleason

Before I was old enough to go to school, I went to "The Park." The first few times I was holding the hand of my father. "Let's go over to the park and take a shower bath," he would say early on a Saturday afternoon. It was never a shower. It always was "a shower bath."

Why he wanted to leave the apartment when we had a perfectly good bathtub I couldn't understand. Maybe it was because he had been a baseball player and baseball players always took shower baths after games. Or maybe, as I realized years later, he wanted me to get used to male bodies without clothes.

As usual he didn't explain. And I didn't care, because we were in the most beautiful place I had ever seen. The park, Palmer, was filled with large trees that provided shade in summer, shadows in winter.

Our first time over there together I said, "This is a big park, Dad. Is it the biggest park in Chicago?" Looking down at me, he moved an arm and chuckled. "This is just a medium-size park," he said. "The city has parks that are at least ten times this size. On the South Side, about five miles from here, the city has Washington Park and Jackson Park. On the West Side there is Garfield Park where people can go to look at flowers. And up north there is a place so big that it has a zoo, Lincoln Park. They're all named for our presidents."

"Was Palmer a president?" I asked. After another chuckle Joseph Walter said, "Nope. He was a very rich gink."

During our early shower bath trips, when I was four years old, a man behind a counter would hand a towel and small bar of soap to my father and me. "On the house, kid," the man always said. When I was eight years old my dad had to pay twenty cents for our towel and soap. A year later there were no towels, no soap. Dad had to bring towels and a bar of soap wrapped in pages from the *Herald-Examiner*. "It's this damn Depression," he told me. "It better end before all the parks go to hell."

I was sure Palmer would last forever. It had to. It was my park. Just a half block west of Grandma O'Brien's two flat at 11251 S. Vernon Avenue. Before I was six years old I was allowed to go to the Park by myself. That was my training for Holy Rosary School just across 113th Street.

Sundays in The Park meant watching the Pullman Panthers and the Bauer Bonnies play football. I also saw a game new to me, soccer. "Our alderman, Shel Govier, was a star soccer player," my dad told me. I was beginning to understand that to succeed in Pullman a man had to have been an excellent athlete.

On weekdays in The Park I sat on the top slat of a bench and watched Irv Gorney, Frankie Moran and my other heroes play baseball. I dreamed of the day when I would be playing with them, instead of watching them.

It was not to be. Grandma O'Brien, a lively and glorious lady, surprised us. She died. Because my mother and her two brothers needed money during the most terrible year of the Depression, Grandma's two-flat was sold. We had to move.

My dad knew how I felt about my park. He knew because he felt the same way. "We'll find another park, Bill," he told me. "One thing Chicago knew how to do was to build parks."

But there was no park awaiting me after we moved into our new apartment at 7218 South Park Avenue. Instead of another Palmer Park I had to settle for a playground called Meyering. It was much too small for "hardball," as we called baseball. I was sure that there would not be another Palmer Park in my future.

Just when I was certain that my dream park would be nothing more than a joyous memory, my mother fooled me. She moved again. This was move number two in what would be a long series.

Helen Genevieve had found a lavish apartment just south of the intersection of 71st Street and Lowe Avenue. Across the street was the "Lily Park," which had real lilies growing in small ponds. But that wasn't it. The real park was a block to the east.

When I walked in through a south gate on 72nd Street, glories were everywhere. There was an outdoor gym with a running track. Just ahead was a library. Off to the left I found a large field house. I read the cornerstone. The park was pretty new. The field house had been dedicated in 1904. It was named for Alexander Hamilton. Hamilton Park was no more beautiful than the park of my childhood, Palmer Park. But I had been too young to appreciate Palmer.

After three years of tiny Meyering Playground, Hamilton Park left me breathless. Walking south from the field house, I saw a vast athletic field, larger than four Meyerings. There were four baseball fields, each with a backstop, and eight softball fields. I was twelve years old that afternoon in August of 1935 and now I could play baseball (hardball) forever. And I would.

Hamilton's playing fields were situated in a bowl between two railroad embankments. The Rock Island Railroad's trains shared the tracks on the eastern embankment with the Twentieth Century. The Wabash, the Chicago & Western Indiana and other railroads ran on the western embankment. Every engineer sounded his whistle as he drove his train past my park.

When late summer shadows were coming down and the Rock Island's new streamliner, the Rocket, came speeding southbound, I felt a strong sense of a past era — Hamilton Park's past, the railroads' past, Chicago's past.

This was my park, or so I thought, until a kid said, "You're new around here. You'll find out that the park belongs to 'John the Cop'." The kid was right. John, large and wide, was a park policeman, employed by the Chicago Park District, not by the city of Chicago. Every park of any size had its own policeman. Palmer Park's cop was known as Mr. Adams. Nobody called him "Adams the Cop." He was tall and slender and looked like a movie actor.

John the Cop looked like a bartender or a butcher or a flat janitor. He was the supreme authority at Hamilton Park. His authority was questioned from time to time but a questioner never won the verdict. If a kid was goofy enough to tell his father that he was in trouble with John the Cop, the kid then was in trouble with his father.

We didn't know John's last name and we didn't dare ask him to tell us.

He talked with my father and other fathers. He even talked with young men, but the only words kids heard from him were "Walk the bike!" and "You're banned from the park for two weeks."

There always are kids who think of themselves as risk-takers. They would jump off a third-story porch if somebody said, "double-dare ya." A few risk-takers were nuts enough to test John the Cop by riding their bikes down the asphalt walkway behind baseball diamond no. 1. They came wheeling, north to south, pedaling furiously. They were so proud of themselves as they waved to their friends.

They were daredevils in their own minds. They had defied John the Cop. Then, they went flying over the handlebars of the bikes. Their bikes careened behind them, rear wheels frozen.

There was a billy club in the wheel of one bike. John's billy club. John was a gifted man. He never lined his club at a kid. He never aimed for the front wheel. He skipped the club along the asphalt as though he were sending a stone across water. When the daring cyclists landed in a heap of contusions, John would say, ever so softly, "Next time, walk the bike." There was no smile. I never saw John smile.

Why "they" instead of "he?" Because foolish kids would try to elude John by roaring up the walk in pairs and sometimes in threes. He foiled that tactic by bringing down the bike in the lead. The other ones wound up in a pile of spokes, wheels, tires and handlebars. And if the cyclists tried to elude John more than once, they would hear his other order: "You're barred from the park for two weeks." He didn't mean ten days.

John the Cop was a five foot nine, two hundred and forty pound legend in his own park.

Bill Gleason is a print and media journalist who was born and raised on Chicago's Southwest Side. He has been a sportswriter for the *Chicago Herald-American*, *Chicago Sun-Times*, and the *Southtown Economist* for over 50 years, as well as a member of the "Sports Writers" program on radio and television. Born in the Depression in the Pullman neighborhood, he became an avid 16-inch softball player at a young age, and was the founder/coordinator for the Chicago 16-Inch Softball Hall of Fame. He served his country in World War II in Europe and earned a Silver Star for his gallantry in action. He lives with his wife in Oak Brook.

Parks in the Neighborhood
Bill Jauss

People my age, who grew up in Chicago in the 1940s, spent the first part of that decade going to grammar school, the middle of it in high school and the final years in college. Regardless of where we were in school, we spent huge chunks of that time in our neighborhood park.

For many of us, two forces dominated those years: World War II and our park. Mine was Sauganash Park, bounded on the north by Peterson Avenue, on the west by Kostner, on the south by Rogers and on the east by the tracks of the Chicago & North Western Railroad line.

We were too young to serve in World War II. Most of us were in uniform for the Korean Conflict. Many of our dads, brothers, uncles and cousins were overseas when we played in the park.

In fact, in spite of V-E Day and V-J Day celebrations, it didn't dawn on me that the war was really over until the summer of 1946. That's when the ex-GIs returned to the 'hood' — guys such as Jack McNamara, Pete Wilson and Bud and Bobby Osgood. Each evening that summer, a score of them would choose up sides and play 16-inch softball doubleheaders in the park. We younger guys would hang around, hoping to be picked on a team.

The returning GIs came home different people from those who had left. Their agendas called for more than 16-inch ball, and things like jobs, wives, kids, rent or house payments. When those responsibilities claimed their time, the park became "ours" again as it had been while they were away.

People have asked, "What was it like growing up in the parks in the 1940s?" It was like this — I'd leave the house on a summer morning, and my mother would ask, "Where are you going?"

"To the park," I'd reply.

"Be home in time for dinner," she'd remind me.

And that was that. Parents didn't have to worry much in those days about their kids' involvement with gangs, crime, perverts or drugs (except for beers we'd coax from the older guys). Oh, we got into trouble, but rarely in the parks. There, we exercised our own form of justice system.

Parents realized in those days that when their kids were in their neighborhood parks they would play games, make friends, have fights and make up with those they fought. Their kids would manage to scrounge up lunch on most days and manage just fine on lunchless days. They would progress in life by following the widely accepted rule of give and take. All of this was achieved with little or no adult supervision in the park.

I know. The 40s are a bygone age. The Park District runs worthwhile supervised programs these days.

But today everything is so structured. Kids rarely get to choose up sides, hire an ump, draw up a schedule, organize their own league, take care of their own field or devise wonderfully resourceful ground rules to take advantage of their park's own individual "personality."

We park kids in the 1940s quickly learned when we biked to other parks that each park is different. So, it was up to our own creativity to utilize our home field advantage.

At Gompers Park, for example, our center fielder Bob McClure had to learn to run up a sloped embankment to catch "Clinchers" that had been soundly struck. Green Briar Park, like our own, had some very short foul lines.

On both softball diamonds in Sauganash Park, the distance from home plate to the right field fence was extremely short. On the south diamond, one could clear the steel mesh fence that separated the park from the railroad track if he lofted a medium length fly ball down the line. All it had to do to clear the fence was carry the 160-foot width of the football field plus a dozen feet or so of bushes.

Thus, resourceful right-handed hitters such as Hector Andreos, Osgood twins Mickey and Sonny, and especially Richard "Dynamite" Enberg, concocted a scheme to achieve cheap home runs.

Dynamite was the master of this scheme. First, using his spikes as Carlton Fisk would do decades later in Comiskey Park, he would obliterate all traces of the chalked or drawn-in-the-dirt right-handed batters' box. Next, Dynamite would plant his right foot deep in the "bucket," swing late and loft weak fly balls down the line and over the fence.

This technique produced some of the cheapest home runs west of the Polo Grounds in New York.

Visiting players squawked so much that we finally enacted an unusual ground rule. Any ball that sailed over the fence from the foul line well over into right-center was ruled a ground rule single.

Hector, Mickey, Sonny and Dynamite didn't complain. Each was still able to pad his batting average with cheap singles, even on nights when his girlfriend did not keep the scorebook.

Now it was time for our left-handed hitters to complain. Jim Fegen, Vern Funk and McClure beefed that they were being limited to singles on some tape measure drives they socked atop the railroad tracks.

The configurations of baseball and softball parks always favor certain types of hitters. But football fields are all 100 yards long, and baskets always hang ten feet above the floor or ground. So, these standards should provide an even chance to all. Right?

In most places, yes. But Sauganash Park had its own personality in football and basketball too.

There was not enough room in the park to have 10-yard end zones behind the goal lines. So, late every August when the College All-Star Game approached, and goal posts were erected in our park, they went up on the goal lines like they were for the Bears in Wrigley Field, not at the back of the end zone as they were in college ball.

As a result, there was much more emphasis on place-kicking and drop-kicking in Sauganash Park. Kids practiced kicking at the invitingly close goal posts. Pete Wilton was one of the best. He and the parks' band of kickers may have been forerunners of foreign soccer players who would come to our shores saying, "I'll keeek a touchdown!"

Of all the sports played in our park, basketball benefited most from local rules.

Guys played hoops on one of the outdoor tennis courts that was rarely used for tennis. Half-court three-on-three games. First team to make 10 baskets wins. Winners remain on court. Losers wait their turn to play again. Call your own fouls — if the bleeding exceeded one pint.

Outstanding high school and college players from around the North Side took park in these three-on-three games. The local guys who hung out on the courts lacked the reputations of the outsiders, but the "chemistry" among them was good. And they had a few rules in their favor too.

Hector Andreos and Steve "Buddy" Rebora would shovel snow from the court to work on their games. Before and after military service, John Anderson made any three-man team he joined a good bet to remain on the court. Eddie "the Mailman" Wiloff could neither shoot nor dribble, but when he put his mail sack on the park bench and took the court wearing those Lil' Abner shoes with their steel-tipped toes, he was a painful rebounding force.

Finally, there was Dynamite Enberg and his patented "water fountain shot."

Dynamite was a pretty good player for the Land Juniors. He became unstoppable when he deftly hopped atop the water fountain in the corner of the court, thus improving his effective height from 5-feet 8-inches to something close to 8-feet 5-inches.

Then, Dynamite would accept passes from us and fire set shots down at the basket.

The hotshots from around the North Side would protest that the shot was illegal. I would point out that the area all around the bubbler was in bounds, so the fountain had to be in bounds too. It was located about eighteen feet from the basket between what would have been 3 o'clock and 4 o'clock in a game of H-O-R-S-E.

We never lost an argument about the legality of the water fountain shot. All we had to say to close the case was, "You're playin' in our park — so you follow the rules!!!!!"

Bill Jauss spent twenty years with three papers, *Neenah-Menasha, Wisconsin Twin City News Record*, the *Chicago Daily News*, and *Chicago Today* before joining the *Chicago Tribune* in 1974, and where he is still a sportswriter. Born in Chicago in 1931, Jauss grew up in Sauganash before graduating from Northwestern University in 1952, serving in the US Army, and then becoming a sports writer. He was an original member of the "Sports Writers" show that ran for 20 years on WGN Radio. He and his wife live in Wilmette, Illinois.

Parallels Between the 1940s and Today
Sandra Pesmen

The more things change, the more they stay the same. Accept that premise and you see many parallels between two time periods: The 1941 attack on Pearl Harbor followed by World War II, and the 9/11 attacks followed by the War against Terror in 2001. You also will be in a better position to understand that those traumatic events brought many similar changes to the lives and attitudes of ordinary people.

In both cases, Americans felt shocked, grieved, frightened and insecure. In both cases, the US presidents made stirring speeches reassuring the public not to be all of the above. Flags began flying, people rushed to join the armed forces, and patriotism ran high. In both cases, people made extreme efforts to remain calm and live their lives as normally as possible as they soldiered on.

As children did on September 12, 2001, children also reported to Chicago Public Schools the day after Pearl Harbor. We too felt confused, sad, afraid and unsure about what would happen next. We too had a sense that America was no longer the safe place we knew. We too thought bombs might fall on us.

But there were some obvious differences between that time and today. No therapists were brought in to comfort us or give us group therapy, and none of us was taken to a private counselor. Nobody I knew ever heard of such a thing. Instead we lived that golden rule President Richard Nixon quoted many years later: "When the going gets tough, the tough get going."

Our principal at De Witt Clinton School on Chicago's North Side was a feisty lady named Anna L. Cronin. She turned on the loudspeaker in her office and barked into the mike, "Attention, children! This is a practice air raid drill! Line up in single file behind your teacher. Walk to your designated place in the hall. Face the wall and sit down, lower your face, and cross your arms above your head. When you hear the all-clear bell, you will return safely to your classrooms!" You can't imagine how comforting that was. As we marched down the hall behind our fifth grade teacher, Mabel E. Twitty, we all were greatly relieved to know for a fact that this war was being handled very efficiently by Miss Cronin and Miss Twitty. We didn't have to worry about it anymore. We were probably more calm than today's kids are after their grief therapy sessions.

As people did in 2001, our families put forth an effort to win the war. Instead of giving millions of dollars to relief funds for 9/11 victims and others around the world as people did in 2001, we threw ourselves into different kinds of activities. One dad on each block became a Civil Defense Warden. He paid a visit to every home, and sat down to smoke a cigarette while he warned us to buy dark window shades and pull them down for a "blackout" when we heard a siren. Only dads smoked, of course. It was a macho thing. Also, cigarettes became very scarce because, as ads on billboards and in streetcars told us, "Lucky Strike Green Has Gone to War!" Our Hershey bars went too, disappearing from candy store shelves. Both were sent from the factories directly to servicemen overseas.

The purpose of the blackouts was to fool the enemy, so he couldn't see where to drop bombs. We also were supposed to go into the basement while the brave Air Raid Warden remained on a rooftop with binoculars, searching the sky for trouble, and ready to blare his siren when all was clear. Fortunately, we never had to do that. Instead of sending children to expensive overnight camps in summer as parents do today, our parents sent us outside with our little red American Flyer wagons to fight the war. We trekked up and down the neighborhood sidewalks collecting old newspapers and magazines. We took them to used paper centers. I still don't know what they did with them. We also collected tin cans that housewives filled with fat rendered from everything they cooked. We turned those tin cans in to the local butcher, who in turn was supposed to hand them over to the War Department to make bullets and bombs. Recently we learned that never happened, and we realized that then, as now, our government didn't always tell us the whole truth.

One big difference between the 1940s and 2001 is that today there is plenty of everything for everyone, with or without a war. During the 1940 war years several necessities were rationed. Wealthy friends and relatives continued to have everything they needed or wanted by buying it through the "black market." We didn't know exactly who or what that was. Regardless of how much money our parents did or didn't have, they considered such actions to be "un-American!" They used that example in lectures about honesty, morality, civic duty and/or patriotism for many years.

Our parents also sold our car when they couldn't get gasoline, and we all rode public transportation. When our mothers and aunts couldn't buy silk stockings because silk came from Japan, they drew brown lines with eyebrow pencil on the backs of their legs to look like seams and went bare-legged. Occasionally the word went out that the Florsheim Shoe Store on Devon Avenue had received a small shipment of silk stockings, and every woman in the neighborhood ran to join the line that wound around the block in hopes of getting her hands on a pair. Meat was carefully rationed. Each member of the family qualified for stamps in a ration book that was replenished every month. There were different colors for adults and for children. The families with the most people in them had the most stamps and probably ate better than our small family of four.

As we moved on to high school, the effects of WW II continued. Our skirts became shorter because manufacturers used all their time and fabric to make uniforms. In 1948, after the war had ended, I went off to college. Factories got back to making women's clothes and our hemlines dropped dramatically. My older brother used to joke that you could tell incoming freshmen girls because they wore new college clothes with long skirts. Upper-class women still wore their old, short ones.

Both short and long skirts were worn with pastel sweaters, a single strand of pearls, brown and white saddle shoes, and "bobby sox". (In those days we didn't mind being called girls instead of women.) We wore our hair as long as it would grow, cut bangs in front and made curls around the edges with perms or curlers if it didn't do that by itself.

All the boys wore slacks and sweaters or plaid cotton or wool shirts to public school. They wore Levi's with T-shirts and sweatshirts after school, and most of them had one dark suit, or a sport jacket with slacks, to wear to church, synagogue or for special occasions. Girls in most Catholic schools wore black, navy or plaid jumper uniforms with white blouses from first grade through high school. In winter they added thick, long, tan, lisle stockings to keep warm. Catholic schoolboys wore dark pants and dress shirts. In contrast, today's girls of all ages go to school wearing low-rise jeans and midriff tees, baring their navels. They add jewelry to several pierced body parts, expensive makeup and straightened hair of many colors. Boys of all ages do all that too, with the latest addition being short, spiky, bleached blond hair.

But the one thing that remains constant in every era is the love and loyalty all of us feel for our country. During all our tragic times, our eyes fill with tears and our voices tremble as we watch our flag wave and place our hands over our hearts. We all feel the same resolve to keep America safe as we say the Pledge of Allegiance and sing *The Star Spangled Banner.*

Sandra Pesmen, a former reporter for Lerner Newspapers and the *Chicago Daily News*, was also features editor of *Crain's Chicago Business*. She now syndicates the weekly Career News Service, and in 1997 was inducted into the Chicago Journalism Hall of Fame. She and her husband live in Northbrook, Illinois.

The Old Chicago Neighborhood

During the 1940s, life in Chicago's neighborhoods was very different than it is today. Each neighborhood was self-contained, and all the necessities of daily life were within walking distance or a quick streetcar ride. Municipal, social, and religious services were close by, including churches and synagogues, public and parochial schools, libraries, police and fire stations and post offices. For shopping, there was a combination of small and large business districts nearby, including groceries, department stores, dime stores, delicatessens, butcher shops, bakeries, drugstores, and restaurants. For recreation, there were numerous parks, beaches, playgrounds or school yards. There were also many entertainment options, including first- and second-run movie theaters, nightclubs, and ballrooms. Other opportunities for socializing were always nearby, at the local tavern, coffee shop, delicatessen, or at activities sponsored by local fraternal or religious organizations. And when needed, all city residents had easy access in and out of their neighborhoods by various means, including diesel and electric commuter trains, elevated trains, buses, trolleys and streetcars.

Chicago neighborhoods were so self-contained they could almost be considered as small towns within the limits of the city. Except for a few trips downtown for shopping, movies, or museums, most Chicago residents found everything they wanted in their own neighborhoods. South Shore

Opposite: *Roosevelt and Halsted, 1944.* Near West Side
(Courtesy of the CTA.)

resident Andrew McKenna could be speaking for all of Chicago when he says, "We didn't wander very far away because everything was nearby. The stores were there, the movie theaters were there, your friends were close, and you did mostly everything on foot or by bicycle."

Many residents remember the '40s as a great time to have been living in Chicago, and have a strong sense of nostalgia about the "good old days." These are strong statements, given the struggles they had to endure during the Great Depression and World War II. The geographic changes that were yet to come, like the movement to suburbia and the introduction of larger centralized shopping areas, would not happen until the '50s. With those shifts, the feeling of community would begin to suffer due to the breakdown of neighborhood boundaries and the increased sense of mobility. To many, the '40s were more than just another decade. It was the time of World War II, of post-war change, and of "the old Chicago neighborhood."

Ethnic Enclaves and Religious Institutions

While many of Chicago's neighborhoods included a diverse combination of residents, some were ethnic, racial or religious enclaves with distinct "boundaries" that provided shelter for those living within. These enclaves date to nineteenth century Chicago, when immigrants and newcomers settled in neighborhoods comprised of people from their own backgrounds. In these enclaves they found the freedom to practice their own religious and cultural customs, as well as make a smoother transition into their new surroundings. From Irish immigrants settling in Bridgeport to Swedes settling in Andersonville, the pattern could be found across the city. This tradition was the foundation for many of Chicago's neighborhoods in the 1940s.

Leonard Amari grew up in the Cabrini neighborhood, an Italian enclave on the Near North Side. "The Italians who settled in Chicago were not unlike other immigrant groups. Many of them came between 1900 and 1920. Why then? It was mostly because of economics. And when they arrived the concept of *quintadina* applied. This meant that when you moved to a foreign land you moved to the neighborhood of somebody from your town. In Chicago, there were historically five Italian neighborhoods, including the Taylor Street area and down at 24th and Oakley. The neighborhood that I am from is on the Near North Side; it's now called the Cabrini-Green projects. It was predominantly Sicilian when I lived there. The actor Dennis Farina was from the Cabrini projects, and his father was the first pharmacist/doctor who had an office in the Cabrini projects. There were a lot of prominent people who came out of my neighborhood."

On the Northwest Side, Polish immigrants settled near St. Stanislaus Kostka Church at Noble and Bradley. Former U.S. Representative Dan Rostenkowski grew up in this Polish enclave right across the street from the church. "This was a Polish section of the city, and Noble Street was the Polish "Broadway" for a while. You have to remember that at one time St. Stanislaus Kostka was the largest Catholic Polish church in the United States. I went to that school, my sisters went to that school and my children went there. In those days, they would have a procession on Palm Sunday and you would have 10,000 people. There were 2,300 children in the school at one time. It was an all-Polish community."

Ethnic culture could dominate a neighborhood, and Bernie Judge remembers how it could even determine status in Our Lady of Peace Parish in South Chicago. "The marvelous thing about the neighborhood was that it was the complete reverse of a class system. My father was born in Ireland — the old country — so I had more status. It was a point of pride to have immigrant parents, because that really tied you to Ireland and its ways. It meant you really knew more about your history and were more inside the real Irish culture. It wasn't an intellectual exercise, but it was a perceptual thing. So, the fact that I had an Irish father who had the gift of gab and a real Irish brogue was a real plus when I was growing up. It gave me a lot of cache in the neighborhood, especially since we both had the same first name. It was important. Judge is an Irish name, a county Mayo name, from western Ireland."

The experience of growing up black in Chicago was very different from that of whites. Most were segregated to a small area on the South Side because restrictive covenants prevented homeowners from selling or renting to blacks. As a result of the waves of black migrations from the south, there was a large population of blacks in a narrow belt on the South Side that came to be known as the "Black Belt." Also known as Bronzeville, the Black Belt was a city unto itself. Except for a small area around Harrison Street on the West Side and in the Cabrini-Green section on the Near North Side, nearly all of the black population of Chicago was concentrated within Bronzeville's borders during the 1940s.

Author Dempsey Travis grew up in the Black Belt and remembers, "In the '40s, the safe boundaries for us were as far north as 22nd Street and as far south as 60th Street, but south of Washington Park was a dangerous area. Although we lived at 59th and Prairie, we didn't go to that end of Washington Park. We stayed closer to the area from 55th to 51st Streets. The boundary on the west was the Rock Island railroad, and on the east it was Cottage Grove. It was a narrow strip that stayed that way until the 1950s and the end of restrictive covenants. We knew that we couldn't cross Cottage Grove, or you were subject to being picked up by the police strictly because you were African-American. I learned early in my life not to cross Cottage Grove. So, we did everything on the west side of Cottage Grove and nothing on the east side."

DuSable Museum founder Margaret Burroughs recalls living in the Black Belt after moving to Chicago in the '20s. "I lived in a thriving neighborhood and there were many black businesses at 35th Street, 43rd Street, and 47th Street, including grocery stores, drug stores, tailor shops and shoe shops. All those streets were thriving areas, and black folks traded with each other. For entertainment, there were places like the Regal Theater, the Vendrome, Forum Hall, the Savoy Ballroom, and the Club DeLisa." Dr. James Carter describes his South Side neighborhood as, "a combination of middle-class and working-class people. We were near 63rd Street and Stony Island — that was the end of the line of the elevated. My neighborhood was mostly brick bungalows with some wooden houses, and although there was a slight mixture of racial groups, it was almost all African-American. Although the area was both middle- and working-class, it wasn't a blighted neighborhood by any means. In those days, people were still migrating out of the south and coming up north looking for jobs with the Post Office and various industries. People had decent jobs in those days and there were some professional people like my dad who was a doctor."

Religious institutions in Chicago, including Catholic and Protestant churches and Jewish synagogues, were powerful forces in the lives of

63rd and Loomis, ca. 1948. West Englewood   (Courtesy of the CTA.)

24th Ward Alderman Louis London, ca. 1942. Lawndale (Courtesy of Richard Elrod.)

Edward M. Burke
New City

I grew up in Visitation Parish, which if you want to talk about a village, it was a village. Visitation was the largest Catholic parish in America in those days with some 2,400 kids in the grammar school, 1,200 girls in the all-girl's high school, and 400 kids in the kindergarten. The boundaries of the parish were 59th Street on the south, 52nd Street on the north, the railroad tracks on the east, and about Union Avenue to the west, which would have been the border with St. Basil.

The neighborhood was basically single-family, although we lived in a courtyard apartment building at 5240 S. Peoria Street. It was known as the Holly Oaks Building, which probably had 36 apartments. We lived on the second floor, and the Houlihans lived on the floor below us. There was no air conditioning, only one bathroom and one telephone. At that point, a five-person family lived in that one bedroom apartment. My two younger brothers slept in the bedroom where my mother and father slept, and I slept on a pull-out sofa bed in the dining room. We would move the dining room table and chairs over and pull out the sofa bed and that's where I slept. Back then we didn't think that we were entitled to our own bedroom, bathroom and car at sixteen years of age.

All my relatives lived in the neighborhood, including my grandmother and two aunts, who lived at 745 W. Garfield. Everything revolved around the church and the school. There was the Holy Name Society, the Catholic Daughters, and the Society of the Blessed Sacrament. The rectory basement had meeting rooms and there was a meeting going on every night of the week. I can remember that the Holy Name Society put on a show for which I played the piano. People "joined-in" in those days. Our local Knights of Columbus was Leo XIII. It had its own clubhouse on Garfield Boulevard with a bar and meeting rooms. People actually joined things — nobody joins anything anymore. I belonged to the Cub Scouts and the Boy Scouts, and Mrs. Houlihan was our den mother. I could stand in front of church on Sunday and say hello to 2,500 people whom I knew. If I didn't know them personally, I knew their sister or their brother or their mother or their father. In those days, there was no television, so people sat out on their porches and socialized. Future historians will determine whether television was our great boon or our biggest bust.

As to neighborhood parks, Sherman Park was our country club. We did everything in Sherman Park. That's where I took my first dog for training and obedience, where we learned to swim and where we played 16-inch softball. It had a beautiful lagoon where I probably fished for the very first time. During winter, the lagoon would freeze over and we would go ice skating and sledding in the park.

For movies, we would go to the Halfield Theater and the Radio Theater, and then you could go to 63rd and Halsted, which was the largest shopping area outside the Loop in those days. Sears, Wieboldt's, and Hillmans were there. Hillmans was in the Wieboldt's building and you would have to walk downstairs to get to Hillmans. Halsted Street had a string of little businesses all the way from our neighborhood to Morris B. Sachs at 67th and Halsted. There was also Bond's Men's Store, and if my recollection is correct, my father took me there to buy my first suit.

As for the White Sox, we could hop on the Halsted Street bus and get off at 35th, and either walk over or take the 35th Street bus to Comiskey Park. I was young when I went to my first Sox game, and it seemed as if we were allowed to travel on public transportation at a very early age. Our parents didn't have to worry about our safety. We used to take the Western Avenue streetcar straight down Western, all the way to Riverview.

My fondest memory of growing up in the neighborhood in the 1940s was the real sense of security. I don't think that anybody felt at risk. We didn't feel like we were poor — everybody was in the same "boat." Not everybody had a car. In fact, in those days it was rare if somebody had a car. People walked. I walked to school in the morning, and I walked home for lunch and my mother was there. She fixed lunch and we listened to radio serials. At one o'clock I walked back to school until three, and then walked home again. We lived at 52nd and the school was at 54th Place, so it was an easy walk down Peoria Street. Mother was at home during the day, and very few of our friends' mothers worked. It was rare. I can remember that Mrs. Houlihan worked because Mr. Houlihan died and there was nobody else to support the family.

Dan Rostenkowski
West Town

I will tell you about my youth. I was born in 1928 in an all-Polish community. Everyone here was either a saloonkeeper, tailor or a grocer, and they all used to meet at the tavern to discuss the politics of the day. My grandfather had a savings and loan here. It was a "home" savings and loan because it was in part of our home. He used to loan money from the commercial part of the building and customers would pay $.25 or $.30 cents a week, like on an insurance policy. Mind you, he would put receipts in all the cubbyholes for the people who were his clients, and if he wasn't there, they would come in and put their $.25 in. He knew who was paying by the receipts that were gone. Can you imagine leaving a store all day long and having people come in and deposit money and take their receipts? There was a high level of closeness and trust in the community — nobody would steal.

I remember once going to St. Stanislaus Kostka, and Sister DeClana, my teacher, told me to bring my mother to school. I knew I was in deep trouble. I came home and told my mother that she had to come to the school. She said, "You embarrass me! What did you do?" My mother whacked me around, although she couldn't hurt me because I was such a big kid. So, I went to the school with her — and both the sister and my mother beat me! It was discipline, but you would never think of striking a nun. I remember my mother chasing me until she laughed when she was so mad at me. The rule was that everybody's kid better behave, and everybody knew everybody. They built St. Stans' in 1847. My grandmother was young enough to have watched the Chicago Fire from the steeple of that church. The church didn't burn down in the fire, although the fire did go to Fullerton Avenue, but on the east side of the Chicago River.

The neighborhood is called East Humboldt because Bucktown is north of North Avenue. You might even call it the Pulaski Park Area. There was such community spirit. There were more activities in that park — the park district used to come here and put a wooden sidewalk over the cement so that you could walk with your ice skates on the wood to go into the park to warm up or walk to the ice. They used to flood that park. I remember my mother bringing big urns of hot chocolate for all the kids when we were outside all day. You are talking about community spirit, and it was fantastic.

As for entertainment in the summertime, there was none organized by parents. We were out there organizing ourselves. Across the highway, Morton's Salt off Elston Avenue used to be a ball field. Everybody played 16-inch softball in those days, and we played ball in fields. There were ten men on a team — the ball cost $1.20 for a Clincher or a Harwood, so it was $.06 a man and we played for the ball. So, the best teams were the ones that had all the softballs.

This community was very, very active in the war. Every kid in the neighborhood was gone because they all volunteered to go at the beginning of the war. You would've been amazed at all the blue and gold stars that were in the windows. Because of the rationing, you didn't get butter and sugar, and everybody felt the conflict. In those days, if a neighbor was sick, everybody was over there with chicken soup. Nobody went to the hospital, so neighbors took care of each other.

I remember my father, who was the alderman, and Ed Kelly, who was then the mayor of Chicago, going into the park across the street and taking things my mother had baked. The ward headquarters was at our house, and the precinct captains would bring in bread, biscuits and bakery goods to take down to the Servicemen's Center. Ed Kelly had one of the best Servicemen's Center in the world. Whenever a kid came through Chicago, and nearly every train came through here, they would go to that Servicemen's Center. They were treated like royalty there.

I went into the service from 1946 to 1948 after graduating from St. John's Military Academy in Wisconsin. Then, I came back to Chicago in 1948 and went to Loyola University. The neighborhood began to change by the end of the decade when the Polish displaced persons came in. There was a tremendous shortage of housing and many families had to live together. All the mansions in Wicker Park became rooming houses. The kids would come home from St. Stanislaus and teach their parents how to speak English. If you wanted to make a living, you better speak English — you learned how to speak English in order to communicate. I remember that if an Irish cop came out here to arrest a neighbor, my father, the alderman, would be screaming at the cop to get away. If necessary, he would then go down and bail out his constituents. That was what the alderman did in those days. It was a combination of neighborhoods and fraternal organizations that helped foster the new citizen.

When my dad, Joe Rostenkowski, was the alderman, he used to have a citizens' class in ward headquarters. When they were asked who the President of the United States was they would say, "Joe Rostenkowski." He was everything to them.

Irving Park and Seeley, 1944. North Center   (Courtesy of the CTA.)

Angel Guardian Orphanage, Devon and Ridge, ca. 1940. West Ridge (Courtesy of the Rogers Park/West Ridge Historical Society.)

Lee Stern
Uptown

I was born in 1926 at Michael Reese Hospital. I first lived in Lake View on Roscoe, then we moved north to Thorndale and Winthrop, and then we moved to the Grandeur Hotel on the southeast corner of Granville and Winthrop. My mother was a millinery buyer at the Fair Store, and my dad was with a company called Ross Federal Service, a theater-checking agency, so he traveled a great deal.

The neighborhood really centered around Swift School and the playgrounds. If there is anything to write about Chicago and its neighborhoods, it is that the playgrounds were where we "lived." The little asthma I had was caused by what we called the "dust bowl" at Swift School, at Thorndale and Winthrop, right along the "L" tracks. They had a big playground at the south end of the school, and a small one at the north end. In those days, the playgrounds had a male and a female instructor. There was a field house there, and they had wrestling, tug-of-war, and softball games. It was just an exciting time in the 1930s and 1940s.

We saw movies at the Devon Theater on Broadway, the Granada, the Uptown, and the Bryn Mawr Theater. We didn't go to the Riviera because that was where you might end up getting in fights. Once in a while, we would go to the Nortown Theater on Western, south of Devon. We also had a great spot called the Glenlake Bowl on Broadway, between Glenlake and Granville. In those days, you had pin boys, usually drunkards, who we were paying $.10 a line. Every once in a while, if they didn't have pin boys, a couple of guys from our group would go and set pins and we would see how quickly we could roll the balls down the lanes. You always had some guys who threw the bowling ball 100 mph. We spent a lot of time there before and after World War II.

We went shopping on Granville and Bryn Mawr, and there was also shopping on Broadway. The local hangout for high school kids, even after we got out of high school, was Al's Tic Tock. Al's was about three or four stores north of Thorndale on the east side of Broadway. It was a place with about half a dozen booths and counters. This was the hangout. We would go there after we left the Swift School playground. That was our place. We would go to the movies and then go to Al's Tic Tock.

South of there was the Edgewater Beach Hotel. The pier at the hotel extended into the lake, like a small Navy Pier, and they would have speedboats out there. The beach walk was a place to walk along the lake and go dancing. I remember hearing Xavier Cugat and all the big stars of the day there. As a kid, I would creep around the fence and sneak in — I remember drinking mint juleps at the Edgewater Beach. There was a tennis club next to the hotel and Bobby Riggs was there.

I started at Senn High School before the war began. You could eat in the lunchroom there, but there were also a lot of stores around the area. One of them was called Nagle's, and that was where all the athletes hung out. I had $.25 a day for lunch and that paid for three ham sandwiches, a bottle of Coke, and an ice cream. There was also Harry's, but the bad kids hung out there. We always heard about all the terrible things that happened there, including smoking pot. We formed a club at Senn called the "Green and White" that focused on the betterment of the school and of the community. I was never in a fraternity at Senn, but I played center on the football team for four years. We started dancing on the stage at Senn during the lunch period, and I was the DJ. I loved high school, and I think that my high school days were the greatest days I ever had.

Life in the 1940s was special because you could go out as a kid and never worry about whether somebody was going to beat you up, shoot you, or anything else. You could go downtown, to the park, or hang around the beaches until 11 o'clock in the evening. You could take your date to the park and you could stay until whatever hour you wanted. It was a wonderful time in my life. I remember getting on the bus as a little kid, I think about it now and it amazes me. I remember when they opened the new bridge over the Chicago River on the Outer Drive and President Roosevelt was there. I think that I was thirteen or fourteen years old, and I got on the bus by myself and went there to see him. You could do all of those things and not really worry. The best thing about the early '40s was the ability to get around and not worry about things. All you had to worry about was a local bully.

neighborhood and parish residents. These institutions, through a variety of religious services, educational opportunities, and fraternal groups, influenced the daily lives of the residents by setting the standards of behavior, morality, and ethics. In addition, they provided a sense of unity and camaraderie during the many national and international challenges of the 1940s.

Those Chicagoans who grew up in Catholic parishes often went to parochial elementary and high schools, attended masses daily, participated in social events at their churches on a regular basis, and were encouraged to live their lives according to the rules of the Roman Catholic Church. They felt a strong sense of community and neighborhood because of their parish lives.

Bernie Judge recalls that, "As a Catholic, other than your family, the church was the center of your life. That was where you did everything. It dictated your conduct and everything revolved around the school and the church. The celebration of young life was tied to your religious institution. It was the dominating influence of your early years and your pastor was more the emperor than the prince because he tended to rule with a strong hand. You were expected to support the parish financially, and to follow its dictates to the letter. Our church, Our Lady of Peace Church, was magnificent. We had ten masses each Sunday and three masses every other day of the week. It was a large parish and the school had about 700 students."

Mary McCarthy O'Donnell was raised at 5158 S. Morgan near her church, St. John the Baptist. "You could walk to seven churches in the neighborhood. St. John the Baptist Church had Irish Catholic parishioners, while St. John of God Church, further west, was predominantly Polish. At St. John the Baptist we had St. Anne's Novena. At the end of the Novena, there was a parade, and the marchers would go by our house all the way from 50th Place and Peoria to 55th and Morgan. All along the way, most every house would put out some kind of lovely statue. As they were going by, everyone was singing, '*Oh, good St. Anne, we call on thy name.*' It was just beautiful."

Beverly was Jim Casey's neighborhood during the 1940s. "Beverly was a very tightly knit neighborhood. It was primarily Irish and Italian, but mostly Irish Catholic. This kind of closeness in the neighborhood was not that unusual across the South Side. Christ the King Church was the dominant force in the community, and everything revolved around it." Morgan Murphy also grew up in Beverly. "In the 1940s, the neighborhoods and parishes meant close and caring neighbors. Your life revolved around your home, your school, and your church."

Dick Jaffee remembers life in South Shore and the importance of religious groupings. "I think that South Shore was roughly one-third Jews, one-third Irish Catholic and one-third Anglo-Saxon Protestants. I didn't know until I was fifteen years old that you could be Catholic and not be Irish. I really thought that all Catholics were Irish because the only Catholics I knew were Irish. Of course, the question about where you went to school was always whether you were 'Catholic' or 'public.' That was the way we thought of the neighborhood."

Irving Park resident Sheila Morris Williams remembers how a Catholic education could dominate one's life. "I went to both Catholic grammar and high school during the '40s. It was an excellent education, and very demanding. A typical school day was highly structured, and would always begin with a 30 minute mass. Of course, the school was filled with nuns. If we ever did anything wrong — like spoke out of turn — we got a rap across the hand with a steel-tipped ruler. If we did it again, we had to 'pay a dime for the missions.' Now, students in those days would never think about speaking out of turn, it just didn't happen. We were always perfectly behaved. We just lived in fear of the nuns — Sister Trinita in particular — she would hit the hardest and was as mean as could be! But we did learn discipline. Our world back then was dominated by the discipline of the church during the school day, and then reinforced at night by our parents, relatives and the community. We didn't have TV or any negative influences in our lives."

Those residents who grew up in the Jewish faith during the 1940s were influenced by the leaders of their synagogues and the teachings of their religion. Most Jewish children attended public elementary and high schools, but often attended after-school religious instruction, including Saturday Hebrew school and Sunday school classes. Most Jewish families wanted their sons to be bar mitzvah as a sign of manhood at thirteen. The tradition of bat mitzvahs for girls had not yet been established in the 1940s. Except for Jewish enclaves on the city's West Side, most Chicago Jewish families lived in mixed neighborhoods on the North, Northwest and South Side where they were a minority group.

For Art Berman, his religious education was an important part of life on the Far North Side. "I went to Ner Tamid Synagogue on California Avenue in the North Town neighborhood and attended Hebrew School there, which meant that when I was done at public school in the afternoon I would be at Ner Tamid four days a week. I even went to Hebrew High School for a couple of years, and that was the synagogue where I was bar mitzvah on the day of Israel's independence. It was the biggest synagogue in the area. The neighborhood was substantially Jewish, and it had evolved

North and Pulaski, ca. 1948. Humboldt Park (Courtesy of the CTA.)

Jim O'Connor
Gresham

I was born in 1937 and grew up in the Gresham neighborhood at 79th and Ashland, but it was really known as Little Flower Parish. Back then, pre-television and pre-mobility, your life was pretty much determined by the parish, particularly on Chicago's South Side. The parish you were in told volumes about you. You knew where people hung out, what they did, and where they played softball. Our neighborhood was defined by the railroad tracks at 75th Street, Ashland Boulevard west to Damen, and up to about 83rd Street.

Our parish dominated most everything. We had a tremendously powerful pastor, Monsignor McMahon. He walked through the neighborhood with two St. Bernard dogs wearing a silk suit with a homburg and cane, not because he needed a cane, but a walking cane. Every now and then, it was like God was coming down the street. He was a dominant character. He took a little basement church back in the '40s and built it into something that came as close to a cathedral as you could find on the South Side. It was a magnificent church, and so much activity revolved around it. They had the Sodality, the Altar and Roses Society, the Knights of Columbus, and McMahon must have had at least five associate pastors. It gives you an idea how large the community was. I would imagine it was probably 80% Irish Catholic — just a huge Irish Catholic population.

Being an altar boy was a major assignment when I grew up in the parish. Where you stood in the pecking order — at midnight mass, or the big weddings — determined how you were regarded by the pastor and the other priests in the parish. Almost all the boys were altar boys because there were so many masses. That was important. I had nothing but nuns as teachers, and I don't think there was a lay person in the school.

It was required that everyone pay something for school. Every month, my father would give me a dollar to give to the principal as payment for tuition. The tuition was $10.00 a year. Of course, you had nuns who were probably getting paid $30.00 or less a month, so you had very inexpensive labor. Every month I got this same lecture: "This represents a sacrifice and you owe something back. For this dollar we expect that you are going to do your homework on time and not goof off." Every kid got the same lecture. I've always felt that in life you don't get something for nothing. There was really built-in discipline.

During the drive to build the church, the pastor determined how much each family should give and what was expected from them. He would say to my father, "Okay, I expect $100.00 from you." The pastor ran the numbers and figured out what everybody was expected to give — and everybody did. He also put a list in the back of the church showing what everybody had committed. He got you to contribute because of your conscience and notoriety, not because of your good faith. Everybody's name and how much they had contributed or pledged was up there. It was phenomenally successful, and the new church was magnificent. Ceremonies around church activities were major, whether it was Good Friday, Easter or Christmas. Midnight Mass was spectacular — that was a large part of life in the '40s.

I was eight years old when the war ended, so barely in second or third grade, and during that time my life didn't change a lot. I remember things like the Texaco man, and how he would race to the car, wash the windows and check the air and oil. The biggest store in the neighborhood was the Hi-Lo Store at 79th and Paulina. That's where everybody shopped for groceries. I was their delivery boy. I would get a dime for carrying the groceries three blocks. It was the first job I had, and I was very, very young.

Milk was delivered on wagons drawn by horses in the '40s, and even up to the time we left the neighborhood in the middle '50s. We lived in an apartment that had an alley behind the building, and I remember the ragman shouting, "Rags a lyin!" Our back door was always open during the years we lived there. We had landings or back porches, and during the winter we would always pile the snow up and jump off the second floor landing. We did not have an iceman there, but we had an old GE refrigerator with the circular top. I never remember having an appliance changed in the eighteen years we lived in that apartment. The washing machine was the crank-type, and it was in a little room off the kitchen. Then they would put the clothes out on the lines to dry. In the basement, we had tubs where the heavier laundry was done.

The thing I also remember about the '40s was that most Christmas gifts were war surplus, such as large target kites, pill boxes, little ammunition cases, small hatchets, or Army-issue shovels. That was very common. There was a big war surplus store on 79th Street near Halsted. I remember a lot of the parents going shopping there in '45 and '46 — that was Christmas. There was not a lot of wealth during that period, and so much of the fun was do-it-yourself.

Rev. Thomas M. Sampelinski, St. Wenceslaus Church, ca. 1948. Near West Side (Courtesy of Special Collections and Preservation Division, Chicago Public Library.)

Chicago Home for Jewish Orphans, 62nd and Drexel, ca. 1940. Woodlawn (Courtesy of the Jewish United Federation.)

Mel Pearl
Lawndale

I was born in 1936 at Norwegian American Hospital and lived in an apartment building at 1537 S. Kolin, at the south end of Franklin Park. I had never been in a single-family home until we built our house in West Rogers Park. On the West Side, we lived in a courtyard apartment building with four entranceways. There were many kids in our building. When the weather was bad we used to go into the vestibule of the building and play all day long. You could have made a life out of that apartment building.

We went shopping and to movies on 16th Street, that was the big commercial street. All the stores were operated by old-world merchants, including Galler's Drugstore with a soda fountain and D&W Delicatessen at 16th and Kolin. There were all kinds of kosher stores, and it was a neighborhood that was a true ghetto. It was an old world ghetto. When my folks moved to the North Side, I stayed back on the West Side to graduate grammar school. During that time, I lived with my grandmother who also lived in our building. She had been in this country for 30 years, but spoke very little English. She spoke Yiddish and Russian, but mostly Yiddish. So, the year that I lived with her, I had to learn to understand and speak Yiddish. All the merchants on the street in our area, maybe eight to ten square blocks at that time, were Jewish and spoke Yiddish. Surrounding us was a Bohemian area, a Polish area, an Italian area, and there was no real trouble. You knew what streets to stay on and where not to go. There were Catholic schools around us, and, of course, the Hebrew schools and all the synagogues. My parents spoke fluent Yiddish because they were born in Europe, but they also spoke English. I would go to the store with my grandmother and my mother, and they'd converse in Yiddish. My grandmother had no real reason to learn English because everybody spoke Yiddish. It truly was a ghetto and there were all tenements. I remember so succinctly that every night in the warmer weather, all the kids would congregate on the corner. The mothers would open the window and yell, "Come on home, dinner's ready. It's time to come home and go to sleep!" Your whole life was on the streets. Franklin Park was a key for us, but it was just as important to hang out on the street corners.

We had a lot of little synagogues in our neighborhood, but the big, fancy synagogues were on Douglas Boulevard, including KINS. The little synagogues were connected to European shtetls, and they were named after little towns that the Jews came from. They were Orthodox, of course, and they would seat 100 people with the women sitting upstairs. I went to Hebrew school and cheder in a guy's kitchen. He was an old world rabbi on Kolin Avenue. He used to sit there with a ruler and give me a whack if I missed something. When I was bar mitzvah, I gave my speech in Yiddish. That was the environment — a little community of old world Jews. If you missed Hebrew school, it was like a crime against mankind, but I used to ditch all the time. On the West Side, we stayed in our own ghetto. When we moved and I went to Evanston Township High School, my first year was really tough.

At fourteen I moved to West Rogers Park. You talk about culture shock! We had built our house on Francisco and Estes. At that time, on our block, there were only four houses and prairie all the way to the clay pits. I had just come from a tenement where there were 700 kids in the yard to this prairie with four houses and you can't see a soul. I'm ready to kill myself and my parents. It was horrible. I went to Evanston because the kids across the street were going there. I only knew three kids, and there weren't any other kids around. You couldn't find a soul. So, I went to Evanston. They had never seen a Jew in Evanston at this time. You talk about culture shock! I had come from a strong Semitic neighborhood to Evanston Township High School. It took me about a year to deal with it. Anti-Semitism was very strong there. In a class of 1200 kids, there were seven Jewish kids. It was a very tough time for me — the Jews and blacks hung out together.

I'm telling you that it was great growing up on the West Side. Nobody had better growing up years than I did on the West Side. It was fantastic, and I loved every minute of it. What made the '40s unique was all the first-generation Americans, and the strong camaraderie in the neighborhood. You didn't get out of the neighborhood because you didn't have your own cars. You were circumscribed by the lack of transportation. You didn't get out of your eight square blocks because you were going into foreign territory after that. There was a very strong sense of closeness, of congregation of people, and everything was out on the street. I really cannot think of any negatives from the perspective of a kid.

Jerry Petacque
Humboldt Park

I was born in Chicago in 1930. We lived in Humboldt Park on Crystal Street, near Division. I have an older brother, Art, and we lived in that area until I was about five. Humboldt Park (the park) was kind of the dividing line. If you lived east of the park, you were considered lower in the social stratification. If you lived west of the park, you were in the higher stratification. We moved from the east side of the park to the west side of the park on Cortez near Kedzie, around 1935.

In the late '30s, the neighborhood was basically Polish, Italian and Jewish. There were probably four or five grocery stores and a kosher butcher shop in the neighborhood, all located on Division Street. We had local barbers who competed with each other — Hymie the barber on Division and Louie the barber on Spaulding. There were competing delicatessens, including Itzkovitz and another across the street, kiddy-corner to it. There was Brown and Koppel on Division and Damen. Many of the area luminaries would go there, including Mike Todd and the Pantzko brothers. The restaurant was in front, but if you walked through a door you would be in a gambling casino where people played cards.

Division Street itself was profoundly interesting. Beginning at Kimball Avenue there were the delicatessens and grocery stores. Then you would go through Humboldt Park and on the corner was Stelzer's Restaurant — that's another vignette. We had Levinson's Bakery, and Levinson was related to the Banowitz family. The Banowitz bakery was on Division near California. Louie's Poolroom and Nate the barber were on Division Street. You had a bunch of Hungarian card places as you worked your way further east. A little further down you had the famous Turkish baths — the schvitz.

I can think of 50 friends I had growing up in Humboldt Park. We knew each other's families, and the families knew each other. They played cards, played Mah Jongg, shopped together, and those connections continued all the way to Damen Avenue (Robey Street). Everybody knew each other. The corner of Spaulding and Division was the meeting place for the people I knew. For the adults, it would be Brown and Koppel or maybe Stelzer's Restaurant, and everybody knew each other. It was a warm, friendly atmosphere, and there was no stratification. You could be a police captain or work in the Turkish bath. They knew each other and they talked. There were no walls that separated them.

I think that the '40s were special because of the interactions between people and the lack of stratification. It was a warm, friendly and fuzzy kind of place to live and grow up. The camaraderie of family, friends, and neighbors made it an open community. My peer group of guys were from Jewish, Polish and Italian families and all got along well — it didn't matter their ethnic or religious heritage. We probably did identify ourselves psychologically, as being from Humboldt Park. We were a little sensitive about being from a community that was different than the affluent, lakefront neighborhoods along Lake Shore Drive.

My earliest negative experience in the neighborhood happened at the schul on Spaulding and Division. The German-American Bund had come to our neighborhood and threw bricks with swastikas through the windows of the synagogue and the delicatessen. My father, Dave, was the second Jewish police captain in Chicago. He was very active in his Jewish orientation and had his own group of vigilantes. There was a pool hall on Division near California and my father would get his group together, including some Jewish policemen, and they would reciprocate to the Bund. Instead of throwing bricks, they would throw fists. That was my earliest memory of negativism in the neighborhood.

In one other situation, there was Gerald K. Smith, a rabid anti-Semite. He gave a speech in Chicago in the early '40s, and when it was over my father and his vigilantes picked him up and took him to the police station for the weekend. Mr. Smith didn't sleep for a few days because my father poured cold water on him to expiate him out of his anti-Semitism. Whether it was successful or not, I don't know.

As for anti-Semitism on the police force, the way it worked was kind of circular. My brother worked at the Sun-Times and he was a Pulitzer-prize winning reporter. The anti-Semitic letters would come to him, not directly to my father. They would say things like, "How did that Jew become a captain?" Most of the people in the police department were Irish, so the anti-Semitism was unspoken. Occasionally, I would go to the morning lineup of policemen at my father's station. He would say, "Gentlemen, good morning. Do you have any complaints this morning? If you do, see your monsignor and don't bother me." They all burst out laughing, because the power in the police department was based on your connections to the parish.

Once my brother Art took me for lunch to a restaurant. Of course, he was a leading authority on crime and the Syndicate in Chicago. We walk into the restaurant — of course, all the hoodlums in Chicago would sit at the back of the restaurant because they were concerned that someone was going to come in and assassinate them. As we walked into the restaurant, these hoodlum-types in their shiny suits waved at my brother and said, "Hey, Art, come here and sit down with us!" So, Art introduced me to these people. Then someone asked, "Hey, Art can we drive you home?" He said, "No, your trunk is not big enough for me and my brother!"

in the '40s from a mixture of Swedish and Luxembourgers. In the '30s, most Jewish people were living in the old 24th Ward on the West Side. Since Ner Tamid was a conservative synagogue, it addressed the middle-class in the neighborhood, and they found comfort there, as well as great leadership. It was a very important institution in our community."

Like many kids, Sheldon Rosing had mixed feelings about attending after-school religious programs. "I was bar mitzvah behind a store next to the Ray Theater on 75th Street in South Shore. My folks were fairly conservative Jews and we had to go to Hebrew School several days a week from 3:30 p.m. to 5:00 p.m. right after grammar school, as well as on Saturday morning. I wanted to be out with my friends who were playing ball." Arnold Scholl echoes that experience. "I went to the Austrian Galician Congregation in Humboldt Park from the time I was seven or eight years old until I was bar mitzvah. It was an Orthodox congregation and it was not that enjoyable going there five days a week. We would have our recess each day and sometimes a couple of us would go into Humboldt Park and play ball. The teacher or the rabbi would come looking for us in the park and guide us back to class." U.S. District Judge Marvin Aspen remembers his Jewish education in Albany Park. "Most of the Jewish boys would go to Hebrew School several afternoons a week in addition to public school. We didn't really enjoy it because the rabbi ran the school the same way he would have taught the children in a European shtetl. We had some problems relating to it and many of us just wanted to finish our bar mitzvah and be done with it. Going to Hebrew School on all those afternoons didn't threaten our Jewish faith or identity. Yet, by the time that we became adults, most of my friends and I became members of Reform or Conservative synagogues, thus failing to emulate the Orthodox practice of Judaism that many of our parents had practiced. That was more a reflection of a new generation of Jewish children in a more modern world than a comment on our parents or on our religion."

Bruce Bachmann recalls the influence of the religious leaders in his Austin neighborhood. "I remember the time three of us stole punch outs from the dime store, and we got caught. In those days, who did you call? They called the rabbi! I got a visit from two older members of the synagogue who scared the heck out of me — all for $.40. I didn't need the money. We just swiped things because it was something to do. I can remember the two men coming up the stairs. I thought it was the police! I never stole again."

U.S. Magistrate Judge Ian Levin remembers growing up in Rogers Park. "The neighborhood was very interesting, and it seemed to be half-Irish-Catholic and half-Jewish. The two religious groups seemed to live separate lives and be in their own special worlds — and not bother each other. There were two different islands of people. We did have interactions when I played at Touhy Beach — a lot of the Catholic kids came to play there or be lifeguards for Sam Leone. But, on the whole, each group went their own way."

Neighborhood Ethnic, Religious and Racial Mixtures

In the 1940s, a broad mix of ethnic groups were represented in neighborhoods throughout Chicago. In some areas, there were enclaves of residents who desired to live close to others of similar backgrounds, but in most neighborhoods a mixture of ethnicities lived together. Some experienced occasional conflicts with other groups, but most discovered that they could live together with a relatively high degree of harmony even if their backgrounds were quite dissimilar.

In sportswriter Bill Jauss' Sauganash neighborhood, two community religious leaders worked hard to avoid divisions between Protestants and Catholics. "Reverend Richard and Father Dolan had similar backgrounds since they both started their churches in the community when it was new. In the 1930s, they were young men just out of ministerial studies, and they didn't have permanent church structures yet. Diversity was something they stressed and they abhorred divisions within the community. They worked together and the young families just getting established in Sauganash saw Father Dolan and Reverend Richard as role models and tried to emulate the standard being set. So we had minimal public vs. parochial divisions as compared with other neighborhoods in the '40s."

Jim Dowdle grew up in South Shore. "In the 1940s, South Shore was a very comfortable neighborhood. The dominant groups were Irish Catholics and Jews. We played softball at O'Keeffe Elementary School, and it was always the Irish against the Jews. It seemed like everybody south of 71st Street was Jewish. Everyone north was pretty much Irish Catholic, but I think that South Shore was a very cohesive neighborhood. There weren't any fights, or anything like that. I think softball is what really brought the two groups together. It was a great neighborhood to be raised in."

Shirley Ochs Simon grew up in Humboldt Park and doesn't recall major conflicts between ethnic and religious groups in her neighborhood. "I don't remember any conflicts in the neighborhood. I had Polish girlfriends and it didn't matter that I was Jewish. In fact, we had one or two black families in our neighborhood. Although we were aware of differences between ethnic groups, it was really the older kids who were involved in struggles and it had nothing to do with us."

Sandy Bank remembers the diversity of Hyde Park in the '40s. "The

Service Guard, 1948. West Town (Courtesy of the Chicago Park District.)

Henry McGee, Jr.
Douglas

I was born in 1932 on the site where Lake Meadows Housing Development is now situated, but I grew up in a two-story apartment building near Garfield Boulevard and State Street. My earliest memories are of my playmates, and attending Sherwood Elementary School. Like many people, I remember my kindergarten teacher, Mrs. Goodman. She, like all of my school teachers from kindergarten through graduate law school, was white. To this day, I have never had the privilege of having an African-American teacher except for my first violin teacher, Mrs. Lucille Davis, who lived in Woodlawn.

I did very well in school and received the American Legion Award for being the best student in my grade school graduating class. Of course, I have many childhood memories of playing with my friends, but I also remember having to pass through the white neighborhood near us to reach both my elementary school and my high school. My black neighborhood ended abruptly at the Rock Island railroad tracks, a half block west of my house. At that time, Negroes did not live west of the tracks, but that was where my grade school was located. There was a sense of great danger in walking beyond the tracks, but I don't remember ever having been beat-up. However, I do remember instances of dodging stones being thrown as I walked or ran to school. The school was at 57th and Princeton, which was some four blocks west of the tracks, deep within white-held territory. There was less trouble and danger walking to Englewood High School, but we always came and went to school as much as we could through the black sections of the area.

We were able to journey downtown, to the center of Chicago, but throughout most of my school years we could not comfortably go north of the Chicago River. As late as 1958, an attempt was made to run me off the road after I returned from dropping a friend off near Amundsen High School. There were some black settlements near and about downtown, like Old Town, where there was a small enclave which is now the site of Cabrini Green Public Housing projects. But most of the North Side was off limits to blacks, and on the West Side, there was only a very small black enclave which formed a "L" with the South Side black neighborhoods. Later, I married a woman from that enclave whose family lived at 2037 Warren Boulevard, which paralleled Washington Boulevard. She went to Marshall High School in a formerly Jewish area. Earlier, my mother and father attended a West Side junior college, Crane, which is now called Malcolm X. Today, as it

has come to pass, the West Side is now exclusively black. But at the time I lived there, blacks did not go to any of Chicago's West Side. All through the time I was in high school and college, those white areas were completely off-limits.

My parents were deeply involved in the struggle against segregation and racism, but I was sheltered by them in ways that precluded much consciousness on my part about such restrictions as these. We lived in an entirely black world for most of the period I was growing up. My family moved to Hyde Park/Kenwood in the mid-fifties after I left home, and I believe that we were one of the first families to move east of Cottage Grove. Before that, blacks were subject to arrest if spotted east of Cottage Grove after dark. Our world was defined by Washington Park, where they had the Bud Billikin Day Parade on South Parkway.

My father was a postal clerk at the time I was in high school, and he ended his career as the Chicago Postmaster, appointed by President Johnson as the first black Postmaster of a major facility in the United States. He was also Chairman of the Board of Education and President of the NAACP. I remember that after the war, my dad and some of the NAACP people owned firearms because there was a lot of trouble in Chicago between 1946 and 1950. My dad was head of the NAACP during that exact period. We came from a middle-class family where we were able to avoid some of the horrors of segregation and discrimination, and we escaped some stuff that other blacks had to endure. My dad and sisters looked white, and at one point my sister had to pass for white to get a job at Marshall Field's. I looked like my mother, discernibly brown and African-American, what we called "colored" in those days.

I grew up with a consciousness that Chicago was not safe outside of black areas, but I really didn't think about coming into contact with whites. I was not conscious of racial prejudice until I went to college in the 1950s at Northwestern. I was among the first blacks in 1952 permitted to live in an integrated dormitory on the main campus of the university. Previously, blacks had to live off-campus. I remember a white guy from Kentucky trying to talk my Jewish roommate from New Jersey out of being my roommate. That, and other events, made racism personal for me, and I became more and more conscious of racial conflict and what it meant to be black or white. Today, when I go to visit my sister and walk around the North Side, there is an air of unreality for me. It still seems amazing to me that blacks can walk freely about the streets of the North Side of Chicago. I guess that Chicago is so changed now that people don't remember that.

Maxwell Street Market, 1941. Near West Side Photograph by Russell Lee. (Library of Congress)

Phil Holdman
Near South Side

My first recollection of Maxwell Street was going to the Irving Theater with my mother when I was five years old. The Irving was located about four houses north of Maxwell on Halsted. It cost only $.05 and that's why it was called the "Nickel Show." My mother never paid for me, telling the ticket-taker that I'd sit on her lap so as not to take up another seat. I would read the captions for her from those great silent movies of the '20s.

My family was very poor. We lived in the rear of my Uncle Jake's house on 13th near Blue Island Avenue. The heart of Maxwell Street was only two blocks away and we did all our shopping there, with the meager salary of my mother's "dollar-a-day" job. My father, Philip Holdman Sr., died two months before I was born.

Shopping with mom on Maxwell Street was really an experience. She knew all the stores and where one could get the best bargains. "Kingfish" Levinsky's fish store was on the south side of the 700 block. The live chicken store was on the same block. The shochet next door slaughtered your fowl for $.10, and an old man "robbed your chrane" (pulverized your horseradish) for your Friday night gefilte fish. I don't think that English was spoken on this block, only Yiddish. My mother was a live chicken maven and she always picked out the one with the most schmaltz.

In later years, when we moved to the more modern West Side, we would take streetcars back to Maxwell to do the weekly shopping. Mom didn't trust those fancy new stores on Roosevelt Road, with their cash registers. Coming home after buying her usual Thursday shopping specialties (a live chicken and a live carp or buffalo fish for gefilte fish), her linoleum shopping bags would wander to and fro because the live beings in them were getting frisky. Passengers in the streetcars eyes popped out wondering what was in those bags. Mom and I always laughed about those incidents. The only thing I didn't like about the live carp was that I'd lose my sleeping place for one night. I slept in the bathtub when it wasn't in use.

Another remembrance in later years was buying my first suit, at the age of twelve, for my forthcoming bar mitzvah. It was back to Maxwell Street to Shloimes Clothing Store with his bargains galore. I wound up with a $4.00 purple suit with one sleeve shorter than the other. If I bent over to one side, like the actor Henry Armetta, the suit would fit perfectly. Anyway, the price was right and my bar mitzvah was a huge success.

dominant groups in the area were older German-Jews, German refugees who moved into the area after the war, Eastern European Jews, and lace-curtain Irish Catholics who sent their kids to parochial schools. There were also Protestants in Hyde Park, but they were really a minority. For Jewish residents, there were a couple of Orthodox temples in the neighborhood, as well as a couple of Conservative temples, but the dominant ones were the Reform temples. When I went to Kenwood grammar school, the entire economic spectrum was represented at the school. There were people on relief as well as kids who were picked up each day by chauffeurs."

Occasionally, there were conflicts between Jews and Catholics, especially those who attended public and parochial schools. Ron Michaels grew up in Austin on the West Side. "My neighborhood was very diverse, but it was predominantly Irish Catholic along with some Jewish, Greek and Polish families. There were unwritten boundaries, and my problem was that my route to public school went past Resurrection Parish. Some of the older Catholic kids would stop me on a regular basis. They threatened me, hit me, and charged me protection money in order to get back on my way to school. I complained to my father about the treatment and I didn't want to go to school because it was such a terrible experience. I remember that he said to me, 'Good for you. When you get beat up enough maybe then you will learn to defend yourself. I'm not giving you money to pay those kids.' Sure enough, I decided to fight back and it became almost a vendetta for me. In the following years, I managed to fight every single one of those tough guys who had given me such a hard time. I also remember that one time I was playing basketball at Resurrection with my shirt off because it was a very hot day. Two nuns came over and told me that I had to put my shirt on. I recall saying to the Sister, 'If I put my shirt on, I will only keep the heat in and that would be detrimental to my health.' She said, 'My son, you should be a lawyer someday.' They let me keep my shirt off."

Harriet Wilson Ellis lived in Logan Square. "The neighborhood was a combination of different kinds of ethnic groups, but there were very few Jewish families in our part of Logan Square. Up around where we lived there were mostly German and Polish families. Although I experienced some anti-Semitism in the '40s, I did have many non-Jewish friends. However, some kids would actually let you know that you weren't invited to come to their parties because you were Jewish. They would say that the Jews had killed Christ and that topic was very common in many neighborhoods and all over the country and the world. My parents also encountered problems when they wanted to rent an apartment. Our last name was Wilson, but it had been Anglicized from the original Russian name when my great-grandfather had come to America from Vilna. Most people didn't know that I was Jewish, and when they found out they thought that I was trying to hide my true heritage. That was not the case since my family was very proud to be Jewish."

Howard Rosen had similar experiences in his Humboldt Park neighborhood. "My earliest brush with anti-Semitism was when we used to hear about the fights between the Jews and the Polish kids. There was a big Polish population on the east side of Humboldt Park — that was the Tuley High School side. The side where we lived was the Lowell grammar school side — it was more Jewish. We would hear about fights where they used fists and clubs, but never guns and knives. The first significant anti-Semitism that I ran into was when I was living in Albany Park. A friend and I were living about a quarter block from a small neighborhood church, right on the corner of Sunnyside and Spaulding. My friend and I were probably two of the only Jewish guys in our neighborhood. I remember being told that I had killed Christ, and I used to be called the 'Yid' and stuff like that. But I would never back down or anything like that. My father infused me with the idea that you stand up for your rights, and I did stand tough."

Lou Roskin also grew up in Humboldt Park. "I was born in St. Louis, and when I came to Chicago we moved to Humboldt Boulevard and Armitage. I was a tough kid and when my new friends told me that Jewish kids weren't allowed to go past Bloomingdale Street, I resolved to change that. During the 1940s, anti-Semitism was very prevalent in the neighborhood. I remember one time when we got news that a group of Polish lads was going to come over and do damage to our temple. We waited in hiding for them and when their car pulled up we jumped out. I grabbed somebody and one of my friend's father yelled, 'Louie — hold them.' While I was holding the fellow, my friend's father accidentally punched me right in the face."

During the 1940s, blacks found it uncomfortable and even dangerous to travel out of the Black Belt into bordering neighborhoods. Taunting, rock-throwing, and physical violence were all real threats that had to be dealt with. Ted Saunders recalls, "As a black man, there were neighborhoods where we didn't go. Usually we never went on the other side of Halsted, and we only went to South Shore every so often. As for downtown, middle-class blacks could go there. It was a matter of whether you were known or came from a prominent family, then you could mix and go anyplace."

Henry McGee grew up in the Douglas neighborhood on the South Side. "There were things you could and couldn't do, but I don't remember

David Cerda
Near West Side

I was born on Damen (Robey) at Roosevelt in June 1927. A midwife came to the house and I was born there. That was the popular thing to do at that time, so it was nothing out of the ordinary. My father was a laborer. He started coming across the border during the Mexican Revolution in 1915. At that time some revolutionaries came into his small village and took the young men, and they killed his older brother. Later, all the men came across the border and worked on the railroad, fixing the tracks, while the women stayed behind. My father arrived in Chicago in 1922, just to work, and he stayed with his brother.

My mother was always at home and never worked. There were only two kids in my family, including my brother who is four years younger. That is in contrast to my grandfather on my father's side, who had twenty-five children and outlived three wives. I never met him because he died before they came up here.

I attended kindergarten in that area around Polk Street and was baptized at Our Lady of Pompeii. We didn't stay there too long, because my mother thought that the schools would be better elsewhere — but the Mexicans were really being chased out of that area. So, we moved to about 1800 S. Kedzie, where some of my other family members were living — like my uncle Manuel, my grandmother and her two children. It wasn't a Mexican community. It was a Jewish area, and there were Jewish precinct captains. There were also some Irish, Polish, German, one black family and another Mexican family in the area. There used to be a Greek ice cream parlor on the northeast corner of Kedzie and Ogden, and across the street was the famous Douglas Park Yiddish Playhouse where Paul Muni performed. That was where I really grew up.

There were problems being Mexican in that neighborhood. They would call us derogatory names and make statements about my heritage, but the neighborhood was really a mixture of people and we were on the border of a variety of ethnic and religious groups.

We would go to Douglas Park on Sundays for family picnics. We would load up the cars with family and friends and go out to the Cantigny Woods around Route 66, where the McCormick estate was located. The kids would play baseball and everybody would bring food. The men would sing songs and my father played the guitar. When it would get dark, we would burn some logs and sing more songs. The families stayed close, and it seemed that we had picnics every Sunday.

Chicago Stockyards, ca. 1940. New City (Courtesy of the CTA.)

Hugh Hefner
Montclare

I was born in 1926 at a hospital at the University of Chicago. The hospital was located on the South Side, but I actually grew up on the Northwest Side of Chicago. The neighborhood was called Montclare. It was adjacent to Oak Park, and bordered by Harlem Avenue to the west, Oak Park Avenue to the east, and Grand Avenue on the north.

When I was four years old we moved into a house at 1922 N. New England. I went to Sayre Grammar School, which was just a block from where I grew up. The major business center for that area was Grand Avenue, and the Grand Avenue streetcar ran from Harlem Avenue all the way to Navy Pier. That was our major transportation downtown, but there was also the Lake Street "L." The streetcar was vastly superior in my mind. There was something quite romantic about those streetcars.

Grand Avenue was our main shopping street. The Montclare Theater was on Grand, just one block east of Harlem. There was a park located about two blocks immediately to the north of us called Sayre Park, and the railroad ran through it. A lot of my memories are related to those trains, which were both freight and passenger. You had to pass the tracks to get to the movies, and we went to the movies two or three times a week. That was the major center of my dreams and fantasies.

I grew up in a very typically midwestern, middle-class, Methodist home. My folks were farm people from Nebraska. They both were college educated and both were teachers at one point in their lives. But there was also a lot of repression, in the sense of the inability to really show emotion. It was very typical of the time. The movies were for me the escape into another magic world where dreams, fantasies and the romantic possibilities were all there.

As for shopping, the drugstore was right across the street from the Montclare Theater. There was a soda fountain that was kind of a hangout, a place where my folks would take my younger brother and me. It was on Harlem, half a block to the north of Grand. Sabbath's Department Store was on Grand, and the first girl who I went steady with worked in the electric department of that store. We bought our Big Little Books when we were kids at Woolworth's and Kresge's, across the street on Grand.

As for the ethnic mix in the Montclare neighborhood — I wasn't particularly aware of any, except that it was totally white. I don't think that there was any particularly dominant racial or ethnic group, as far as I was concerned or aware. The Montclare neighborhood was very homogenous. I was not aware of any bigotry during the 1940s, and was raised in a family that was very liberal.

The Second World War began at the very time I was about to graduate from grade school in 1939. I was at Steinmetz High School in December 1941 when America got into the war. The Depression and the war were, in many respects, an intensely romantic time. I grew up during the time of the World's Fair in 1933 and 1934, and we went there. I'm a kid who developed all kinds of creative games that we used to play, and a lot of them came from movies and things of that kind. I created a game called "Clay," which is actually an improvisational game that we played with modeling clay on a tabletop in which we would create murder mysteries, haunted houses, cowboy towns, and a lot of things inspired by movies. Then, I started drawing comic books and creating mystery stories and things, and a lot of what I did was, in a real sense, a rehearsal for what came later. I started a club and a magazine connected to it called the "Shudder Club," which was related to my fascination with murder and horror movies and radio shows. The magazine contained reviews and short stories that I wrote. It was part of a very inventive and imaginative childhood.

One of the major impacts from the war, particularly during high school, was the fact that I didn't have a car. One connects the teen years with a time when you become very mobile with an automobile, but during the war everybody had gas limitations. I only used the family car on special occasions, but most of the time I couldn't. I wrote a song called "The A Car Blues" that reflected the fact that I was wearing out the leather of my ration shoes. You had to go without certain things because of the war, but at the same time, it was a period in which America really was very homogenous and believed in what it was about. There was a strong sense of neighborhood. People knew their neighbors and tended to hang out with people who lived in their neighborhood. People tended to become romantically involved and to marry people in their own neighborhood. I think that was very much the way of things in the '40s, and I grew up with the same group of young people from kindergarten all the way through high school. I didn't interact too much with kids from other high schools.

It really was a small town community in Montclare. Growing up on the Northwest Side was almost suburban. In the '20s and '30s, it was almost rural. There was a tremendous amount of prairie, and as a boy, I loved that. As I said, my parents were originally farm people in Nebraska. There was a forest preserve just a few blocks west of us that was almost a woods. And, growing up in the late '30s, there were still horse-drawn milk wagons, coal wagons and rags and old iron peddlers roaming the alleys. I *didn't play many sports in the alleys or the streets because I wasn't a big sports-person. I was much more interested in games of imagination.*

I think that the '30s and the first half of the '40s, particularly during the Depression and war years, was a very romantic time. The popular music of the era was very romantic, and the most popular music of that time was Big Band Swing. It's a music that I still relate to and still play at the Playboy mansion when friends gather here on the weekends. I grew up on jazz, and one of the things that I loved about the music was that it spoke to me in a special way. It was black music, and very American, and for me there was something quite special about that. I had strong feelings about integration. The jazz clubs on the South Side were the only place where you really saw mixed audiences. I was a very liberal kid, and it was the beginning of the Civil Rights movement. Even when I was in the Army, the men whom I served with were all white. There was no bigotry in the neighborhood when I grew up, but I became aware of it when I was in the Army.

The late 1930s and early 1940s were a special time for me. Once I began Playboy, I began living in a world all my own that I created. For me, it is connected to the dreams that came directly out of childhood. It is the '30s and early '40s that are the most intensely romantic times for me, and a time that I remember with the greatest fondness.

Lincoln, Belmont, and Ashland, ca. 1940. North Center
(Courtesy of the CTA.)

any mistreatment — as long as you lived within your normal Negro existence. I wasn't aware about the status of blacks in the military, even though my father tried to join the Navy and they wouldn't let him do it. They had what was called the 'Negro Navy' and he refused to join it, but he didn't tell us that. So, my parents kept a lot of things from us, which I guess is how black, middle-class parents did things with their children. So, my biggest memory of the white world was the danger of going through a white neighborhood, or the fear of getting attacked because we might go through a white neighborhood to get to or from high school."

Former Alderman Leon Despres recalls the integration efforts in his Hyde Park neighborhood during the '40s. "I have lived in Hyde Park ever since 1908, except for two years from 1922 to 1924. I remember that in the '40s housing was very difficult to find in the neighborhood and there were rent controls during those years. As for integration, black families did start moving in, but there was no radical change. A lot of people moved out of Hyde Park, including German refugees, and there were some very distinguished people moving in, including many distinguished African-Americans. The remarkable action of the Hyde Park/Kenwood Community Conference was to welcome African-Americans into the neighborhood and to say that we wanted to have an interracial neighborhood of high standards. Hyde Park had a wonderful atmosphere in the '40s and '50s. It still has a great atmosphere of tolerance and there is a much greater sharing of social values than in most other communities."

The Sense of Community

Today, Chicago neighborhood life in the 1940s is remembered as a special time. Many aspects of life just seemed to be better — the clothes, music, movies — the list could go on and on. But for most who grew up then, the overall sense of community found in the neighborhoods is missed most of all. This sense of community unified the neighborhood, which was very important during the Depression and the war years, when people needed to work together, and depended not just on their families, but their neighbors, too. This helps explain why there is so much nostalgia for the "happier times" of the '40s, despite the fact that so many suffered hardships during the decade.

During the '40s, there were rules of behavior that governed neighborhood life, and neighbors worked together for the betterment of the community. Residents were expected to behave in a way that reflected positively on their families, and for children in particular, there would be consequences if they disobeyed. Montclare resident Chuck Chapman remembers, "I think that the '40s were unique because of the moral code

---

Hiroshi and Dorothy Kaneko
Near North Side

Hiroshi: *Until the time of the Pearl Harbor attack in 1941 we were farming in Oregon near Salem. After being sent to a temporary camp, we were moved to the Tule Lake Internment Camp in northern California in May of 1942. We couldn't get out unless we could find a job and a place to live, which could be very difficult. The best situation for us would be to find a domestic job where we could live and work together. In July of 1943 we found a domestic job working in Barrington, but after Dorothy got pregnant we had to move on. So we moved to the South Side of Chicago to 6404 S. Ellis Avenue.*

Dorothy: *I'll never forget that place. It was so hard to find a place to live. We would see a vacancy sign and they would always say, "We don't want any Japanese here." We would always tell them that we are not Japanese, we are American.*

Hiroshi: *Because it was so hard to find a place to live we decided to find an apartment building and rent to people coming out of the camps. In 1944 we leased a large, 150 room building at 1039 North LaSalle, it's called the LaSalle Mansion. It quickly became a gathering place, almost a community center for Japanese-Americans. People would come from all over to meet their friends and stay. Eventually we leased two other buildings, as well.*

Dorothy: *I had to cook for them all because there weren't any Japanese restaurants around back then. But soon other Japanese stores started opening there and that's how the Japanese neighborhood started at Clark and Division.*

Hiroshi: *It was a real rough neighborhood when we got there, and one of our buildings had a prostitute living in it — the police arrested me for prostitution and took me to the Chicago Avenue Police Station! My precinct captain, "Dinger" Maloney, heard about my arrest and came to the station. He talked to the officer who arrested me, "Hunchback" Kelly, and told him, "Don't ever bother that man again!" Maloney was a powerful man in the neighborhood and he got me released right away. He knew that there were a lot of votes in our buildings and he treated us well.*

Dorothy: *He brought us twenty-five pairs of nylon stockings one election year to give to the ladies. They were very scarce back then. Another year, he gave free breakfast "passes" to everyone that voted. That's the way it worked in those days.*

Hiroshi: *There were strip clubs and lots of taverns in the area back then. There even was gambling in the barber shop next door. Of course, the barber shop was just a front, with gambling going on in back. It was raided so many times! You would hear "bang-bang" and know it was being raided again.*

Rainbow Market, 218 W. North, 1949. Lincoln Park (Courtesy of the Japanese American Service Committee Legacy Center, Mary and James Numata Collection.)

99th and Halsted, ca. 1940. Washington Heights (Courtesy of the CTA.)

Lake Shore Drive Access, Foster and Sheridan, ca. 1945. Uptown (Courtesy of the CTA.)

Anna Marie DiBuono
Near South Side

I was born in 1938 and I still live on the same block where I was born, Vernon Park Place and Aberdeen. In 1946, we moved across the street. The boundaries of the neighborhood are Racine, Morgan, Harrison and Polk Streets — the neighborhood is called Little Italy.

It was a very united neighborhood. Different regions of Italy settled in different sections of Chicago, and most of the people from my father and mother's town settled in this section. It was called Accerra, and it is a province of Naples. They all settled in this section from Ryland to Loomis Street, from Harrison to Taylor Street. I think that it was the biggest or second biggest Italian section in the city. The Sicilians settled around Oak Street in the Cabrini area. The Tuscany and Venice regions settled around 24th and Oakley. The Neapolitans all settled around where I am located. It was a wonderful era, and it was wonderful growing up here because everybody was so close. There were strong bonds between families, and the majority of families all sponsored one another at baptism and confirmation. It seemed like all the families chose godparents who were close friends.

As for shopping, in the old days we went to Roosevelt Road. There was a variety store called the 12th Street Store that sold groceries, served root beer from the barrel, and they had hot waffle sandwiches with vanilla ice cream. Everybody still talks about the vanilla ice cream and hot waffles.

We had two movie theaters — the Villa Theater on south Halsted Street was a small theater where Greek Town is now — the Garden Theater was on Taylor off Racine. Everybody went to the Garden. It was a small show and it was loads of fun because the whole neighborhood would be there.

There weren't many Italian restaurants in those days. There was Granata's Restaurant on Taylor and Newberry, and Tommy Granata owned that restaurant. Mrs. Ferrara had Ferrara Bakery on Taylor and Halsted. We had all the stores on Halsted Street, including Conta di Savoy, which originally started out on Halsted near Taylor. In those days you had the baskets of snails and the snails would be walking all over. You had all the cheeses and the beautiful prosciutto and capicola and buffalo mozzarella. There weren't many restaurants in the old days, so people ate at home. There were a few other little restaurants near Halsted Street, but for me that would have been a little too far to walk.

My grandmother and grandfather had one of the first Italian bakeries in the city. Because people in the neighborhood didn't have much money they mixed their bread at home and would bring it to the bakery — and for a penny my grandmother would bake the bread for them. Everybody put their initials in the dough so they knew whose bread it was.

I can remember when my parents opened their restaurant — Tufano's. In those days, kids would take pizza from the bakery and walk a half a block to the restaurant. I remember all the celebrities who would come to the restaurant — Frank Sinatra, Tony Bennett, Dean Martin, Jerry Lewis, Jerry Vale, the Crosby Brothers, and the McGuire Sisters. People still talk about the crowds that formed outside to see the McGuire Sisters because they were in their prime. In the old days, it was the Italian restaurant for the Italian stars to visit.

We used to have the feasts on Morgan Street. The people from my parent's town would have a procession, and you would donate money by pinning it on the saint. If you made a nice donation, they would shoot a firecracker in front of your house. The bands would play happy music, and all the Italian men and women would be singing. It was just a different time. It was just a safe, happy time. Our parents wouldn't have to worry because they knew we were in the neighborhood.

We didn't get into trouble like kids do today. Our time was much happier. We didn't have things like children have today, but we were happy as larks. We played volleyball and the boys played basketball. It was such a happy time, and I cannot remember violence like there is today. We had everything at our fingertips. We had a tightly-knit neighborhood and we could go to all of the places we wanted to go. We always felt safe and we never locked our doors. We were never afraid, because nobody would harm us. You slept with your windows open. But, before you knew it, the University of Illinois came and the neighborhood went. We were fortunate because we lived on the right side of the street, but everything else went down.

Reading Time, Chicago Public Library, Austin Branch, ca. 1940. Austin (Courtesy of Special Collections and Preservation Division, Chicago Public Library.)

that applied at that time. By and large, there was a sense of community, of neighborhood, and a feeling that it was important to look out for each other. There was such a feeling of safety that when I was a little kid, I could stay out until late at night and my mother didn't have to worry about me. The condition of the neighborhood was such that all the kids were obliged to behave in a certain way so that if you saw another parent they were allowed to correct you if you did something wrong. It was just like having your own parent stop you if you misbehaved. In that way we sort of had a greater regard and an acknowledgment that this was a larger community family."

According to former Chicago Park District Superintendent Ed Kelly, there was also a strong sense of trust in his Cabrini neighborhood. "When I would go down to the Cipolla Grocery for milk or food, Mr. Cipolla would always write the cost on a brown paper bag. Then, I would go back on a Saturday and pay him. They trusted the families in those days. We would help each other and support each other, and that was going on through the whole neighborhood."

Marvin Aspen also remembers the closeness of his Albany Park neighborhood. "Most of the people in the neighborhood were first-generation Americans, and the second biggest group were immigrants. There were a few families who were fairly well off, but most were middle-to lower middle-class, although I'm sure I didn't know it at the time. You had no sense of lacking anything of substance, and there was a tremendous closeness. You knew everyone who lived there, and not only did you know them, you interacted with them. In those days, relationships were geographically-oriented to the neighborhood and within walking distance. You just knew, socialized and grew with everyone."

The lack of affluence during the era kept family life simple and focused on what was important — perseverance. According to Jim McDonough, "I think that life in the 1940s was a simple life and people learned to endure hardships. As a young kid, I never went hungry, but we certainly never had any luxuries. I think that you learned principles of life and an appreciation of the simpler things. I never felt any fear during those years, but I did learn 'street smarts.'" Mike Perlow would agree, " In our generation, most of us came from 'poverty,' although I hate to use the term because it really wasn't poverty as we think of that term today. Apartment living, especially for those of us who grew up on the West Side, was typical, and most of the kids came from first- and second-generation immigrant families. Coming through the Depression, jobs were valuable, although I never really felt that uncomfortable about money. I think that everyone had about the same standard of living through the 1940s."

In spite of all the challenges of the times, neighborhoods were special places to live in the 1940s. As Burt Sherman remembers, "I had a wonderful childhood, and even though I didn't realize it, we were going through very tumultuous times during the '40s and World War II. Life was so different than it is now. It was much simpler and less competitive. People were very nationalistic and families were very close. And the concept of neighborhood was very strong at that time. When I look back, I feel I would prefer it that way, but then I am looking at it from a biased viewpoint. There were inequities at the time that I wasn't aware of, and I feel bad about it now. But I had a good time during those years. I was fortunate enough to have wonderful parents, a good family, and we were close. It was a much more family-oriented time."

Finally, Jack Hogan recalls, "I think that camaraderie was the unifying force that kept the neighborhood so strong. The people got along so well, and we relied on that social interchange. I think that everybody believes that their neighborhood was the greatest neighborhood in Chicago, because we were all feeding off the same experiences. Everybody got along with everybody.

"Whenever I think back to what I enjoyed most about life, I look back on the '40s. In spite of the war and the struggles that came from it, it was the greatest time in the world."

Chicago Park District's "Save the Lawn" Contest, 8318 S. Rhodes, ca. 1940. Chatham (Courtesy of the Chicago Park District.)

The War Years in the Neighborhood

America entered World War II following the attack on Pearl Harbor by the Empire of Japan on December 7, 1941. For the next four and one-half years residents of Chicago, like the rest of the country, had to deal with many changes in their daily lives. Life on the home front required citizens to adapt to new necessities that included paper and scrap drives, food rationing, Civil Defense preparations and air raid drills. Chicagoans participated in each of these efforts with an unmatched patriotic fervor and learned how to unite to meet the challenges. In addition to new governmental requirements, citizens became involved in the war effort by creating Victory Gardens on empty lots and prairies, purchasing War Bonds to support their country and help finance the war, and hanging flags in their windows to recognize family members serving in the Armed Forces. The Great Depression was over and World War II had begun.

Pearl Harbor Day

War in Europe and Asia had already begun by 1939, but most Americans hoped to avoid becoming an armed participant in the growing war fronts. Then, on Sunday, December 7, 1941, in a surprise attack, the naval and air forces of the Empire of Japan hit the American military on the island of Oahu in Hawaii and decimated the US fleet in Pearl Harbor.

Opposite: *Mrs. Harry Riley and Children, ca. 1944.* Near North Side (Courtesy of the CTA.)

World War II had begun for America. Many Chicagoans first learned of the attack while tuned to their radios on that early Sunday afternoon.

After the attack on Pearl Harbor, West Ridge resident Sandy Zuckerman Pesmen had concerns about what that event really meant to herself, her family, and America. "I was ten years old in 1941 when the war started and I remember saying to my aunt, 'What is this? Is this scary?' And, she said, 'Oh, no. There's nothing to be afraid of. We had the other war in 1918 and your dad was in the reserve. We knitted socks and afghans for the soldiers and that's what we'll do now. There's nothing to be concerned about. We'll all have to help America.' She just dismissed it. That was calming until we got to school the next morning. Anna L. Cronin, our principal at Clinton, said over the loudspeaker, 'Do not be afraid children. We are going to have an air raid drill, and you will be safe. Now, we will all go single file into the hallway. This will be our air raid shelter and you will all sit down next to the wall and you must not make any noise. Now sit down in the corner and your teacher will be in front of you.' We were doing this as her voice was bravely coming over the loudspeaker system from the office. We sat down along the wall, and felt that we were perfectly safe. We felt we would be safe throughout the war, no matter what happened."

On the Northwest Side, Bill Jauss felt the same impact. "I was ten years old when Pearl Harbor happened, and my first thought was 'Gosh, I guess my dad has to go.' But my dad didn't go into service because he was too old and had two kids. He was very fortunate because he escaped both World War I and World War II, just by the accident of when he was born."

Marvin Aspen, who grew up in Albany Park, recalls the limited understanding he had about the war. "I had three uncles who were in military service, two in Europe and one in the Pacific. My mother had one of those flags with three stars in the window. I was seven years old when the war began, and, to be honest with you, the impact on my life during the war years was very little because I was at an age when I was just becoming aware of the larger world around me. The war itself was somewhere out there in Europe, Africa and Asia. At my young age I didn't understand the consequences and certainly not the meaning that it had when I became a little older."

Home Front Efforts: Rationing, Scrap Drives, and War Bonds

One of the responses to the war on the home front was an effort to save and conserve materials that were in limited supply, including scrap metals such as aluminum, tin and brass, and raw materials such as silk and rubber. The city's response was huge, and eventually residents recycled materials ranging from newspapers to kitchen grease. As it turned out, the scrap metal that was saved would have a limited impact on the building of armaments. It would, however, be valuable in the making of consumer goods and allowed critical materials such as "virgin" aluminum to be used for the construction of aircraft.

Although there was some uncertainty by citizens about how newspapers and kitchen grease were actually used for the war effort, the evidence is clear that both materials were used to help the military. In the case of kitchen grease, homemakers would take the waste cooking fats to their butchers and receive a cash payment for the cans of fat. The fat was then turned into glycerin that became dynamite. As for the newspapers, they were used by the military to make waterproof supply cartons. Rationing of meat, sugar, butter, eggs, shoes, nylons, tires, and gasoline was necessary to preserve the supplies and redirect them to the military during the war.

The rationing of daily necessities was difficult for many, and often seemed to be administered unfairly. West Ridge resident Sandy Zuckerman Pesmen recalls, "There was meat rationing, but rich people somehow had as much meat as they wanted because they had more red ration stamps than we did. I don't know how they got them, but they would go to butchers and get steak. We didn't have a whole lot of steak, but lamb was available, so we had a lot of lamb chops and fish. We managed okay, and nobody was ever thin or hungry in our house. I do remember the limited availability of silk stockings. My aunts were upset because they didn't have silk stockings

and they would paint lines on their legs with make-up that was available."

Dick Jaffee also remembers the effects of rationing in his South Shore neighborhood. "When rationing started, meat and gasoline became scarce. There were A, B, and C stamps that were used for rationing. My father needed to get around because of his business, so he got a C stamp for gas rationing. One of the things about shopping that I remember was that my mother would take me to the store because of the meat rationing. She would put me in line to get a pound of ground beef, the allocation for the week. I would stand there and wait until I got to the front of the line and use the coupons to get the meat for the week."

For children, the lack of bubble gum was a problem during the war. Lawndale resident Mel Pearl recalls, "I remember that we could never get any bubble gum. I do recall that once my father somehow got a box of bubble gum. We treated that gum like it was gold. I went out and gave my friends a piece of it and told them that they had to chew it very slowly because they would never see it again."

Jerry Petacque's father was a Chicago Police Captain who had to deal with people who "lost" their ration books. "In the '40s, after the war had started, a lot of people fictionalized that they had lost their ration books. They had to report the loss to the local police station. My father, who had a fantastic sense of humor, would roll up a piece of paper and put it to his ear to make believe that he had a loss of hearing. So, the word was you didn't go to Captain Petacque if you lost your ration books."

Children were particularly valuable in the effort to collect scrap metal and paper. From roaming the alleys to going door-to-door, their enthusiasm and competitive nature could yield large amounts of material. U.S. District Judge Charles Kocoras recalls, "We were always having paper drives at school. Because my father had a truck, somehow, we had access to more paper than anybody else. We would go around collecting it and bring the paper to school, and I distinctly remember that with my dad's help we always had the most paper. There was always some kind of recognition for that good deed." Gerald Bender was also actively involved in helping the war effort in the Lawndale neighborhood. " I remember picking up all the newspapers from peoples' back porches, dragging them to school, and looking through the pile to see if there were any comic books. We had these giant paper drives at Bryant School, and I can remember carrying paper off the back porch and almost dying because it was so heavy. I remember that we were also collecting old pots and pans.

Competition was also a factor in the selling of War Bonds. Grand Crossing resident Frank Rago recalls, "Every Friday we would buy War Stamps or War Bonds at school. We didn't have much money, but when

Pearl Harbor Day

Fr. Andrew Greeley

Pearl Harbor is as fresh in my mind as September 11, 2001. I remember it very clearly. I was sitting by my family's Philco radio listening to the Bears playing the Cardinals. I remember the Bears were losing when they interrupted the broadcast — the Japanese had bombed Pearl Harbor and the battleship Oklahoma had caught fire — then they switched it back to the football game and the Bears were winning. My reaction was one of astonishment. I knew where Pearl Harbor was because I was a geography freak. I thought that our world was in a state of collapse and that we were at war, but I had no idea what that would mean.

Dan Rostenkowski

I was playing ball in the alley alongside of our building that had a tavern on the corner. Somebody came out and said, "The Japs are attacking Pearl Harbor!" I didn't know what that meant. I went upstairs and told my mother, "The Japs are attacking Pearl Harbor!" "Where is Pearl Harbor?" she asked. It happened on a Sunday afternoon, and my dad came home that night. He was the alderman at that time, and I'll never forget that he had a white hat on. He said, "We'll kick their asses in three weeks! Those sons of bitches, we'll kick their asses in three weeks!"

Bob Kennedy

I was sitting in the upper deck right below the announcer's box on December 7, 1941, during the Cardinal/Bear game. Bob Elson saw me sitting there, opened the window and hollered down to me, just before the half, "Hey, Bob, the Japs just bombed Pearl Harbor!" I said to my buddy, "Where the heck is Pearl Harbor?" I had no idea where it was located. So, some of the fans around me said, "What did they say Bob?" "We're going to war," I said. Then the fans started leaving and it got real quiet in the ballpark. It was amazing because the players stopped on the field and looked around and didn't know what was going on. People were driving away. No horns were blowing. There was no noise, and we were all aware that we're going to war.

Estelle Gordon Baron

On December 7, 1941, I slept in. We were living with my folks in an apartment on Paxton, and I got up late. It must have been around 11:00 am when I woke up. I walked into the front of the apartment and my husband said to me, "Would you believe the Japs bombed Pearl Harbor?" I had never heard of Pearl Harbor. Hawaii seemed so far away and so foreign to us. We weren't really on top of the news the way we are now. We have breaking news now, and can see events as they are happening. So, we were dependent upon the radio and the news commentators, like Edward R. Morrow. We hung onto their words because it was current and what was happening.

Ray Meyer

I'll always remember when Pearl Harbor was attacked. We were living with my wife's parents because I was out of work. Her sister and brother-in-law lived upstairs in the two-flat. We were eating lunch that Sunday, and, all of a sudden, they came running down to tell us the news — Pearl Harbor was bombed. We were shocked, and we listened to the radio all day, and heard Roosevelt's speech the next day. The war affected all of our lives in so many ways. The military started calling up people to join the war effort. I was about 25 at that time, so I went down with "Moose" Krause, who was going to join the Marine Corps. I was planning to join the Marines with him, but at the recruiting station they asked me if I had ever had an operation, and I had had one on my knee. They told me good-bye. I got a letter from Dr. Danny Leventhal indicating that I was in perfect shape, but too much cartilage was taken out, so I never served in WW II.

Howard Rosen

I was listening to the Bear football game on the radio with my dad. They interrupted to say that Pearl Harbor had been bombed. The next morning I went to school and my 5th grade teacher, Mrs. Evelyn Carlson, brought a radio to class and we listened to the Roosevelt speech. I felt afraid about the war. I remember my father putting his arm around me and saying, "There's nothing to worry about. They don't know who they're messing with!"

Jack Hogan

Everybody thinks about where they were on December 7, 1941, but I don't remember where I was on that Sunday, although I do remember the next day very vividly. I remember hearing Roosevelt deliver his Declaration of War speech to Congress on the radio. My mother cried during the speech because she knew what was going to happen. I was totally oblivious to it. I was in high school, and it was too remote for me. I didn't understand that I would be in the service in a couple of years. My mother knew. Her brother had come from Ireland and served in World War I, and he was gassed and it ruined his life. So, she immediately saw the possible consequences.

Wayne Juhlan
Portage Park

I grew up at 5527 West Irving Park Road, right across the street from Portage Park. I was four to fourteen during the 1940s, and the biggest thing during this time was the war. Everything seemed to be geared around the war effort, like the rationing. There was no bubble gum! If you were a kid this was a tragedy! We chewed it once or twice, but we couldn't get it. The other big thing I remember were the stars that hung in the front windows of homes. If you had a son who was in the war you'd proudly hang this blue star, and we were very aware of them around the neighborhood. Every now and then we'd see a gold star, which meant someone had been killed.

My dad was handy with wood and he built a large display case that he placed at the southwest corner of Irving Park and Long Avenue. It had the names of all the people in the neighborhood who were serving and what branches of the military they belonged to. He was very proud of it. It was for the whole neighborhood. And us kids did things that made us feel like we were doing our part for the war effort too, even though we were only six or seven years old. I had a Victory Garden where I grew tomatoes and beans. It really made me feel like I was doing my part.

Of course, all the games we played would be war games. Instead of cops and robbers we were GIs. One of the things we did was take cans filled with saw dust and play war. We'd hurl these cans and when they'd hit the target sawdust would scatter like a hand grenade. We would wear plastic helmet liners so the kids would never get hurt, but everything had to be about the war. Even trading cards were war cards. They were just like baseball cards except they had actual battle scenes on them, and kids would collect them like baseball cards. Kids collected War Stamps, too. We would keep them in a little book and when you filled the entire thing you could turn it in for a War Bond. It was about $17.00 for a bond, and the stamps were about $.10 apiece, so it took us awhile to save. We were so proud while we were doing it, comparing notes with the other kids, and asking, "How many stamps do you have?" This stuff kept us kids involved, and made us feel like we made a real contribution.

The funny thing about being a kid, you know, is that your imagination runs away with you. For example, we never saw many commercial planes flying during the war. When an airplane did fly over we would be kind of nervous, even though we knew the war was thousands of miles away. For a minute, we didn't know. And listening to the newscasts at the time could be funny because kids take things literally and don't know the language. We'd hear about a battle between us and "guerrillas with small arms" and imagine a bunch of apes fighting with little hands.

American Legion Scrap Drive, Devon and Ashland, ca. 1942. Rogers Park
(Courtesy of the Rogers Park/West Ridge Historical Society.)

Waste Paper Drive, Sherman Park, 1945. New City (Courtesy of the Chicago Park District.)

CITIZENS OF CHICAGO!

This harmless piece of paper was dropped from an airplane. It COULD have been an enemy's bomb bringing death and destruction, or a propaganda leaflet spreading disunity and bewilderment among us. That it is neither, is due to the skill, courage, and sacrifice of our fighting men now invading Europe.

When the War Bond Warden in your block calls, during the Fifth War Loan Drive, welcome him in. Then dig into your savings and buy EXTRA war bonds! Your block has a quota. Watch the thermometer on your corner. Put it over the 100% mark! If you have bought war bonds since June 1st where you work or anywhere else, fill out the Red, White and Blue Credit Slip which the War Bond Warden will have. Then your block will receive full credit for all bonds you buy, wherever you buy them!

Chicago and Cook County War Finance Committee. 5th War Loan

Philip R. Clarke,

Chairman

National Printing & Pub. Co. 31 2150 Blue Island Avenue

Handbill Dropped From Airplane Over Chicago, ca. 1944.
(Private Collection.)

the teacher called your name you would say how many War Stamps you wanted. The stamps were $.10 apiece. One day my dad gave me a dollar and I felt so important because I would be able to buy ten War Stamps at school. The teacher called out my name and she asked me how many stamps I wanted. I called out ten, and it made me feel great until the girl behind me bought a $25 War Bond. That upset me for a while."

Victory Gardens

Many empty lots, prairies, and Park District grounds in Chicago's neighborhoods became sites for Victory Gardens. Millions of pounds of fresh vegetables made their way to Chicagoans' tables from these gardens, allowing farmers to focus their efforts on growing fresh foodstuffs for the men and women of the military serving around the world.

Fr. Gene Smith recalls the Victory Garden in his South Side neighborhood. "I remember Victory Gardens at a place called the 'cornfield' that was a vacant lot between Dorchester and Blackstone on 72nd Street. On one side of the street, people grew corn, and on the other side, people grew tomatoes and other vegetables. I remember coming home with a lot of tomatoes one day, and my mom asked me where I had got all of those. I told her that they were free and you just go to this vacant lot over there and help yourself. Well, my mom told me that the vegetables weren't free and belonged to somebody else."

Radio historian Chuck Schaden remembers the Victory Gardens in his Norridge neighborhood. "My family had a Victory Garden north of Montrose Avenue on some vacant land. It must have been farmland at one time. They probably were going to develop the area before the Depression because they had put in sidewalks, but the 1930s changed everything. I guess there was a source for water, but there weren't any buildings under construction there in the early '40s. People just took over that land to build Victory Gardens during the war."

On the South Side, Dick Jaffee remembers the Victory Gardens in his South Shore neighborhood. "We had a Victory Garden that was a plot of ground on a Jeffrey Avenue empty lot, on the east side of the street. We would go there and cultivate the land, plant seeds and harvest some of our own food. I guess that we got some corn and other vegetables from that garden during the war."

Civil Defense

Immediately after December 7, there was fear that the Japanese and Germans might launch an invasion of the United States. This led to the creation of a Civil Defense effort that would impact every American. In

Chicago neighborhoods, thousands of citizens volunteered to serve as Civil Defense Wardens whose responsibility it was to be certain that Chicagoans were prepared for any eventuality. Residents were expected to learn a variety of activities, including how to survive an air raid, make sure that apartment and house windows were light-tight, and how to spot and identify the various types of enemy aircraft.

Frank Rago was active in the home front efforts in his Grand Crossing neighborhood. "I remember being a Junior Air Raid Captain — I assisted an air raid warden. Those were intriguing and eerie times because we would have to go around at night and check that people had covered their windows during the mock air raids. We would have to report people who had light showing from their windows. And planes would drop bags of white flour. If they hit anywhere on your block, then your area was considered destroyed because they had the so-called 'block-buster' bomb at the time. People took it very seriously."

Ron Davis has clear memories of Civil Defense and air raid drills in West Rogers Park. "On every block was a bulletin board that listed all of those who were in the service, and those injured and killed. And there was a Civil Defense warden for each block. He would wear a helmet and armband that had a CD on it. We would have blackouts, and on certain nights we were told that everybody had to turn off all the lights in their home, unless they had light-proof shades. The blackout would usually last half an hour. All the lights were out in the whole neighborhood except for the gas tank near Kedzie and the canal. Nobody ever questioned how airplanes could fly to Chicago from Germany or Japan."

Rick Fizdale recalls how the father of his friend and neighbor, Steve Zucker, was an Air Raid Warden in the North Town neighborhood. "Sometimes during the war Steve and I would go with him when he made his rounds. Everybody had to pull their curtains and make sure that no light was getting out to the incoming planes. Steve's dad would walk through the alley and look into stairwells and basements. It seemed frightening that this could happen so close to where I lived and played. How absurd that we were looking for enemy soldiers in what was the center of my universe! At some level I understood, because the news was so global at that point. Every time, throughout the entire war and deep into my adolescence, if I heard an airplane overhead at night I assumed it meant that there might be bombs. On one hand, I knew it wasn't so, but on the other, I couldn't stop my pulse from beating faster. So, I was conditioned by the air raid warden, by the blackouts, by the radio, and by the movies I saw at the Nortown Theater to believe that war kills people."

Chicago Civil Defense Flyer, ca. 1944.
(Private Collection.)

Children's War Games

Patriotism came in many forms during the war years. For children, one way of demonstrating support for the war effort was through games that they played. At the extreme, these games led to harsh stereotyping of Japanese- and German-Americans. But to most children, these games were just another variation of the "good guys versus the bad guys."

Burt Sherman remembers the patriotic games that he used to play during his childhood on the Far North Side. "I was born in 1936 and was only five years old when the war began, so I remember those years from the perspective of a kid. The main thing that kids played was 'war.' That was very common. At that time, we were either playing the good guys or the bad guys. The bad guys, of course, were Hitler and Mussolini. We used to make fun of them, and we had songs about Hirohito and Tojo. We sang popular songs that poked fun at them. All the children knew and sang the songs. At the same time, we would imitate the American soldiers — the good guys against the bad guys. We also played cowboys and Indians, and it was the same kind of thing. The lines were clearly drawn between the good guys and the bad guys. I didn't have a sense of fear during the war years. Even though we saw the newsreels, it probably didn't sink in the way it should have. As far as we were concerned, we were far enough away from the war. When you were a kid, the only thing that touched you was when you lost a relative."

Window Flags

"Son in Service" flags were first hung in windows to commemorate those Americans serving in World War I. The tradition continued during World War II, when each family who had a member in active service was entitled to hang a white flag with a blue star in their window. The blue star would be replaced with a gold star if the service member was killed. Often companies or organizations would fly multi-star flags in factories or meeting halls to support large groups of service people.

Author Fr. Andrew Greeley remembers the impact of the flags in his Austin neighborhood. "When the war began, my father was in his middle-40s, so there was no chance of him going into the service. I had cousins on my mother's side who did go into the service. I remember seeing the service stars in people's windows, including the blue stars and the gold stars. There were twenty-two young people from the parish who were killed during the war, so our parish flag had hundreds of blue stars and twenty-two gold ones. I remember being an acolyte at the funeral mass for one of the deceased."

The issues on the Southwest Side were the same for Tom Doyle.

"My father was about 35, so he missed serving in the military. But a lot of our neighbors served during the war, and some got killed. So, they would put flags in the front windows with gold stars on them. I also remember the memorial signs at the end of every block with the lists of neighborhood people who served in the military. Our neighbors were close, and we knew each other well."

For Belmont Cragin resident Chuck Chapman, patriotism had many meanings. "Some of the guys in my neighborhood were killed, so I remember seeing the gold stars in the windows. There were also a lot of blue stars, for those who were in the service. There was an optimistic view of everything at that time, and a high level of patriotism and American spirit. There was the strong belief that if we just put our minds to it we could do anything."

USO Shows

Chicagoans from every neighborhood served in the military. Many of those who couldn't serve supported the armed forces by participating in the USO (United Service Organizations). When servicemen could get a furlough to visit Chicago, or be in the city on layovers as troop trains came through, they would visit the USO Servicemen's Centers. The Chicago centers were very successful in providing the servicemen with a wide range of entertainment and recreational activities throughout the war.

Morgan Murphy, Jr. remembers gathering pies and cakes in his Southwest Side neighborhood that were brought to the USO. "Daniel Flaherty was head of the Chicago Park District at the time, and with that designation he became head of the USO. My job was to use my Red Flyer wagon and pick up all the pies and cakes in the neighborhood and take them to Mr. Flaherty's house. He would put them in his car and take them downtown. The USO Servicemen's Center at Union Station had 5,000 model planes hanging from the ceiling. I used to wish that Mr. Flaherty would take me with him so I could see them, but I was too young to go, although I always begged my parents to let me go with him."

Dan Rostenkowski's Northwest Side neighborhood put forth a similar effort. "I remember my father, who was the Alderman, and Ed Kelly, who was then the mayor of Chicago, going into the park across the street and taking things my mother had baked. The ward headquarters was at our house, and the precinct captains would bring in bread, biscuits and bakery goods to take down to the Servicemen's Center. Ed Kelly had one of the best Servicemen's Center in the world. Whenever a kid came through Chicago, and nearly every train came through here, they would go to that Servicemen's Center. They were treated like royalty there."

"Save Your Tires" Display Panel, ca. 1944. Loop (Courtesy of the CTA.)

School Children's Victory Garden, Jackson Park, ca. 1945. Woodlawn (Courtesy of the Chicago Park District.)

Victory Garden, 32nd and Keeler, 1942. South Lawndale (Courtesy of Special Collections and Preservation Division, Chicago Public Library.)

Office of Civilian Defense Drill, ca. 1942. Near West Side (Courtesy of Special Collections and Preservation Division, Chicago Public Library.)

Division 4 Christmas Party, 1942. Near West Side (Courtesy of Special Collections and Preservation Division, Chicago Public Library.)

Working for the War Effort

The demand for workers during the war opened up new opportunities for many neighborhood residents. For those who suffered through the Depression without employment, this was a welcome opportunity. As factories switched to the production of defense materiel in Chicago, women, teenagers, and even children could find a wide variety of work if they wanted it.

Richard Lukin of Kenwood remembers working for the war effort at a very early age. "During the war, a friend and I had a sub-sub-contract doing defense work. Here we were in grammar school, twelve- or thirteen-year-old kids, doing steel production and defense work. There was nobody else to do these things. Somebody had a defense contract and needed some hot bodies to do these simple mechanical things. So we set up a workshop in a friend's basement with vices, milling machines and drill presses. We threaded bolts — cases and cases and cases of bolts."

Bill Phelan had a job selling newspapers in the Englwood neighborhood during the war. "I worked at a newspaper stand at the railroad station at 63rd and Wallace. I worked there for long hours, from 4 o'clock in the afternoon until all the trains were out of there at midnight. I was still in school, so I was a pretty tired young man on some of those days. I remember one time when a troop train came through. For some reason, there must have been a problem down the line. They stopped the train at 63rd and Wallace, and there must have been 1,000 troops on that train! They let them off the train and they swarmed into the depot and bought out almost everything there — all the candy, cigarettes, and magazines. They cleaned us out!"

Margaret Short Lamb grew up in a little coal-mining town in Southern Illinois, but after graduating from high school in June 1942, she came to Chicago to work in a defense plant. Like many women of the time, she relished her "Rosie the Riveter" role. "My first job was at Harry Davies Plastic Factory on the North Side, where I learned how to operate drill presses, tapping machines and lathes. I was only making $.42 an hour without any benefits, so I left that company and went to work at the big Chrysler plant on South Cicero Avenue around 79th Street. I got a job there working on a lathe and cutting steel off of rocker arms that went into engines for airplanes. It was a huge, noisy place, and in the summertime it was a really hot place to work. In fact, some people would faint. They even had to bring ambulances to the plant. We were supposed to wear a safety hat while we worked, but one girl who had a pompadour wouldn't wear the hat. She got her hair caught in a machine and it scalped her. I worked nine hours a day on the swing shift, from late in the afternoon to 1:30 a.m., six days a week, even on holidays. I earned about $53 a week and thought that I was rich! So, I started sending money to my parents because my father had been disabled in the coal mines. While I was working in the plants, I lived on the North Side near 2800 N. Halsted with my sister's family. It was a long ride back and forth to the plant and sometimes I would have to take a couple buses and the "L" to get there and back home. Since I came from a small town, it was wonderful to live in the big city of Chicago."

Getting News About the War

Most Chicagoans got their news about the war from listening to the radio, watching newsreels at the movie theaters, or reading one of Chicago's several daily newspapers. War-related stories dominated both the airwaves and newsprint, but many residents grew to depend on the comforting voices of their favorite radio newsmen for their information.

Fr. Andrew Greeley recalls hearing famous broadcasters of the day. "I remember Gabriel Heatter saying, 'There's bad news tonight. There's bad news tonight.' And, then occasionally, as time wore on, he would say, 'There's good news tonight.' I remember H. V. Kaltenborn, Edward R. Murrow, Eric Sevareid and Elmer Davis. I also remember John Charles Daly, who went on to be one of the moderators on "What's My Line." Then, there was Charles Collingwood, reporting from London when Edward Murrow wasn't there. The 5:30 p.m. radio news somehow seemed more vibrant than the television news does today, perhaps because so much was left to your imagination. I remember Ed Murrow saying, 'This is London,' with all the portent of doom. Radio was very powerful because you were envisioning what they were talking about. And my memories about the war years are very powerful. I thought that our world was in a state of collapse and I had no idea what that would mean."

Charles Kocoras' father would listen to the war news on the radio in their Englewood home. "My father would listen religiously to the evening news to learn about the progress of the war. The name Gabriel Heatter sticks in my mind, and my father would always listen to him. My father kept up with the events, and Greece, his home country, was very much a participant and was actually subjugated by the Germans. First, the Italians controlled Greece, and then, because they weren't happy with the Italians, the Germans came in and basically took over. We had family back there during the war. Of course, I do remember an enormous sense of relief when the war was over and that exultation was present in all of Chicago."

Fr. Gene Smith was also an avid radio listener. "We listened to radio to hear news about the war. The radio was on the kitchen table and it was

Parade Float, 1942. Woodlawn (Courtesy of Special Collections and Preservation Division, Chicago Public Library.)

Blood Donor Honor Roll, Mundelein College, 1944. Rogers Park (Courtesy of the Rogers Park/West Ridge Historical Society.)

the center of our life while we were studying, ironing, eating or having family discussions."

Mel Pearl relied on the daily newspapers for the latest on the war. "Every day there was a headline about another battle in Europe or the Pacific. As the war came to an end, my first reaction as a kid was that I guess we will never have newspapers again because all I ever saw in the newspaper were war stories. I thought that there would be nothing else to report."

Serving in the War

Over 12 million Americans served in the military during World War II. They all had their own stories of where they were trained, stationed, and served in the states or overseas. For those serving in the country, much of their time was spent moving from camp to camp, occupied by mundane, often monotonous work. For those in combat, the goal was survival, and hopefully a return home to life in a safer world.

After the attack on Pearl Harbor, former Illinois Supreme Court Justice Seymour Simon closed his office in the US Department of Justice and was soon in the Navy. "I went to San Diego for training and shipped off to Pearl Harbor. I spent a year and a half at Pearl Harbor, which wasn't very difficult duty and I ended up becoming the assistant to the Flag Lieutenant, Commander, Service Force, Pacific Fleet. That was a good assignment. Then, I was assigned to the staff of the commander of a force that was organized to go forward with the fleet as they started across the central Pacific. The long-developed plan to fight a war against Japan called for having all the services on ships — flotillas — which they called 'the train.' The train would move forward with the fleet. But when Pearl Harbor happened they couldn't do it, because they no longer had control of the air. They had these slow moving supply ships and the Japanese would have bombed the hell out of them.

"So, they built these big naval bases in the South Pacific instead. Ironically, by the time most of them were built they were obsolete, because the fleet was operating 1,000 miles ahead. So, they decided in the Central Pacific they'd go back to the 'train' that would go with the fleet. When US forces took the Gilbert Islands they discovered that there were no Japanese aircraft closer than Saipan or Guam. So, they decided to leave the whole fleet of big carriers, cruisers and maybe one battleship out there. Overnight, we became the biggest supply base in the Pacific fleet. I was there until May 1945, when we went to Eniwetok and Ulithi, and the Pacific fleet mounted the invasion of the Philippines. It was a sight that I will never forget. We would stand on the deck of the ship and all you saw

was steel mass for twenty miles around you. What a sight that was, maybe the greatest collection of naval power ever assembled anywhere."

The Army put West Sider Phil Holdman's musical talent to work when he enlisted on April 8, 1942. "I went from Camp Blanding to Camp Stewart, Georgia, which was a real hellhole with swamps. They put me in a band because I was a drummer, and I made a lot of money. They used to pay me for dance jobs and for playing at the Officer's Club. My friend Miltie, who was in the South Pacific, got upset at me because I complained that I hated Camp Stewart because they didn't even have ketchup on the table, and he was reading my letter from a foxhole in the Pacific! I never went overseas because I was in the band. I used to play for the troops. One time I played on a program called "Parade Rest," which we did every Sunday night, outdoors, in a big band shell. There would be 10,000 troops on the hills, and they would listen to our band. We had guest stars like Bob Hope and Harpo Marx, and I even participated in skits with Harpo and Jackie Leonard. I was in the Army for four years, and I played in a band the entire time. I got out in December of 1945."

Lakeview resident James Thommes served in both Alaska and Europe during the war. "I got drafted in February 1942, and went into mechanics school in the Air Force. I was sent to the Aleutian Islands and got on a crew that was involved in bombing Kiska and Attu, where the Japanese were located. When I finished that tour, I came back to the States and went to pilot school but I 'washed out' like most of the other guys. Then, I was sent to gunnery school and got on a B-24 heavy bomber. I took overseas training in Mountain Home, Idaho, and was sent to Italy. While I was there, I was on fifty bombing missions that included Germany, Yugoslavia and Romania. As a result, I received three Air Medals and a Distinguished Flying Cross. I was lucky because I did not sustain any serious injuries, although on one mission my plane came back with 147 holes in it! When I finished my 50th mission, the Air Force sent me back to the States as a war casualty. At that time, the war in Europe had just ended. I went to Ft. Sheridan on a 30 day furlough, but then they said that anybody with over 85 points could get released. Since I had accumulated 120 points and fought on two fronts, I certainly didn't want to end up in the South Pacific or in Japan. So, I figured that it was time to end my service."

Jack Hogan left his Auburn/Gresham neighborhood for Europe after going into the military in June 1943. "I served with the 755th Field Artillery Battalion. We saw combat from October right up to May 1945, and our big distinction was that we were at Bastogne at the Battle of the Bulge. Our unit was with the 101st Airborne and we were part of the

Lincoln Park Servicemen's Center, 1942. Lincoln Park (Courtesy of the Chicago Park District.)

Lincoln Park Servicemen's Center, 1942. Lincoln Park (Courtesy of the Chicago Park District.)

Display Window, Chicago Public Library, Hild Branch, ca. 1944. Lincoln Square (Courtesy of Special Collections and Preservation Division, Chicago Public Library.)

Recruiting Center, 1942. South Lawndale (Courtesy of Special Collections and Preservation Division, Chicago Public Library.)

Book Drive for Servicemen, Chicago Public Library, South Shore Branch, 1942. South Shore (Courtesy of Special Collections and Preservation Division, Chicago Public Library.)

Chiyo Omachi
Humboldt Park

I was born on Terminal Island in California. It's a man-made island in Los Angeles harbor and my father was a ship builder there. Terminal Island was the first place that the government evacuated all Japanese-Americans after the bombing of Pearl Harbor. Well, they didn't exactly evacuate it. They told us to get off in forty-eight hours! Can you imagine? And the night before we were to leave the FBI came and took all the men off the island. So, the island was filled with hundreds of women and little kids and no one to help them. We had to get rid of everything, absolutely everything, from our refrigerator to our car. My mother had beautiful things from Japan, which we had to give away. We even gave away our pet cat. It was terrible.

We were moved to an old, abandoned school and lived there while the government built the internment camps. The men and boys stayed in a large gymnasium and the women and girls were in these little classrooms. In May of 1942, there were signs posted that said all Japanese were to go down to the train station with two bags each. That was all we could take. All we knew was that we would be transported to another location, we didn't know where. Soon, we were moved to the first of the camps to be completed in Poston, Arizona.

Poston was one of ten internment camps built, and eventually it was expanded with the additions of Poston II and III. Conditions were bad. People got typhoid and died. We didn't have good medical care, or any medical care really. It was terrible, and it was so barren. We just marched into the camp quietly. We were Americans, and we kept shouting this, "We are Americans!" People wore patriotic badges and things, but that didn't make any difference.

Eventually, a time came when we could leave camp and go to school. I had to fill out a lot of paperwork and get the approval of the local police, the FBI, the Army, the Eastern Command —all sorts of people! I did this and went on to finish high school in Pennsylvania, where my uncle was living. I began college there, but came to Chicago to finish. I graduated from Roosevelt University in 1948. I came to Chicago because this is where my parents came after they were released. At that time, even after the war, Japanese-Americans still weren't allowed to return to California. It wasn't until a few years later that the okay was given.

We lived on Whipple Avenue on the West Side, near the Lake Street "L". I started working for the Japanese Resettlement Committee on LaSalle Street, which was helping to find jobs and homes for those coming out of the camps and starting a new life in Chicago.

Recruiting Center, 1942. South Lawndale   (Courtesy of Special Collections and Preservation Division, Chicago Public Library.)

Bill Gleason
Greater Grand Crossing

On November 16, 1944, which was my birthday, we went into attack for the first time. I was the second of two scouts. We were up in the attic of this French farmhouse overlooking a field — and I had never read The Red Badge of Courage.

The 442nd Regimental Combat Team was in our area, most of them Japanese-Americans from Hawaii, and many with parents who were in the Internment Camps. It was the most vicious outfit in the United States Army and they just frightened the Germans to death. This short sergeant, about 5'6", is standing there listening to our preparation. He tugs on my jacket and pulls me over. "Are you sons of bitches going to go across that field at 9 o'clock in the morning? Is that what I heard?" "That seems to be right," I said. "They'll shoot the crap out of you!" So I asked him, "What would you guys do?" "Well," he said, "we'd go over there at night and kill them in their foxholes."

Oh, God, was he right! That day, the two of us scouts got out there and made a very interesting discovery — they didn't fire on us. They let us proceed because they wanted all of the other guys too. So, I'm on one side of this field, and this town that we were supposed to take is about 3/4 of a mile away. The first scout is on the other side. I'm under this sapling, and it was mid-November, so there were dead buds on the tree. And I suddenly became aware that somebody was shooting these buds off the tree over my head.

"Holy Christ," I thought, "how am I going to shoot back at this son of a bitch even if I can find him?" You see, I made a discovery when I was about 12 or 13 years old, when I began playing kissing games. I realized then that I was the only person who could not wink his or her left eye. So, now I'm in the Infantry, and I can't wink my left eye. They tried to turn me into a left-handed rifleman but that didn't work. We would go down to the firing range, luckily I had a number of sympathetic guys who were down in the pits, and I would miss the target. Not only miss the bulls-eye, but miss the whole target! But they'd ring up that I had hit something, so I got to be a rifleman.

Well, after awhile I decided that I would go over to where the first runner was located. We were talking back and forth across the field and then some of the guys from our platoon came up. There was a clearing to cross, and our lieutenant was there. He was a big guy, he played football at Minnesota, and was the biggest man on the field. He had a lot of courage, too, because he was such a big target. So, he was up, and with about five other guys, two scouts joined them.

Oh, the other thing, I was wearing a white patch that I had cut from something and was using it over my useless left eye. One of the guys came to me and said, "Gleason, what in the hell are you doing with that white patch." So, I explained to him, and he replied, "Oh, my God, you're in combat and you can't fire. You better take that thing off because some Kraut is going to shoot you right in that eye." I cut a new patch from my gray gas mask container, and I used it instead.

As we were crossing this clearing, there was a big guy from North Carolina with us, a real rascal whose name was John L. Wilson. He saw too many WW I movies. So, he gets out in this clearing and he wheels around to fire and he is hit in his big thigh. He needed a medic, and the first scout said, "I'll go find him." So, I'm working on this big ass, and the first scout forgot one of the basic rules — babies creep and snakes crawl. Well, he was creeping and he got one right in his ass. So, now I've got these two guys. I go over to the first scout, and they're firing merrily at him. I said, "Just stay down!" So, I'm sort of on my side and ministering to him. I opened his pack of sulfa — and it was empty! After I cursed for about a minute and a half, I decided to give him my sulfa. He was so considerate that he said, "What are you going to do if you get hit?" I said, "Look, we're going to worry about that later." So, I poured the sulfa in and the medic, who was a tremendously brave guy, came to pull him off the field. I went back, and we got across the clearing and we went on from there.

After these first two days, we finally were taken off the line and were drinking great quantities of wine. The whole thing seemed so romantic. I realized quickly that I was a "war-lover." I just enjoyed the whole damn thing. While we were resting there I heard, "Gleason, you've got to fall out." "What the hell is this for?" I asked. "You're going to get a medal. You've got to be out there now." It was our captain calling. Joe Bell from Pittsburgh, Kansas, said, "If you're not out there, Captain Bell will get your ass." So, we scrambled out on a slope and there was Major Yao, who was second in command of the battalion. He was a guy who knew how to treat the men. I remember one time when we were coming down a road and Yao was there passing out apples to the men. He was in charge of this decoration. So, I figured, I'll probably get the Bronze Star.

But, it's funny, because the Silver Star kind of appealed to me. When I came up the first time, me and this other guy had been on a special assignment on a little trail in the Voge Mountains. This valley that *we had to cross was at the foot of the mountain. It was a narrow pass, and a GI came by and said, "Do not sit on the ledge. Do not sit down. Just go where you were going, and you'll soon see what I mean." Well, we soon learned what he meant, because two guys sat down on this little ledge, and one sat on a mine and killed them both. In other words, it was covered with mines — and we knew that war was earnest and real. Later, guys were talking about decorations, and some said that they didn't want any medals. I'm listening to this, and I figured that as long as I was over there, I might as well get a decoration. I thought that a Silver Star would be nice because it was for gallantry in action. I loved that. So, I said to myself, "I'll get the Silver Star."*

So, I walked up to the major, and it was so simplistic. He thrust this little thing into my hand and he gave me a little ribbon. I said, "What is this?" He said, "How the hell do I know what it is?" So, I opened it, and it was the Silver Star. And, it went on from there.

Thank God, we didn't have many days like that. We only had one other day like that first day. If we had more we would never have had any reunions — there would have been nobody left. We wound up in Austria on V-E Day, then they moved us back into France. We were in a tent camp near Rheims being staged for the Pacific until little old Harry dropped the bomb. I was discharged by September 1945, and then I was back in the neighborhood.

group that was surrounded. When I reflect on it now, I didn't think that I would be here today. We knew that we were encircled and were being attacked on an almost hourly basis, but our friend, General Patton, broke through and we survived. That was a very, very trying time. We stayed in combat until the American soldiers broke through and across the Elbe River. Some of our unit did meet some Russian soldiers up near the Elbe River."

When John W. Creighton graduated from Tilden High School in 1943 he went directly into the Army. "I went through basic at Camp Wallace, Texas, and from there we went to New York City and on a boat to England. We were in England for a while as part of the 480th Anti-Aircraft Division, and we were using 40 mm guns to shoot down Nazi planes. Then, on June 9, 1944, three days after D-Day, we landed at Normandy Beach. In Europe, we went in as a strafing unit and went across the Cherbourg Peninsula and all the way up the French coast until we finally got to Paris, just after it was liberated. The French gave us wine and liquor and were so happy to see us. I came home in January of 1946."

Ed McElroy was an accomplished athlete throughout high school. He was a White Sox bullpen catcher in 1943 until he entered the service. "I went from the Sox to the Army Air Corps in 1944. I enlisted in the Air Corps when I was just eighteen years old. First, I went up to Ft. Sheridan. They kept me there six weeks playing basketball. Then, I went down to Shepard Field in Texas, where I had basic training. I played on the baseball team there until I hurt my knee and I couldn't play ball. So, they shipped me out to Air Corps Intelligence at Chanute Field in Rantoul, Illinois, near Champaign. Next, I went to B-29 school in Patterson, New Jersey, and they kept me there until they sent me to Randolph Field, where I was a catcher on the baseball all-star team."

Playboy Magazine founder Hugh Hefner was also transferred multiple times during the war. "I enlisted in the Army in early 1944, right after graduation from Steinmetz High School. I was in service from the spring of 1944 until the spring of 1946. I went in when I was just turning eighteen, and I did basic training at Camp Hood in Texas. I went to a couple of other camps and ended up at Camp Meade in Maryland, between Baltimore and Washington, DC. I was going to be shipped overseas to the European Theater, but I had done some typing, so I was stationed in the Replacement Depot Headquarters at Camp Meade. When the war in Europe ended, I was shipped to the West Coast and had a similar job at Camp Adair in Oregon, just outside Eugene. Later, I wound up at Camp Pickett in Virginia and finally went back to Camp Meade for discharge."

Many Chicagoans have memories of family members serving in the military. West Ridge resident Ron Davis recalls, "I had a cousin who was

Alice Fink
Hyde Park

I was born in Berlin, Germany, but I had a side trip before I came to America. You see, Hitler came to power in Germany in 1933. With him came new restrictions on Jewish people every few months, little by little. I was still able to go to school until September 15, 1935, the day the Nuremberg Laws were passed, which among other things, meant I could not go to public school. These kind of things went on and on. You could only go shopping certain hours. Then you couldn't go to the theater. Then you couldn't go to the park and sit on the benches. When the Nazis went into Poland it was one big sweep. We, on the other hand, went through this process step by step.

My father, like many others, thought Hitler would not last. And like many of his friends who were soldiers in World War I, thought nothing would happen to them. These men would say, "I have the Iron Cross, they are never going to touch me." Unfortunately, a lot of people felt this way.

By 1938, everybody was trying to get out, but it was very difficult to leave. A cousin of mine in England made arrangements for me to go to nursing school there before the war started, and luckily I got my papers to leave. I was fortunate to get there, because the rest of my family did not get out. In the early 1940s, when the deportations began, many in my family were picked-up. My father, mother, and brother all died in the camps. You see, many of the things that happened during that time, we did not know about until much later.

So, I lived in England during the war. I did my training and then I worked. Sometime around 1943 the Jewish organizations in England formed a group to help Holocaust victims at the end of the war. In May of 1945 the first relief teams were able to begin their work. I did not go until September of 1946.

My husband, John, had been sent to Aushwitz, and a number of other places, and he ended up in Bergen-Belsen. That's where he was liberated from on May 15, 1945. When I returned to Germany in 1946 with the Jewish Relief Unit, I was sent to the Displaced Persons Camp at Bergen-Belsen, and that's where we met. We got married there in 1948. John did not want to stay in Germany. Many DPs went back to the towns and places they lived before, but some went back and found that there was nothing left to return to. A great many people just wanted to leave, one way or another. I was ready to go back to England, but my husband did not want to do that. I had distant relatives living in Chicago who would give us the papers needed to come here. We also applied to Australia and South Africa, but those did not come through. So this is what we did, we came to Chicago, and we came with nothing. Because we had a private affidavit, we were not eligible for assistance, so we started from scratch. We literally had to buy one piece of dinnerware at a time, having only two cups on the table, because that is all we could afford. Not like it is today.

My relatives lived in Hyde Park, and many of the German-Jews who had come before and after the war settled in that area. All we got was a small basement apartment — you just could not find a place to live in those days. It was pretty awful. There were thirteen different families living in the basement of that building. We had one small room, the smallest you could think of, and a bathroom down the hall that we all shared. My daughter was born four weeks after we arrived. It was very difficult. John would have a very long day at work and a bus ride, and in such a small room if the baby cries you do not get much sleep. We really did not do too much back then. We had enough to do just to make it day by day.

It was not easy. We did know a couple who had come to America a few months earlier, and there were other people we knew. But Americans, and even some Jewish people, questioned our past — Why did you survive? How come you did and everybody else didn't? You must have done something crooked. You did not necessarily get a friendly reception.

The Holocaust was not a subject that was talked about. It was something that you wanted to leave behind. Immigrants today get a lot of support and assistance. We were looked at very differently, especially if you were German. People just didn't realize that there were German-Jews who survived. The picture seemed to be that nobody was left. So if you somehow managed to survive people would ask, "How come?" It was very difficult.

After moving to Andersonville and living there for a few years we moved to Rogers Park in 1958. In those days this was a Jewish neighborhood (the Devon Avenue area). We moved here because we wanted our kids to go to Hebrew school and live in a nice neighborhood.

Anti-Defamation League Advertisement, ca. 1949. Loop (Courtesy of the Jewish United Fund.)

Flag Dedication Ceremony, 1942. Uptown Photograph by Jack Delano. (Library of Congress)

Sheila Morris Williams
Irving Park

World War II started when I was six years old. I remember my parents sitting hunched over a radio listening to reports of the attack on Pearl Harbor and worrying out loud. I felt the fear in their voices, even though I didn't understand what was happening.

Soon, children were involved in the war effort in our own little ways. We saved tin foil, rolling it into giant balls and competed for who had the biggest one. We saved newspapers and string, and pulled a red wagon around the neighborhood asking people for their donations of paper. We also helped by covering all the windows of the house in dark, heavy blankets to keep all light from shining through during the blackouts. Every block had an air raid warden who checked each house. If any light shone through, they would be fined.

Entire families worked in Victory Gardens. We grew seasonal foods we could eat right away, and canned foods for later in the winter. Mom stretched every dollar during the war by making her own bread and rolls twice a week and by canning the tomatoes she bought from the fruit man, who came through the alley with his horse and cart. We lived on ground meat and vegetables. I hated ground meat after the war.

When President Roosevelt died, I again sensed the profound sadness of the adults and remember sitting on the curb in front of my house, crying for our loss.

The end of the war is still clear in my memory — everyone outside cheering and dancing in the street, and throwing toilet paper over all the trees. We kids stayed up very late those nights. We all talked to everyone, even people we were not friends with.

The boy next door, who was about eighteen, joined the army and was gone for the entire war. I worried so much about him. I had a crush on him. When he came home, walking down the shady street in his uniform, I ran to meet him and jumped into his arms with joy and cried with relief.

My Aunt Pat was my hero of the war. Even though she was 40 years old when the war broke out, she joined the newly formed WAVES, for women in the service. She served in Hawaii and sent me a grass skirt and a funny top with two gigantic flowers on it. I thought it was great. But the most special thing of all was the WAVES navy blue trench coat that she let me have after the war was over. It was huge on me, but I wrapped it around me a couple of times and I became "Wonder Woman." It wrapped me in courage.

killed in the Pacific, and everyone had relatives who served in the war. My uncle, who was a doctor and almost 40 years old, had to go in as a Captain. He was in the South Pacific and served in the battles at Leyte and Guadalcanal — he operated on both American and Japanese soldiers. I remember that he sent my mother a bracelet made from a piece of a Japanese Zero airplane. He even put her name on it." Lawndale resident Mike Perlow's father also served in the Pacific Theater. "I remember missing my father, and it was tough on my mother. My father was overseas for a couple of years, so he wasn't around. He was in the South Pacific on Guam, Eniwetok, the Philippines, the Marshall Islands, and Japan. He didn't get injured during the war, but he was right there — because he was a surgeon and he was going into battle with them. My father, his brothers and cousins, and one of my uncles, many of whom were overage, all enlisted in the service. They couldn't get in there fast enough. I think that was very typical and they were very patriotic."

Many young men entered the service just as the war was ending. For them, life in the military meant helping the transition to a post-war world. David Cerda went into the military after graduating from high school in June 1945. "I volunteered when I was seventeen, right around the time that Germany surrendered. They were going to take me right after graduation, and soon we were on the train to Great Lakes. They were training us to go to Japan. We were learning how to identify Japanese airplanes and ships, but during boot camp they announced that the war was over. I knew how to type, so they decided to send me out to California and I spent time typing discharge papers. I would add up the points to see how fast they could get discharged. I was in the military from June 1945 to August 22, 1946. I got one check for $52.20 and that was my unemployment check."

George Mitsos' service in the Army also occurred toward the end of the war. "After I graduated from Amundsen High School, we went on vacation in northern Wisconsin and I registered for the draft up there. When I came back all my friends were getting drafted, but I wasn't called. So, I went to the draft board on Montrose at Damen and asked why I hadn't been called. A lady, who was a customer of my father, told me that since my father had lost one son already, she was delaying it. I told her I wanted to go, so they drafted me. I went up to Camp McCoy, Wisconsin, and helped to discharge the veterans who were returning home. After the first month, I only had one point — I figured that I would have to be in the Army for twelve years before I would be discharged! From there, I ended up coming to Ft. Sheridan, and I worked discharge there, too. I got out December 26, 1946. I had one year, twenty-six days of service."

As servicemen returned from the war, many found that cultural changes had taken place while they were away. Writer Jack Mabley returned to Chicago in the fall of 1945. "I walked into the offices of the *Chicago Daily News* to get my old job back and their attitude was, 'Oh, you've been away?' I had been replaced at the paper by a woman, which was unique at the time because before the war women had been confined to the society and cooking sections of the paper. There were only one or two women reporters on the news side then. But when we came back, they were holding most of the positions for us. There was a lot of shuffling, and I hoped to get my old job back. I had been getting $42.50 a week when I left, and four years later when I came back they offered me $65, although they were paying the women $75 a week. I leaned on my bosses and I managed to get $75 a week and my old chair. After the war, the city was really upbeat. The guys who came back were so glad to be alive and to be home. While I was overseas, I told myself that if I ever got home I was never going to leave again. There was a pretty good feeling in the air. The war had cured the Depression and there was a rush for college enrollment under the GI Bill, since the government picked up most of the cost. There were jobs and spirits were high because we'd survived that damn war. It was good times and they got better."

As African-American servicemen returned home, there was hope that the small movement towards integration in the military would be rewarded in American society. Grand Boulevard resident Truman Gibson recalls, "Everything changed after the war. You see, when the war began and the draft was instituted, southerners protested that blacks would be included in the draft at all. The Army had a big problem. We went from strict segregation to integration. President Truman was the one who integrated the military. In fact, I was on two presidential commissions and helped draft the desegregation order."

For many African-Americans, however, change did not come fast enough on Chicago's South Side. Dempsey Travis recalls, "The neighborhood didn't change at all as a result of the black soldiers coming back from World War II. The neighborhoods were just like the Army — Jim Crow. If I listened to my father — he had expectations that things were going to get better because we had served in the war. He and my uncles would say, 'You fought in the war and now you are entitled to more things.' But, if it was an entitlement, then the government was never forthcoming. That was something in my father's and my uncles' heads, but not in my head. The neighborhood didn't change a great deal after the war because there were restrictive covenants in 1948 and title policies

Remembering the End of the War

Howard Rosen

I remember that it was a mob scene downtown. On Madison at State they set up a huge platform from the north to the south side of the street. They were giving speeches and playing music. Thousands of people were just milling around cheering and dancing. Servicemen were hugging and kissing the people in the street.

Bernie Judge

I remember the end of the war in 1945. We climbed onto the roof of Jeffrey Food and Liquors that overlooked 79th Street. We went up with buckets of paper and we threw the paper to celebrate the end of the war on V-J Day. It was a big celebration and everybody was in a terrific mood. I was only five years old, so I shouldn't have been up on the roof. I had an older brother and sister, and we had a lot of freedom and could do a lot of things that kids can't do now. But it was okay, my parents knew what we were doing that day because it was a celebration. I remember that it was a very important event.

Chuck Schaden

When the war ended, we were living across the street from the fire chief, Walter Schoenfeld, of the Norwood Park Township Volunteer Fire Department. On V-E Day, he came out of his house with a gun and shot into the air a couple of times in celebration. I remember that kids on their bikes were riding up and down the street of our block ringing their bells and blowing their horns. People who had automobiles would drive up and down the streets blowing their horns. It was a totally unorganized expression of joy that was repeated on V-J Day, which was a little better organized and a little more solemn.

Steve Zucker

I remember my mom yelling out the window, "The war is over!" My friend Rick Fizdale and I went to the mailbox at Western and Rosemont and we sat on top of the green, metal mailbox waiting for the troops to come home. We waited for hours and hours because we thought that the troops were going to come marching down Western Avenue.

Joesph Lamendella

All the neighbors came out on the street and were banging pots and pans on V-J Day in 1945. I was eight and my brother was five at the time. We each got a bottle of white wine and a cigar and got drunk and disgustingly sick in the middle of the street. I have not had white wine, with rare exception, to this day, and I don't think that my brother has ever had another cigar.

Mayor Edward J. Kelly Reads News of President Roosevelt's Death, 1945. Loop (Courtesy of the Chicago Sun-Times.)

required a signature. There were 'no blacks allowed.' If you violated the law, you voided your deed."

The Aftermath

The impact of the war on the Chicago home front was complex. Passions raised during the conflict often encouraged bigotry and racism, perhaps most harmfully to the small but growing Japanese-American community. While only a small number of Japanese-Americans lived in Chicago before the war, many were relocated here from the West Coast both during and after the war. While violence was rare, war-time propaganda had created an atmosphere of fear and mistrust, leaving many Chicagoans unwilling to give jobs or rent apartments to the newcomers.

The Jewish-American population in Chicago was particularly impacted by the death and destruction caused by World War II. During the war, there was very little information coming out of Europe about the persecution of Jews. For many, it was only after the war that families learned of the Holocaust and the fate of their loved ones abroad.

Lawndale resident Gerald Bender had family living in Poland during the war. "The most important impact of World War II on my family was when we learned that my grandmother, aunts, uncles, and cousins were all murdered in Poland. They were put in a pit and buried alive in Lomza, Poland, near Bialystock. They were among 7,000 Jews murdered in that town. So, the war had a profound effect on my life because it let me know what a Jew was." Bruce Bachmann's Austin family was also touched by the Holocaust. "The most traumatic experience concerning the war was that a cousin of mine was in a concentration camp in Europe — he didn't escape Europe in time. He did survive, and he showed me the numbers on his arm, but he didn't talk much about his experience. His wife also survived, and my uncles sponsored them when they came to America."

Arthur X. Elrod, President Harry Truman, and Mayor Martin Kennelly at Union Station, 1948. Near West Side (Courtesy of Richard Elrod.)

Daily Life in the Neighborhood

In the 1940s, the routine of daily life in Chicago was similar to that in other major American cities. It centered around going to school or work, shopping for daily necessities, listening to the radio, reading the newspaper, getting together with friends and family, and relaxing or playing in parks. Once in a while, people would eat out at a restaurant or go downtown to see a show, but with limited funds available to most families, these luxuries were saved for special occasions.

Most families were close, both geographically and emotionally, during the '40s. Members of extended families, including parents, children, and grandparents often lived in the same buildings, or within a few blocks of each other. As a rule, families ate dinner together and children were expected to be at the supper table at a specified time each night. If a mother wanted the children to come home, she could open the window and her voice brought a quick reaction. Children rarely disobeyed their parents, and if they did something to break the rules, there was swift punishment "as soon as dad gets home."

There were also the continual issues of dealing with the Great Depression and the impact of World War II, as well as the changes that occurred after the war. By the early '40s, however, jobs were easier to find and that meant money for more than the bare necessities. The shortage of adequate and affordable housing was always an issue throughout the decade. Across the city, residents commonly lived in two and three flats, apartment buildings, working man's cottages, or if they were lucky, "modern" brick bungalows. Often, extended families lived together in apartments, two-flats and single family homes. Chicago Mayor Richard M. Daley tells of how he shared his Bridgeport bungalow with members of his extended family during the '40s.

As for shopping, there were few full-service grocery stores available during the decade. Thus, residents of Chicago neighborhoods bought their daily necessities at local neighborhood stores that were no more than a few blocks away. It was an era of small, independent shops that were often owned by first- and second-generation immigrants. In many of these shops, ethnic specialties were the focus, including meat, poultry, fish and baked goods. Daily shopping was also necessitated by the lack of reliable refrigeration to preserve food, the overall lack of storage space for large supplies of food, and the lack of funds available to families to purchase groceries for the entire week.

Many modern conveniences had yet to arrive. Air conditioning was available in movie theaters, but not yet in homes, so during the summer many residents would sleep outside on porches, grassy sections of boulevards and parks, or at the beaches along Lake Michigan. Transportation was also vastly different. With few people being able to afford automobiles and a limited supply of new cars available during the war years, neighborhood residents walked or rode buses, streetcars, trolleys, or the elevated trains.

Opposite: *Chicago Park District's "Save the Lawn" Program, 6342 S. Greenwood, ca. 1940.* Woodlawn (Courtesy of the Chicago Park District.)

For most people, life in the 1940s is remembered as a safer and happier time, despite the tremendous negative impact on lives caused by the Depression, World War II and its aftermath. It was also the last decade to still have nostalgic links to the nineteenth century — an era of ice men, waffle vendors, and value still counted by the penny.

The Depression

The Depression was still in effect at the beginning of the 1940s, and there was a constant struggle to find jobs, affordable housing and enough money for daily necessities. Adults and children adjusted to the severe economic hardships and tried to make the best of the difficult times. Interestingly, many Chicagoans do not remember themselves as "poor" because it seemed that everyone was in the same economic situation. Then, at the beginning of World War II, there was the sense that economically, things had begun to take a turn for the better.

Writer Bill Gleason grew up in on the Southwest Side of Chicago. "The '40s — that was my decade. I graduated from Parker High School in 1940, and, in September of 1940, I got lucky and found a full-time job. So, I finally had some money to spend. Everybody says, 'We weren't poor.' Well, we weren't, because my father worked everyday during the Depression. He was a blacksmith in the post office garage. But we still had to scramble, like so many other families. I got a job and I no longer had to go to the dime store and buy new soles that you put over the old soles of your shoes. I had money to spend. It was a glamorous job — I worked for the ticket broker in the Hotel Sherman."

Northwest Sider Bill Jauss has similar memories of the Depression and its effect on his family. "During the Depression, my dad worked at the Fulton Market in a meat packing plant, so we always had plenty of food and meat. I really thought that there was a barter system going on and that meat was money. I remember one time my mom took me to Klee Brothers down on Cicero Avenue at Six Corners to buy me a new suit of clothes and a pair of high-top boots — with a little crevice to put a knife in. My mom gave the clothier a bacon in exchange. You know, doctors made house calls in those days, and I remember my mom giving the doctor a ham for coming to take care of us kids. I think there must have been a barter system going on. I guess nobody had any money during those years, but we never missed any meals and we always had a roof over our heads. I never felt deprived and we always had everything that we wanted. It was an interesting time to grow up, and I think that families were closer."

Nancy Bild Wolf remembers the impact of the Depression on her family in West Rogers Park. "My mother worked as a stenographer, mostly because my father only worked on and off during the 1930s. She also worked as a salesperson at the Wieboldt's store in downtown Chicago. So, I would come home from grammar school and open the front door with the key that we left under the mat. Since my mother was willing to feed anybody in need of a meal, I would sometimes open the door and find a stranger eating lunch at my house. She would provide food in exchange for doing work around the house. During one period, we had a handyman named Hunt and he would come every summer and do carpentry work and painting. One day, a man came to our door who was an itinerant photographer and offered to take pictures of my family. My mother told him that she didn't have any money to pay him, but when he smelled food cooking he offered to take the pictures in exchange for a meal. He had all of his photographic equipment with him and he set it up and took family pictures. I was only seven years old when that happened, and because of his photographic skills we have many lovely pictures of my family taken during those years. It was obvious that during the Depression people did almost anything as a way to survive."

The Depression had a dramatic impact on real estate development. Land values dropped, foreclosures jumped, and many open lots and even some unfinished buildings could be found throughout the neighborhoods. Sandy Zuckerman Pesmen grew up in North Town. "There were many empty lots between houses because of the big Depression. We first lived in Albany Park in an apartment and then moved to North Town in 1940, when my father had enough money to put down on a little bungalow. Next to us was an empty foundation where somebody had started to build another bungalow, and the Depression had come along and they stopped. During the winter the foundation would fill with snow, and my friends and I would go out with a little sled and just jump in. Nobody watched us, and when we got cold we'd go inside. It was a safe place to play and it was a good neighborhood, with families all around us."

Apartments, Bungalows and Houses

It was a challenge to find housing throughout the 1940s due to the lack of new construction during the Depression. In the more densely populated neighborhoods, the dominant form of housing was apartment buildings, many of which were in a courtyard configuration. Although families lived close together in those arrangements, many Chicagoans have fond memories of living in apartments because of the camaraderie and community feeling among neighbors. Those lucky enough to afford their own houses, whether wood frame or brick bungalow, also have strong positive recollections about their living conditions.

Shirley Ochs Simon
Humboldt Park

I was born in 1927 and I lived in Humboldt Park at 1438 N. Maplewood Avenue, two blocks south of North Avenue. The neighborhood boundaries were Division, North, California and Western. My earliest memories are of playing in the street in front of our house. The house was a strange building because a tailor shop fronted it, with a big window, and we were in the attic above the tailor shop. The tailor's family lived in back of the store. Our entrance was at the back of the house and we had to go through a cinder path and then up some stairs. It was a rickety, unpainted, rat-infested cottage. It was terrible.

My parents met and married in Fall River, Massachusetts, and came here for work. My aunt lived next door, and she said that there was work in Chicago. My father was in poor health, and that affected his ability to have steady employment, so it was very hard for us. He struggled during the Depression. My mother worked at a hospital supply shop where they made doctors' and nurses' uniforms. It was a low-skilled, piecework job where they did sewing, and she worked very slowly. It was a very bad period in her life. There were just two kids in the family, my brother and myself.

My memories of those years are only partially positive. When I look back, I wonder how we survived it. We were always cold and always hungry. It was really bad. For example, we would play outside in front at night, but we knew that we could not walk back to the house through the passageway without mother because she would take her shoe off and hit the sides of the building to scare the rats away. And I'd hear rat's scratching in the wall. It didn't seem to bother me much, but she used to cry. It was rough for her, but I was a happy kid. I played all the time. We rarely saw an automobile on our street. When they came by, it was a big deal, and everybody had to watch it. I remember just hanging out a lot. My mother worked and I was on my own, even before school.

I went to the movies all the time, and the park was very important to me. Since my mother worked, I was at the mercy of older children to take me places, but they were willing. My brother was two years older, but I had very little to do with him in those years. He'd run the alleys and steal potatoes from our neighbors, making little fires with his friends to roast the potatoes. We would put tin cans on our shoes and run around. We would make our own toys, like scooters from boxes and skates.

I remember the milkman allowing me to hold the reins of the horses on his wagon. He'd stop and we would go half a block while I'd hold the reins. We had to stand up because there were no seats. Then I would get off at the corner because I wasn't allowed to cross the street.

The special thing about life in the '40s was the freedom. Oh, the freedom! Anything was possible, even during the war. I could go anywhere and do anything and be out as long as I wanted and see anyone. I never felt unsafe. In fact, when my husband and I courted, I remember sitting at the lagoon in Humboldt Park at 2 a.m. on a summer evening without a thought of fear. People slept in the park. Sometimes we slept in the grass on the boulevard on a very hot night on a blanket. Automobile traffic wasn't too bad. We always felt safe, and we walked everywhere and anywhere. At night, at the age of fifteen, I would be on Division Street and would have to walk six blocks to visit a friend. It was nighttime and it was dark, but I never thought twice about it.

I remember the time when we were living on Division and we had to move. They were tearing the building down to build a new dime store, so we had to go. My mother worked, so she said, "Okay, Shirley, find a flat with at least four rooms," and she gave me a rental price. I would look for signs as I went to school and on my way home after school. I would inquire and even look at the apartments, and I was only thirteen or fourteen years old! That was a feeling of freedom! I was working at that time, as well as going to school. There were jobs for kids, and we could go anywhere. I worked downtown at the Boston Store, and I went on my own.

We had our first telephone in our apartment on Hirsch Street, but that wasn't until I was fourteen years old. So, we would have to use my aunt's phone on Maplewood. The doorbells didn't ring, and when my girlfriends would come to visit they would have to yell for me. It would echo through the hall! One could live very easily without these services that we take for granted today.

Old Brace Shop, Michael Reese Hospital, ca. 1940. Douglas (Courtesy of the Jewish United Fund.)

String Instrumentalists, Jackson Park Field House, ca. 1940. Woodlawn (Courtesy of the Chicago Park District.)

Fr. Gene Smith
South Shore

I was born in 1936 and raised at 72nd and Dorchester, referred to as St. Laurence Parish. My neighborhood was blue-collar. We were, for the most part, children of immigrants. My parents were born in Ireland. People around me were, for the most part, born in Ireland, and a few from Sweden, Poland, Germany, and Japan. So, blue-collar workers would get up early to go to work and come back tired. Some people would head for the steel mills, others would go downtown where they had professional jobs.

The day before I began kindergarten, I was in the kitchen with my parents. My dad looked down at me and said, "Well, tomorrow is the first day of school. Bejesus boy, your playing days are over!" I said, "I'm only five years old, and all my playing days are over?"

Life was fine during grammar school. I remember in first grade I was supposed to buy cookies for the class for Halloween because it was my turn to bring them. I asked my dad for some money so I could buy cookies at the store that was next to the school. He reached into his pocket and pulled out a handful of change. As I mentioned, my father was from Ireland and had been a farmer there. He was a big, strong man with really large hands. He said, "Help yourself." So, I took a few coins out of his hand. I thought that with the size of this man's hands he would have been wonderful on Mary Hartline's show "Super Circus."

During the 1940s, most everything was within walking distance. Hardly anybody had automobiles and we could play in the street and not worry about running into a parked car. Everything was ambulatory. If we went someplace, we got on a bus or streetcar to get there or to visit relatives. So everything was pretty "medieval." You didn't get outside of your little community. My friend George Scales and I used to go to the railroad trestle that had tracks that ran from the Loop out to everywhere and anywhere. We would sit and watch the I.C. go downtown and wonder what kinds of jobs people had and what they did there. Then, the I.C. going out to the University of Notre Dame in South Bend would go hurtling by and we would wonder what it would be like to see them play football there. Other trains, like the Broadway Limited, the City of Miami and City of New Orleans would pass by. We would wonder — what it would be like to be outside this community and go to some of those places? We would sit and speculate about that for a long time. What will move us beyond 72nd and Dorchester into the next phase of our lives?

In South Shore, Estelle Gordon Baron and her family lived in an apartment building. "We all lived in six-flat apartments in my neighborhood and we were very close with our neighbors, particularly growing up. We would play in our backyards and in front of the building. The six-flats formed a 'U' shape in the courtyard. There were three apartments on either side of the entrances, and then a central staircase in the middle. We would play cat-in-the-corner and things like that out front. It was a small town life in a big city."

Dick Jaffee remembers living in several different apartments in South Shore before moving into a house. "When I was born in 1936, we lived at 8020 Dobson, west of Stony Island Avenue. I also lived in an apartment at 8227 Clyde. My mother enjoyed having arched doorways and canvassed walls, and they paid about $35 a month rent back then. They were very proud of it, and it was a great place to live. When I was about five years old, in May 1941, we moved to a first floor apartment at 7949 Jeffrey near the corner of 80th and Jeffrey. My first memories of apartment life were the notices on the doors about vacancies, but when World War II began, apartments were very hard to find. My memory is that our neighborhoods were like little towns — a place where I could ride my bike, use my roller skates on the sidewalks, and pretty much do whatever I wanted as long as I stayed within the boundaries of the neighborhood. Later in the '40s, we were able to buy a house. We decided to remove the fence separating our yard from our neighbors, the McCarthys. My dad and Mr. McCarthy built an outdoor cooking area as well as a screened-in summerhouse and the two families would frequently eat dinner together during the summer."

Marvin Levin spent most of his early years in Albany Park on the Northwest Side. "We moved to Albany Park in 1940, when my mother and father rented a one-bedroom apartment with a balcony on Monticello, between Wilson and Leland. It was a big courtyard building, and the landlord lived in the building. He seemed to cut the grass with scissors to keep it trim all the time and he kept the building in beautiful condition. Albany Park was a neighborhood completely filled with apartment buildings, so people were very close together. In fact, my childhood friends became my friends for life. We knew all kinds of people, and we were always hanging out together. We walked to school together, came home together, worked together and played together."

Steve Zucker remembers the special kinship that was established around his West Rogers Park apartment building. "Our building at the corner of Rosemont and Western must have been constructed in the early '30s. It went from the Nortown Theater all the way to Western, and then it turned the corner and went down Rosemont to the alley. There were three entrances in the rear of the building and it backed up onto the Nortown so that you had a huge wall to play around and against — we used to throw balls against it. I remember that there were many kids under the age of eight running around our backyard. We played every game known to kids, and developed friendships that have lasted a lifetime."

Howard Rosen's apartment building in Humboldt Park was a microcosm of neighborhood life. "In those days, everybody would sit on their back porches. In fact, the highlight of a summer day was to sit out there with a pitcher of lemonade. All the parents would be out there, and the older people, and they would be drinking lemonade, playing cards, and listening to the radio." Ron Newman remembers life in his Austin neighborhood in the same way. "I loved the West Side, and our building was like a little community where everybody took care of each other. There were two courtyards in our building. If my parents weren't home, I knew that I could go to dinner at a friend's house. My father, mother, brother and myself lived in a one-bedroom apartment with an inner door bed."

Although he was born in Albany Park, Journalist Joel Weisman moved to West Rogers Park toward the end of the '40s. "I was born in 1942, and grew up during the '40s in Albany Park, at Albany and Montrose. I lived in a three-flat building that was owned jointly by my mother and her family. The big question at that time was where we were going to move — Skokie, Lincolnwood, or Rogers Park. Those seemed to be the main choices, but I could never understand why we wanted to move. My mother used to bring me on walks with my sister who was a baby. She would take us over to Ravenswood Manor, which was just a lovely area, and only a couple of blocks from our house. It started at Sacramento, near Albany, and east to about California. I always thought that we were going to have our own house and I would have my own bedroom. My vision of a home was one of the places in the Manor, an older house with beautiful foliage around it. There was one place that had statues and an iron fence around it. I remember envisioning us living near there, but we ended up moving to a new house in West Rogers Park."

Austin was home for Fr. Andrew Greeley. " I lived in what we called North Austin, near Division Street and Austin Boulevard. My very early memories are of two-flat living, backyards, and playing with other kids in the alley. There was a house down the street that had been moved back toward the alley so that a second house could be built in front of it. I lived in an apartment until 4th grade and went to St. Angela grammar school, located a block north of Division and two blocks west of Central. We eventually moved into our own home, a Chicago-style bungalow, at 1301 N. Mayfield."

Leonard Amari
Near North Side

I was born on the Near North Side. I am from what is now called the Cabrini-Green projects. One of the corners in the neighborhood was called "murder corner" because every so often they would find bodies on that corner. But it was also a neighborhood where I would walk safely down the street as a little boy. All my aunts and uncles lived there. All the people on the block were relatives or seemed like relatives.

In my Italian neighborhood, most of the men of that generation didn't work — they were Damon Runyan characters. My mother was one of six sisters, and only one of the husbands worked. All my uncles lived in my grandfather's apartments for free and hung out at a poolroom at Maple and Clark.

We moved out of the neighborhood to the Lathrop Homes on Diversey. It was mostly non-Italian-American. We lived in three different apartments there, including two high-rises and one low-rise. Our place was at Diversey and Damen, and it was subsidized housing. I can't tell you if the people who lived there felt disenfranchised — I know I certainly didn't. I didn't realize that it was subsidized housing until much later. I remember the sense of community living there, and that people left their doors open. I remember that on Halloween we would be out trick-or-treating until midnight and never felt unsafe.

In the summer, they would show a movie on the side of the building in the main courtyard and we would all bring out our chairs and blankets. The movie was always The Man in the Iron Mask. *I also remember they had community showers along the Chicago River, just under the bridge at Diversey Street, and I remember the snapping turtles, the swing sets and baseball. It was a wonderful place to live.*

My father's parents, and my mother's as well, came from Sicily, where there historically has been less respect for the rule of law, so there was an attitude against authority. I don't remember anybody in my family having a vehicle sticker, let alone insurance. That was just part of the culture. To their credit, all of those parents insisted that the only way to get their children into the mainstream of American society was by going to school. I could steal or fight and it didn't matter, but if I got a bad report card my father beat the heck out of me.

Chuck Schaden
Norridge

I was born in 1934 in Chicago, but my family moved to Norridge in 1939, just west of Harlem, the city's western border. At that time, Norridge wasn't much and almost everything that we did, except for living and sleeping, was done in Chicago. Irving Park Road was the lifeline to the city. Just about everything that we did was either on Irving Park or an easy connection from Irving Park. We lived in a five-room brick bungalow with a living room, dining room, two bedrooms separated by a bathroom, a kitchen and an unenclosed back porch, that later on, was enclosed. The neighborhood was almost all single-family homes. Many of the people were there when the first homes were built, just before the Depression in the 1920s. A lot of people lost their homes in the '30s and I think that the home we moved into had been vacant for some time. I have a vivid memory of a backyard that was way overgrown with weeds. The grass was high and there were hollyhocks everywhere, so it took some time to clear all that stuff.

We had a lot of community activities during the war years. Before there was television, all the neighbors would sit on their front porches in the summer evenings after dinner. Down the street, a family with teenage sons would play music on the big open porch in front of their house. The kids would play music and the whole neighborhood would enjoy it. They played contemporary songs from 1942, 1943 and 1944, which were songs accepted by everyone, young and old. We had block parties and block picnics and everybody knew everybody. This was very important. You knew everybody on the block — up and down. If a new family moved in, you got to know them right away. Everybody looked out for everybody else. In most cases, the women did not work outside the home. Although, as the war years progressed, I know that some of the women were starting to work in defense factories and plants. My mother never worked outside of the home, but had a volunteer job where she was assembling service ribbons that would be awarded to people in the Army, Navy, Marines and the Air Corp. She was also involved in Red Cross bandage rolling projects, as most of the women during the war years were.

The '40s were special because it was a time when everybody had the same interests and concerns, and everybody looked out for one another. We were in the war together, and even post-war, we were still together. We did things for each other. It was a different time. It was an unsophisticated world, but a caring one. If a kid on our block was walking down the street and a neighbor saw the kid doing something wrong, the neighbor would say, "Stop doing that. Quit monkeying around. Don't throw that thing over there or I'm going to tell your mother!" If she did get to the point where she would tell your mother, your mother would not be irate, or tell her to mind her own business. She would very grateful that she told you, and be embarrassed that her kid was doing something wrong.

Do you remember the candy cigarettes with a little red thing on the end? They were called names that were take-offs of Chesterfields or Lucky Strikes. Kids used to eat those things. They loved to play with them, because everybody smoked in the '40s. We weren't smoking, but we were eating these candy cigarettes. In the winter, you could walk down the street with one of these candy cigarettes and pretend you were smoking, and your breath would be visible in the winter. I was walking down the alley one time with another kid. We were doing this, and one of the neighbors called my mother and said, "Charles is smoking in the alley." Boy, I got grabbed by the collar faster than you could say Jack Robinson. I had to prove to my mother that I had the candy cigarettes in my jeans.

I think that was a pretty good time to grow up. We had finally come out of the Depression. The families who had grown up in the Depression, like my parents, were doing better. It didn't affect me at all, and I didn't know that we barely had enough money for an ice cream cone. But the families in the '40s were beginning to be a little more prosperous because of the war. A lot of people who were in wartime industries were making more money than they had ever made before because they were working extra hours.

After World War II, Phil Holdman finally had enough money for he and his wife to move to their own apartment. "In 1947 or 1948, Alberta and I finally found our own place on Augusta Boulevard, across from Humboldt Park. It was a four-room apartment, but in those days it was tough to get an apartment. Part of the deal was that we had to buy the furniture from the people who lived there — it cost me $1,000 for the furniture! We were desperate to have our own place, so I gave them the money and then threw it all out. We then bought our own furniture. We lived in that apartment for several years."

After living in apartment buildings for most of the 1930s and early '40s, Sheldon Rosing's family bought a bungalow in South Shore. "We finally had enough money to buy a bungalow at 7637 S. Ridgeland, two blocks west of South Shore Boulevard. It was the best thing that we ever did. It was ideal because I could walk to school and come home for lunch. The house was a brick Chicago-style bungalow with an underground sprinkling system, and I think that my parents paid around $8,000 for the place. My dad had some money saved and borrowed the rest from a relative, who he paid back in a couple of years. The real estate taxes for the place then were something like $300 a year. It was great for my family to finally get into their own place and out of an apartment."

Transportation

During the 1940s, most Chicago residents relied on walking to get around their neighborhood. Automobile traffic was limited during the war years, due to gasoline rationing and the limited construction of new cars, so public transportation was generally used to get downtown and to other sections of the city. The "L," streetcars, trolleys, and buses were the most common means of transportation, and are remembered fondly for their fun, if perhaps, bumpy rides. For a small number of people, trains like the Chicago & Northwestern, the Milwaukee Road, the Burlington Northern and the Illinois Central were also options. These trains would have cost almost double the $.07 streetcar fare, so for most residents it wasn't a first choice.

On the South Side, Charles Kocoras remembers the "Green Hornet" streetcars. "When I was growing up trolley cars were on their way out. Then we got the Green Hornets, before they changed totally to buses. The Green Hornets were terrific. They were electric, moved on rails and they would zip right along. They ran on the main streets like State Street and they replaced the old red streetcars. I never took the Illinois Central, and only rarely did we take the "L" if we were going downtown. Going downtown was like going to another city, since we had all the shopping we needed in the neighborhood at 63rd and Halsted."

It was not uncommon for children to ride alone on public transportation in the 1940s. Whether traveling to school, downtown, or attractions like Riverview Amusement Park, kids enjoyed an unusual level of freedom. Joe Lamendella lived in the Lake View neighborhood during the '40s. "When I was just ten years old I would take the subway downtown. I used to take the Belmont bus to the "L" and then ride to the Museum of Science and Industry. It was safe and nobody gave a second thought about it."

Ian Levin grew up in Rogers Park and lived near the Morse Avenue Elevated Station. "We didn't have a car until the late '40s, so we would take the train to visit our relatives on the West Side and in Albany Park. Occasionally, my parents would take us downtown for dinner and a movie, but our neighborhood offered everything we wanted, so we remained there most of the time."

In 1943, the State Street Subway was completed. Howard Rosen was lucky enough to get a ride on the one of the first trains. "I remember the day they opened up the subway — not to the public, but for a trial run that would go from State Street to North and Clybourn. In order to get on you had to buy a War Bond. You see, they were offering a pass on one of the first trains as an incentive for the war effort. A lady who had just bought four bonds turned to me and asked, 'Would you like to go for a ride on the subway?' So I took a ride on the new subway. I was really fascinated with it."

On the South Side, Andrew McKenna remembers the transportation that was available in his South Shore neighborhood. "The Illinois Central was the dominant form of transportation and ran down 71st Street near where I lived at 72nd and Crandon. One of the attractions of my neighborhood, particularly for people who worked downtown, was the fact that the I.C. was there. In the 1940s, most people took the train into the city, unlike today where most use automobiles."

Morgan Murphy, Jr. spent his early years in Visitation Parish on the city's Southwest Side. In the 1940s, his father built a new house in Beverly in St. Cajetan Parish. "Beverly was in the city then, but the area was not heavily developed. In fact, the streetcar line only went to 112th Street. I remember that we still had gas streetlights back then, and there used to be an old lamplighter who would come around every night. He had a little ladder and he lit the streetlights. It was pretty far out and there was a lot of prairie in the '40s. The area did not really develop until after the war. My father would go downtown to work each day by taking the Rock Island Railroad from Beverly/Morgan Park at 111th Street. While I was waiting for him at the station I used to watch the big steam engines go by. I got to know the engineers and they used to wave at me."

Bill Phelan
Englewood

I was born in 1932 at 74th and Racine. It was a very interesting neighborhood, called Englewood. I went to St. Brendan's grammar school, at 67th Street, which was a full mile from 74th Street. In those days, they sent us home for lunch, so I would be walking back and forth twice a day, about four miles. We had two other parishes near us, including St. Sabina, which was only four blocks from my house, but I was not within their boundaries. Anything north of the railroad overpass at 75th Place was in St. Brendan's, south of there was St. Sabina. I am the oldest of seven children, and all of us went to St. Brendan's.

On my way to school, I used to go by a German church called Sacred Heart, which is kind of an interesting church. They had no boundaries and anybody of German descent, or anybody who was Catholic could go to that church. They had masses in German in those days, too. The other interesting place that I passed by was the Chicago Christian High School at 71st and Racine, which was all Dutch. So, there were a lot of Dutch, Germans, Irish and a lot of Italians in the neighborhood. I passed through the league of nations on my way to school every day! Many days I would have to fight my way back and forth, with my brothers and my sister. I had to take care of them, too. It was quite a job on some days.

During the war everybody was working. Even though I was young, I always had jobs that included delivering newspapers and working at a ballpark that was two or three blocks from our house. It was called Shewbridge Field, and all the public and Catholic leagues played their games there. On Saturdays there would be times when six to eight football games were played there. They would start at 8 o'clock in the morning and go all day. As for baseball, the women's baseball league used to play there. I know they had a lot of big manufacturing companies that had teams playing there, like the Ft. Wayne Zolmer Pistons, who later became the Detroit Pistons, the Seal Masters from Aurora, the Joliet Seven-Up and other companies that sponsored teams. The Chicago team was called the Chicago Matchmakers, and they were involved with a company that manufactured matches. They had some pretty good games there.

I started working at Shewbridge when I was ten or eleven years old, and it happened like this: one night, the lights were on at the field, and we had nothing to do, so we snuck into the ballpark. We got caught by a policeman. He yelled at us to stop and I stopped, but my friends kept on running. He brought me up to the priest who was running Shewbridge for the monsignor, Fr. Sweeney. He said, "What's your phone number so I can call your parents and let them know what you did." I said, "I'm sorry Father, we don't have a telephone." He said, "You be here tomorrow morning at 8 o'clock because your punishment will be to clean up these stands." So, I was there at 8 o'clock the next morning, and I cleaned up the stands. At 10 o'clock he came out and said, "You're doing a terrific job. You're hired." That was my first job at Shewbridge Field, and all my brothers and my sister followed me there. All of us worked there doing different things over the years. I hung the scoreboard, did the balls and strikes for the baseball games, and cleaned the stands. Then I got promoted to a big job: I was in charge of filling-up the concession stands with beer, pop, hot dogs and candy. I had total access to the commissary where they kept it all, and I had to fill everything up and ice down all the beer before the games. The ice used to come in 50 pound canvas bags, and I only weighed about 110 pounds, so I had a tough time engineering those bags and dumping them into the bins where the pop and the beer was kept. I'll never forget the day when I was about twelve years old, one of the beer bottles exploded and part of it was lodged in my thumb. I still have the scar to this day. I had a handkerchief and I just wrapped it around my hand and kept on going. There was a little blood in the beer and the ice, but I got the job done.

St. Rita High School, 63rd and Western, ca. 1946. Chicago Lawn (Courtesy of the CTA.)

Dempsey Travis
Washington Park

I was born in 1920 and grew up in the Black Belt. By the 1940s, my neighborhood had graduated to Bronzeville. Anthony Ogleton received a proposition about changing the name from Black Belt to Bronzeville. The Chicago Defender picked the name Bronzeville, and it sold newspapers. I say that Bronzeville is wherever black people live.

In the '40s, the safe boundaries for us were as far north as 22nd Street and as far south as 60th Street, but south of Washington Park was a dangerous area. Although we lived at 59th and Prairie, we didn't go to that end of Washington Park. We stayed closer to the area from 55th to 51st Streets. The boundary on the west was the Rock Island railroad, and on the east it was Cottage Grove. It was a narrow strip that stayed that way until the 1950s and the end of "restrictive covenants." We knew that we couldn't cross Cottage Grove, or you were subject to being picked up by the police strictly because you were African-American. I learned early in my life not to cross Cottage Grove. So, we did everything on the west side of Cottage Grove and nothing on the east side.

For me, life was interesting in the neighborhood and there were always people who were making it and were successful. Famous people lived close by, and that meant there was hope. My father was a laborer until he died. He probably never made more than $50 or $75 a week, and that had to be during wartime. I knew that there was a life beyond that, and he convinced me. That was how I got into the music business. He and my mother kidded me and said, "You're going to be the next Duke Ellington," and I believed them. My mother would take me downtown to all the shows, and there weren't a lot of black people going downtown to see shows then. The first time I saw Duke Ellington was in 1931 at the Oriental Theater. I said, "Ooh, that's him!" That experience made the case that he was a big image. He was bigger than God, he was so huge an image to me. He was handsome, articulate, and suave — just a good image for me. It was these kinds of things that kept me awake — they were my role models. It's my opinion that failure is a learned process, and I never hooked into people that I thought were failing.

When we lived on 36th Street, people at 48th Street and Evans were another class. There was Dorothy Donegan, and she lived right across the street, but never spoke to me. I was a little boy, and she was very attractive. I did silly things like playing ball by myself in front of her house with the hope that she would come out and say, "Look at that guy, isn't he wonderful."

Being an only child, you imagine and create your own games, and I think that was an advantage. I could always entertain myself — you become self-sufficient.

I would play at Ellis Park when I was growing up. It was between 36th and 37th, just west of Cottage Grove and east of Vincennes. It was a beautiful park. The West Point Baptist Church was at 36th and Cottage Grove. In the early evening, I could see black people dressed up in gowns and tuxedos, so I knew that there was something other than overalls around. Some people never noticed that there were other kinds of dress. We considered ourselves blue-collar, but with upper middle-class aspirations.

I started playing piano at five years of age, but I became interested in jazz at an even earlier age because my father was a piano player. He couldn't read, but he could play piano. Many black musicians couldn't read, but could play music because they were so talented. There were people like myself who could read, but were not very talented. I didn't realize how inadequate I was in that area until I got to DuSable High School, which was then called Wendell Phillips High School, then Wendell Phillips-DuSable. That too, was based on a newspaper contest like the naming of Bronzeville.

DuSable High School was interesting, because they had an economic mix of people who went there. There would be a doctor's son, a lawyer's son, and a post office worker's son. Back then, post office workers were prominent. In fact, many doctors worked in the post office because the medical profession was slow during the '30s. I also remember when people had difficulty getting an apartment, but it was different for my father because he had a piano. If you had a piano there was stability, because you couldn't move out in the middle of the night. That made you a good tenant.

At DuSable, I ran into the color thing and the shades of black. I hadn't really been aware of that issue when I was younger. My uncles' girlfriends looked as if they could have been white. People played this game of color, and it became an issue of who was the "blackest." When you start fighting with yourself about that kind of stuff, you are really in serious trouble. What damned difference does it make what color you are? There was more status, in your mind, if you were a lighter color. I thought that it was a lot of nonsense! The light girls got the better guys, and they had an advantage in the professions. They got the goodies.

Grocery Store in the Black Belt, 1941.   Near South Side   Photograph by Russell Lee.   (Library of Congress)

Earl Calloway
Near South Side

I came to Chicago from Buffalo, New York, with my mother and sister. I was about seventeen years old when I came here back in 1943. I arrived on the train at the 12th Street Station. We took an old streetcar, the one where you enter at the back door and exit by the front door, to 2020 Roosevelt Road. All along the way, I remember seeing the juke joints, where they danced and drank whiskey and beer. These places didn't have sophisticated entertainment. They jammed all night and sometimes during the day. If they didn't have live entertainment, they would play music on jukeboxes or Rockolas. They had many juke joints on Roosevelt Road.

We lived with this lady by the name of Mrs. Taggert. Her husband was known as "Old Blind" Taggert. He played the guitar, and he traveled all over. He was quite famous. We stayed with him and his family. He was the one who encouraged my mother to come to Chicago. I stayed upstairs in a room, and they stayed downstairs. At first, I slept on the floor and my sister and mother slept in a bed. Then, I got sense to move upstairs to a room with a bed. That was my introduction to Chicago.

I got a job quickly working as a bus boy because I had to make money so that I could get back to school. When I started I didn't know what a busboy was. I thought it was working with a bus, or transportation, or something like that. Finally, someone told me, but it didn't make any difference to me. So, I started working at the Harding Restaurant. Then, I went to the Congress Hotel at Congress and Michigan, and I worked there for about a month. In the meantime, I was looking for a better job. I came here to this building (now the offices of the Chicago Defender), and upstairs on the second floor, was the office of the Urban League. I went up there and told the gentleman what I wanted, and they gave me a job washing fluorescent lights. I had a bucket and rags and went all over the city washing those lights. I went to one of the most fascinating places out in Cicero. It was in the back of the storefront, and man, I spent the entire day washing fluorescent lights where they were gambling, and doing all those kinds of things. I did two or three of those kinds of places out in Cicero. I did that all summer, but you know, it never occurred to me the historical importance of what I was doing.

Shopping

Shopping was an important part of daily life throughout the 1940s. Larger shopping areas, usually clustered around primary intersections and transportation hubs, would include major department stores, appliance stores, men's and women's clothing and apparel stores, confectionery stores as well as first-run movie houses. Each neighborhood had its own local shopping area as well, including a combination of small grocery stores, drugstores, shoe repair stores, dry cleaners, meat and fish markets, bakeries, candy stores, hardware stores, taverns and small restaurants. Many neighborhoods also had small "Mom and Pop" grocery stores, usually located on the corner of the block or on the first floor of apartment buildings.

Estelle Gordon Baron has vivid memories of the sweet shops in her South Shore neighborhood. "I remember that at 71st and Merrill, going east, there was a Fannie May candy shop, and it was the prettiest little place you ever saw. When you walked in, the wallpaper was covered with roses and it had white wrought iron along the walls. The whole store was white and pink with little green leaves all over. On top of the glass counter where the candy was located, they always had a little dish with a paper doily and little samples of Fannie May cream-filled chocolates. They were so delicious, and I remember them so clearly. In those days, the candy wasn't prepackaged so that you could select exactly what you wanted. You had the option of taking the candy in a bag or a box. Also nearby, was another place that brings back strong memories — Newman's Bakery had the most marvelous pastries! They were very fancy, and I can still taste them. There was one shaped like a horn, made of very flaky dough, filled with sweetened whipped cream, and powdered sugar on top."

Andrew McKenna remembers the shopping around 71st and Jeffrey in South Shore. "Shopping was on 71st Street between Stony Island on the west and Yates or South Shore Drive on the east. In a half-mile area between Jeffrey and Yates or South Shore Drive, there were three Walgreen Drugstores: one at 71st and Jeffrey, one at 71st and Paxton, and one at 71st and Yates. Shopping included a drugstore, florist, candy store, shoe repair, and a men's store/haberdasher. There were also a few restaurants, the Hitching Post and the Shore Post. These were not white tablecloth restaurants, and very often the dinner or luncheon menus were much the same."

A few blocks away, on 79th Street, Bernie Judge recalls the places where his family used to do their daily shopping. "For day-to-day shopping, we went to 79th Street, which included a meat market, fish store, a liquor store, drugstore, cleaners and the shoe repair. There was also a Kroger store that opened on 79th and Euclid on the north side of the street, and people shopped for everyday items there. Most of the stores were owned and operated by Jewish people who were primarily first generation. Years after Kroger opened, a Jewel opened in 1953. I also remember a Dressel's bakery and Hackelman's bakery on that street, so we always ate fresh bread."

It seems every neighborhood had a small corner store that stocked the essentials of daily life. Sheila Morris Williams remembers the store at Montrose and Central Park in her Irving Park neighborhood. "Our corner store was the 7-11 of the 1940s. The owners were immigrants who worked very hard, keeping the store clean and open long hours. They lived right upstairs, which made going to work very easy for them. My mother would send me to the store to buy milk or bread. If I had a couple of cents extra I would buy some candy, like the little candy cigarettes you could get in a cardboard box. I would sashay around with one hanging out my mouth, pretending to be cool. The store had plenty of penny candies, which were very tempting for us kids. The store was really a gathering place for kids, and the owners never seemed to complain about all the kids lounging around."

David Cerda lived in East Garfield Park and remembers, "My mother would shop at Goldblatt's Department Store a lot. For grocery shopping, there was a place in the middle of Kedzie, between 19th Street and Ogden Avenue. We would go there or down the street to A&P. There were also some stores on 22nd Street that were predominantly Polish and Bohemian. As for Mexican food, there was a store called Casa Estados on Halsted Street, north of Roosevelt Road, and that was where my family would get Mexican food."

Joseph Lamendella and his family did their shopping on Lincoln Avenue at Belmont. "That was the number one retail center on the North Side, outside of the Loop. My mother would also go to the local grocery and butcher. Kresge's and Woolworth were up the street from us at School and Lincoln, and they used to sell live turtles as pets for a dime. Wieboldt's was also at School and Lincoln, and it had a record store on the ground floor with individual booths to listen to the records. Of course, there seemed to be a tavern on every corner back then."

In the North Town neighborhood, Joesph Epstein remembers the Devon Avenue shopping area. "Devon was one of my favorite streets because it was very grand. During the '40s, it was the 'Jewish renaissance' on Devon, with stores like Seymour Paisin's Dress Shop and Hillman's Stop-and-Shop, an elegant place with the supermarket downstairs and the delicatessen and restaurant upstairs. I also remember Neissner's, Kresge's, Abram's and the Crawford Department Store. My favorite Chinese

Jesse White
Near North Side

I was born in Alton, Illinois in 1934. When I was seven, my family moved to Chicago. We lived on the Near North Side in an area that is now called Cabrini Green. We lived at 536 W. Division in a four-story walkup where we used coal for cooking and heating.

When I was a kid, the area was integrated and cosmopolitan, and was really inhabited primarily by Italians. I worked at an Italian grocery store, Sam Aiello's, where I was a stock boy. I was also responsible for the chickens. I would clean them, take them out of the coop, lock their wings behind them, weigh them, dip them in hot water, and then use the chicken picker to pluck their feathers off. Then I would cut them up and gut them if they needed that done. Of course, I lost a love for chicken because of my close involvement with them.

We got along well in the neighborhood, and we acquired an appreciation for the other person's culture. We had a religious festival, known as the Feast, where they would line the streets with booths and people would sell food. Then they would bring the angel through and parade each day of the three-day festival. The band would play, and they would put dollar bills on the angel. They would have Ferris Wheels and other rides. We would always look forward to the Feast, just like the city today where blacks look forward to the Bud Billikin parade.

We were very poor, so us kids would have to work. My brother shined shoes and I worked in a grocery store. My other brother delivered papers. We were determined to be survivors and to bring money into the house for the family. We were on public aid, so we would get butter, but we would have to mix yellow coloring in it for it to look and taste like butter. We probably ate beans seven days a week. My mother knew how to cook them, and she would take potatoes and mix them with onions and smother them so that we could make a meal out of that. She would also make chili, doing what she could to stretch a meal a long way. She would somehow make nutritious and enjoyable meals with limited amounts of food on a very limited budget.

The neighborhood had a very positive impact on me. One of the first things I learned from growing up in an integrated environment was that you do not have prejudice in your heart. But, when I went off to college, I went to a segregated environment where I would hear black people saying that we should hate white people. I wasn't raised like that. I grew up to believe that we should love each other, work together, and do all we can to live in peace and harmony with one another.

Sheila Morris Williams
Irving Park

Our neighborhood was on the Northwest Side of Chicago. I lived at 4314 North Central Park Avenue, near Montrose. There was a tavern on the corner, of course, all neighborhoods had one. Ours was Goodman's Tavern, and all of the men in the neighborhood hung out there after a day's work. Women never went in, but sometimes children did, if their father sent them out for cigarettes. Imagine that today! I can still remember the smell of stale beer and heavy cigarette smoke. It was like walking into a smelly fog. I never spent more that two minutes in there. Two doors down was the Lincoln Bottling Company, and if you asked the right way on the right day, the manager would give you a free bottle of cola. That really made our day.

The Drake Theatre was only a block away from our house, on Montrose Avenue. At least once a week we went to the movies and saw a double bill, with a newsreel, cartoon, and an action short for the boys. I think it only cost a dime. I remember the bill changed twice a week, but we couldn't afford to go twice. Next door was the local ice cream shop, like on "Happy Days." That was where I had my very first date, at about age twelve.

My brother Bill and I delivered the Chicago Daily News and the German paper, the Abenpost. We were about nine and ten years old at the time and it was really difficult for us to push the huge newspaper cart down the street. We took turns walking up to the second and third floors of apartment buildings and laying the paper nicely on the back porch doorstep. We would be reported to the newspaper agency if we did not deliver the papers perfectly.

The neighborhood was alive with service and delivery men, most of them driving a horse-drawn wagon — the ice man, rag man and produce man. The ice man had a truck with a back that folded down and the kids would scramble up on the truck looking for ice chips on a hot day. There was no air conditioning back then. In the winter we would hitch a ride on the back of the truck and skid on the ice.

We played games in the alley behind our workingman's cottage. Hide and seek and kick the can were our favorites. We even put ash piles from furnaces to good use in the winter. The ashes were usually dumped into a large pile along the fence. We dug into these frozen ashes, which were covered with snow, and made a fort or house out of them. Pretty risky, since we also shared the alley with rats. I remember one year when giant rats ruled the alleys, there was an epidemic of them. They were really scary.

The neighborhood kids were Jewish, Swedish, Polish, and German. We were the only Irish people on my block. I loved to pick up my friends at their homes for a day's play because of the wonderful smells that wafted from their homes. I never found out what exotic foods were cooking, but it kicked off my interest in cooking later in life.

We did all kinds of things for amusement. Our local grammar school, Patrick Henry, had a great playground and gigantic sand pit, which I really loved. We would work together, all ages, to build a giant sand castle. We called it a "ball castle," because we made tunnels and balconies in it and dropped a tennis ball in the top and watched it whiz through the building. I loved ice skating at the local school yard, which was flooded all winter. I never felt the cold. Sometimes we would even put our ice skates on at home and skate down the side street to the ice rink.

My brothers and I also devised a "roller coaster ride" starting in our back yard and ending in our basement. We charged $.02 and put kids in a sturdy wagon near our basement stairs. We put a large piece of stiff wood, twice the width of the wagon and about six feet long, over the cement stairs. We whizzed those kids into our dark basement where we had ghouls and ghosts set-up to scare them. The speed of the ride and the darkness scared those kids to death. It was a popular ride. No lemonade stands for us — we were city kids.

Judges, Chicago Park District's "Save the Lawn" Contest, 1633 N. Mason, 1940. Humboldt Park (Courtesy of the Chicago Park District.)

Raymond DeGroote
West Ridge

I was born in 1930 in the North Town neighborhood, and have lived on Claremont ever since. When I was growing up this was a brand new neighborhood, having been laid out in 1926. This was a typical two-flat neighborhood in that owners lived in one apartment and rented out the other. Many of the corner lots around here were not built on right away, so they were just vacant lots. During the winter, the fire department would clean them out a bit and flood them, and we would go ice skating on these corner lots.

My neighborhood was nice, with good schools, and of course, good transportation. I've always had an interest in transportation. In fact, my parents told me that as early as seven years old I noticed there were different streetcars running in the city. Some had round roofs and some had squared-off roofs. My father insisted that they were all the same, except for "the funny blue cars" running on Madison Street. Those funny blue cars turned out to be the first of the new "Green Hornet"-type streetcars, the PCC car. They were an attempt by the transit companies nationwide to improve the image of public transit, making them more streamlined. Chicago had one of the largest fleets of these cars. They were blue before the war and painted green after. They got the name Green Hornet because they were quiet, fast and because the Green Hornet was a popular character at the time.

I remember going downtown, alone, at seven years of age. A seven year old kid going downtown by himself! That was pretty good stuff! My father made me a map — take the Western Avenue streetcar to the Ravenswood "L" line, get on and go to Quincy and Wells, then walk a couple of blocks west to the Marquette Building. It wasn't scary at all, it was an adventure! I liked riding up front on the streetcar with the motorman. We kids always stood up front and rode with him. It was a grand adventure!

Streetcar fare at that time would have been around $.07, compared to $.15 or $.20 on the Chicago & North Western line. This would have been a staggering difference in those days! The North Western wasn't off-limits, but it wasn't practical. Occasionally, I would ride the Illinois Central trains for special occasions, which were also higher fare. We would ride them to the Museum of Science Industry and get off at 57th Street, which was within walking distance.

Riding the streetcars of the 1940s was not very different than riding the buses of today, except that the ride back then would have been smoother. If the tracks were good at all, it was a smooth ride. The older "Red Rocket" streetcars could be noisy, as they growled along, especially when they stopped. If the tracks were not maintained properly, which was the case during the war, the car would rock back and forth. The Green Hornet style streetcar was smoother and faster, and it could pick up speed rather quickly. These new streetcars performed well, which was one of the objectives when they began production in the mid-thirties — to make a high performance car. These were good pieces of machinery, and they served for years and years.

A critical transportation addition came in October 1943, when the State Street Subway opened. It was pushed through because it was considered essential to the war effort. The congestion in the Loop was pretty bad, because all the trains had to run on the elevated tracks back then, including the North Shore Interurban trains. While they could manage it, service was slow. The subway relieved that congestion. It allowed people to get downtown quicker, which was something that was deemed critical to the war effort.

Kids had a role in this success as well, because if we bought a War Bond, we got a free ride on the subway the day it opened. And I did! Believe me, I was down there! I think I was in eighth grade at the time and I was the Transportation Coordinator at my school. My job was to tell the kids how to ride the subway, and I even gave a class one day! I showed pictures and used a map. I told how to buy a fare and use a transfer, and talked about how not to be afraid of the dark and all the noise.

The other important transportation event of the decade was the forming of the CTA (Chicago Transit Authority) in 1947. It was created to take over the various transportation properties that were near bankruptcy. Public transportation rarely makes money, and this was the case here. The CTA was set-up to buy Chicago's two major transportation systems — the Chicago Surface Line, which was the streetcars and buses, and the Chicago Rapid Transit Company, which was the "L" and subway. Eventually it bought the Motor Coach Company as well, which included the double-deck buses that ran on Sheridan Road. The goal was to merge all these lines together and improve the transportation system in the city. Many of the CTA's changes did help. They cut down the number of local stops, which helped speed-up service. They eventually got rid of all the streetcars, and parts of most of the PCC cars became parts of the 6000 series elevated cars — the green cars.

But the automobile was always the greatest threat to public transportation. Everybody wanted their own means of transportation. It began as early as the 1930s. After the Depression, as more and more people began to get some income, they wanted a car. My father was a good example of this, he had to have his Buick! Public transportation ridership dropped tremendously after the war, for two reasons — they all bought automobiles and they all started moving to the suburbs.

"Green Hornet" Streetcar, Garfield Park, 1947. East Garfield Park (Courtesy of the CTA.)

Clark and Balmoral, ca. 1940. Edgewater (Courtesy of the CTA.)

Ann Gerber
Edgewater

My world really revolved around Clark Street in Edgewater. In the 1940s, I was living at 5705 North Clark Street, in a third floor walk-up. It was a Swedish and German neighborhood back then. My father had a grocery store at 5555 North Clark on the corner of Clark and Bryn Mawr. I remember during the war my father thought there was going to be a shortage of sugar. He put all the money he had, about $5,000, into Domino sugar. The back of the grocery store was filled with little yellow boxes. But the sugar crisis never came, and the sugar got harder, and harder, and harder. My mother used to upbraid him, "Why did you do that?" Because of that, I've never nagged any of my three husbands.

Down the street from the grocery, across from the Calo Theater, there was a big church on Clark. The minister used to stride through the neighborhood wearing a long black coat and hat. I think he was very tortured. He never looked happy, and we were all very terrified of him. His manner was very scary to us. He was probably a very nice man, but I only saw him as a specter walking through the neighborhood.

I also remember the peddlers on Clark, especially the one who made ice cream fudge. It was not cold to the touch and it was not frozen, but when you ate it, it was cold. I don't know if it had menthol in it, but it was delicious. I remember some of the women in the neighborhood would ask, "How do you make this?" And he would say, "I'm never going tell you, because I'm going to make a fortune off of this!" I don't think he ever did.

As a Jewish girl living in Edgewater I remember feeling very left out. There were only a few Jewish families in the neighborhood. I went to Pierce School, and one day after classes I went over to a girlfriend's house and her mother answered the door. She said, "You can't come in. The girl's have formed a club called 'IHS,' that means 'In His Steps,' and we don't want any little Jewish girls coming in." It just broke my heart.

In the summer, on really hot nights, my mother would take two sheets and we would sleep at the Bryn Mawr beach. At that time there was a very big beach at Bryn Mawr. It was very safe, and you would see your neighbors sleeping there, too. And I do remember going to Riverview in the summer. My girlfriend, Dorothy, had a big, heavy father who was a motorman and he took a group of us to Riverview for the rides. I was the skinniest and the littlest, so I got to sit next to him. When we went on the roller coaster I was the only one who wasn't afraid because I was so wedged-in! He was so big there was no possible way I could fall out!

One of my first jobs was working at a dime store on Clark near Foster. I started working at Miesner's when I was around fourteen years old. I was a really scrawny little kid, but I told him I was seventeen. I loved working there! My first job was in the basement making Easter baskets. They had a formula: she would give you a basket, and you would put in twelve jelly beans, three marshmallow eggs, two little rabbits, and then you would wrap it in cellophane with a bow. But they never looked full enough for me. So I would put in extra jelly beans and extra eggs, and things like that. I remember he came down and said, "Our baskets have never sold as well since you have been making them!"

I was very conscious of being poor as a kid. I wanted to be on Sheridan Road in the better section! I always had hand-me-down clothes. My mother had a son and three daughters, and I was the last. I didn't have a dress of my own until I was about twelve. I was very much aware of being deprived, but everyone around me was deprived. I didn't like it. I remember seeing girls at Senn High School with angora sweaters and matching ankle socks, and they could buy French fries at lunch, too. I saved my money.

Back then, it seemed everyone who had money went to Sullivan High School. "Good girls go to Heaven, bad girls go to Senn." That was the saying. Senn was just okay, but we were always in awe of the girls who went to Sullivan. They were better dressed, and people picked them up in cars! I remember one boyfriend who rode me home on his bike everyday. That was as good as it got!

restaurant was the Pekin House, whose owner began to look more Jewish as he grew older. For a while I worked at Pekin House for $.70 an hour, and I could eat anything I wanted for free except the shrimp dishes because they were more expensive."

Rogers Park resident Dr. Ira Bernstein moved to the neighborhood in 1943 after living in Virginia. "We lived at the corner of Columbia and Lakewood, and I went to grammar school, Hebrew School and high school all within a block of my apartment. Since my mother was ill, my sister and I did the shopping. There was a grocery store on Sheridan Road between Columbia and Pratt on the west side of the street. Abe's Delicatessen was on the southeast corner of Columbia and Sheridan, and I also remember Mesirow's Drugstore on the northwest corner of Pratt and Sheridan."

Former Cook County Sheriff Dick Elrod remembers shopping as part of his daily life on the West Side. "Roosevelt Road had many little grocery stores and dress shops and it was like a long shopping mall. The Jewish people tended to stay in the neighborhood for their shopping. In fact, I remember a grocery store on Roosevelt that delivered, and they used to bring our groceries to our third floor apartment at 1323 Independence."

Next to State Street, Maxwell Street might be Chicago's most famous shopping experience. Mel Pearl grew up on the West Side, and when he was just ten years old began working at his grandfather's shoe store near Maxwell Street. "It was on Halsted, just north of Maxwell Street and it was called Brusman's. I used to go there and help by pulling the shoe boxes for the salesmen. The Maxwell Street area was a bustling place, almost like a movie set. Around the corner from my grandfather's store was a little delicatessen in the basement and they used to send me there to get sandwiches for the staff at the shoe store. I remember that there was such a wonderful smell of hot corned beef that permeated the neighborhood. Mexican vendors had come to the area by the late '40s and they used pushcarts to sell their wares. However, during the '40s, Jewish merchants were still the predominant group on Maxwell Street. I remember the street was a hubbub of excitement and it was an incredible experience to be there. It was a great, great time!"

Working Life

From working in the steel mills of the Southeast Side to department stores in the Loop, Chicagoans have always been known for their strong work ethics. And during the 1940s, residents of Chicago neighborhoods found a wide variety of jobs to provide income for themselves and their families. The war provided a big boost to the economy, and many residents who had gone without jobs could now find employment. Children and young adults were also encouraged to work too, ranging from delivering and selling newspapers to setting pins in bowling alleys. It became a family affair to find enough income to cover monthly expenses and still have extra funds for entertainment.

Howard Rosen commuted from his Albany Park home to his job in the Loop during the '40s. "The first job I had was one I got through some friends of mine who were working at Kitty Kelly's Shoe Store on State Street near Monroe. I wasn't allowed to sell shoes on that job, but they had me wrap packages during the Christmas season. When Christmas ended, I didn't have a job. So, I went back downtown to find a new job. I walked into a store off State and Madison called Berland's, another ladies' shoe store. I remember walking up to some guy and saying, 'You don't need anybody to work here, do you?' I was so sure that he wasn't going to hire me. The man's name was Mr. Spiwak, and he said, 'Yeah, I do need someone, as a matter of fact.' So, my first official job was selling shoes at Berland's. They had a downstairs area where they sold the more expensive dress shoes, and an upstairs where they sold the 'play' shoes. I was hired to work upstairs, and although I was a very shy, laid-back kid, somehow I developed a whole new personality and turned into a terrific salesman with a strong personality. I would still be shy when I left the store, but when I was selling shoes it was a new me."

Jim O'Connor's father bought a farm in northwest suburban Woodstock in the 1930s, and the family would go there on weekends. "We would spend our summers there. It started as a dairy farm and then became a beef cattle farm in the late '40s. We also had a lot of chickens. So, the deal was that on Sunday we would collect the eggs, wash them, put them in large cartons, and then bring them back to Chicago. My sisters and I would go door-to-door and sell the eggs to our neighbors. We did this during the '40s, and the three of us would go to all the apartments in our Gresham neighborhood around 79th and Ashland and sell the eggs for $.15 or $.20 a dozen. Our parents let us keep the money. We tried to sell 30 dozen eggs every Sunday night."

Edie Phillips Horowitz lived in Edgewater and remembers, "One of the best jobs I ever had was working for the Chicago Bears and George Halas. I was a receptionist and secretary for Rudy Custer, one of the top people in the Bears organization. They were located at 37 S. Wabash, and Mr. Custer gave me a nice desk in his huge office. It was a very easy job and a lot of fun because it didn't involve a lot of typing. Clark Shaughnessy was the head coach of the Bears at the time. In fact, I had to be bonded for the job because I was asked to sit down with him while he drew the plays on the blackboard — I then copied them down in the play

Chicago Public Library Bookmobile, 115 S. Crawford, 1944. West Garfield Park (Special Collections and Preservation Division, Chicago Public Library.)

Looking North on Clark, South Loop, ca. 1944. Loop (Courtesy of the CTA.)

Charles Kocoras
Woodlawn

I was born in 1938 at 6614 S. State Street. That was an odd structure. I lived on the second floor, and there had to be at least twenty rooms on that floor. The first floor of the building was a huge, barn-like warehouse. My father, who was a wholesale dealer in fruits and vegetables, would sell his produce to horse-and-buggy fruit peddlers. Peddlers kept their horses and wagons on the first floor and lived on the second. Most of these people were Greeks from the old country who came here as young men because the economy in Greece wasn't so good. America was the land of opportunity! So, they came here and lived with my father and mother.

The Greek community concentrated around 67th, 69th, and 71st and State. Like all of Chicago, when immigrants first came, they tended to stay to themselves. There were some a little further west, and there was a big Greek community in Greek Town west of the Loop. There were Greeks up north, but we never crossed Madison Street other than when I went to my first Cubs game in 1948. As people became more successful and more mobile, they felt less of a need to stay among their own kind, so they started disbursing. At one point, compared to Athens, we had the second or third highest concentration of Greeks in the world. There are more than 250,000 Greeks in the Chicago area.

My father came to America around the turn of the century. He was about seventeen years old when he came in 1901 or 1902. Then, as immigrants often did, he worked for the railroad for a while. The railroads were the big employers then, and he was just a water boy. He wound up in Utah someplace, but somehow made his way back to Chicago and got into the produce business at the wholesale end. Once upon a time, he was the premier guy in the south markets around 71st and State.

A very fond and vivid memory of mine was going down to the markets with my father. The daily routine was for him to get up at 2 o'clock in the morning. You have to understand that these were the days before the interstate highways were developed and built. In those days at 2 a.m. there was no street traffic. None. For me, it was fun to be with my dad. For him, it was the beginning of an eighteen hour workday. When you're a kid, you don't understand what these people went through. So, we would get in our empty truck and drive to the market, around 15th and Morgan. I learned to drive about the age of fifteen. When I got behind the wheel of the truck I couldn't hit a car or a building even if I wanted to, because there was nobody on the street. We would come most of the way down State — there was no traffic at all. The street was quiet and the city was quiet.

When we got to South Water Street, my dad would purchase his merchandise and by 6 a.m. the truck would be loaded. We then would drive back down south to his store and unload the truck. All the grocers from "ma and pa" grocery stores would come and buy their morning goods. Then, in the afternoon, my dad would spend time delivering the merchandise to these stores. He would begin his workday at 2 a.m. and wouldn't get home until 6 or 7 o'clock in the evening. Even when he was in his 60s, he kept that schedule.

One of the stores I delivered to is still in business, and the owner is still a friend of mine. In those days it was on Commercial Avenue, and it was called Gayety Candy Company. When I was a kid, Gayety Candy made their own ice cream and chocolates. They would buy bananas from my dad for banana splits, and they would always buy the best bananas. When I was twelve or thirteen years old I always made that trip to Gayety Candy because they would give me homemade ice cream.

I think that the '40s was a time of expansion of ability. The early immigrants worked with their backs and they sweated. Suddenly, the schools were being attended by them and by their children. So, there was an expansion of learning by immigrants at that time. All the Greek parents, even though they weren't formally educated in their own countries, insisted on everybody going to school and excelling in school. We had to bring our report cards home every time, and while some parents couldn't read English, they knew what the grades were. If you brought home a grade that wasn't good, you had to explain it. There was this emphasis on education that is characteristic in Greek culture. There was an understanding that you were Greek ethnically, but you lived in America. So, it was exploring not only your own culture, and being proud of it, but being exposed to different cultures and different races.

It was a marvelous time living in the city and growing up during the 1940s. Crime was much less in those years, and murder was a rare event. There wasn't the sense of insecurity that would come later. There wasn't a sense of fear if you were in a strange neighborhood, but there was little reason to go anyplace else.

book for the team. The funny thing was, I never really understood football, or had much of an interest in the sport."

Hal Lichterman grew up in the Albany Park neighborhood. "To many people, Albany Park was centered around Lawrence Avenue. On Lawrence and Central Park was a very famous delicatessen called Rudich's. People hung out there, and at Lawndale Pool Hall. However, my stomping grounds were on Kedzie Avenue, where there was a bowling alley called Leland Bowl with a pool hall upstairs. I would swing around to Montrose and I'd set pins at Monte Cristo Bowl and Drake Bowl. They had leagues at that bowl, and I was probably one of the only Jewish kids who set pins there."

Otho Kortz grew up in Englewood and has memories of the nearby stockyards. "Englewood was a fantastic neighborhood, and in those days almost every family had someone working in the Union Stockyards. I worked there, so did my dad and my grandfather. My dad worked in the stockyard business from the time he was fourteen — and he died in the stockyards in Joliet. He was weighing some cows, and he had a stroke. He was happy to die there." Another resident of Englewood, Bill Phelan, remembers the work ethic in his neighborhood. "It was a great, interesting neighborhood, and I wouldn't even call it middle-class. They were all hard-working people — blue-collar people. My father was a Chicago streetcar man for many years, and later became a policeman during World War II. He was born in Canada, and when he was eighteen years old he came to Chicago with some of his other brothers and sisters and got a job at the Rock Island Railroad. He also worked for the Chicago Surface Line, and then the Chicago Police Department, from where he retired. My mother worked a good part of her life as a housewife, and she also worked outside the home a great deal to help the family, because it had to be done."

Sheldon Rosing's life changed when his father had a heart attack at age 38. "My dad had been a life insurance salesman for Metropolitan Life and worked in South Chicago. We lived in South Shore, and when he couldn't work, my parents opened a grocery store downtown near State and Van Buren. They sold fruits, vegetables, candies, nuts and stuff like that in their little store that near the Dearborn Street Station. When people traveled on the trains, they would stop in for cold cuts and other food. Our rent was about $140 a month in 1941 because of rent controls, but when the war ended, the rent skyrocketed to $900 a month and we just had to close the store."

Young people had to be versatile when it came to finding a summer job. Mike Perlow, who grew up in Garfield Park, recalls, "I have always had a very strong work ethic, and when I was a freshman in high school my father suggested that it was time for me to get a summer job. I had come

Kay Kuwahara
Near North Side

My beauty shop was at 111 W. Division, inside the Mark Twain Hotel. When we got here in 1945, the neighborhood was pretty rough. Many of my customers were waitresses, strippers, showgirls, prostitutes, and "26" girls. Back then, all the taverns had "26" girls. The girls had to be very attractive and dress provocatively, and run the dice game called "26."

The hairstyle back then was "the more the merrier" and the "bigger the better." That was our specialty, making hair larger. And back then women would come in once a week to get their hair done. They didn't wash their hair everyday like they do now. They would come and get a shampoo and set, and then maintain it during the week. The hair wouldn't get dirty because the dirt couldn't penetrate all that lacquer!

At first, people would come to the beauty shop, but after they saw that I was Japanese, they would never come back. But the nightclub girls and waitresses didn't care, and kept coming back. They liked my specialty — blondes. I loved blondes and could make their hair a platinum blonde, which was very popular back then. We got really good word of mouth and pretty soon all the waitresses would come in. Then, because their hair looked so good, all the strippers started coming in. Then the prostitutes started coming in! It was a real wide-open place back then!

When we got to the Mark Twain we didn't know of its bad reputation, but we soon learned. I was told the prostitution was run this way — you gave a tip to the porter and he would get you a girl. These were our clients! Not all of them, but a lot of them were.

We also had all of the big-time syndicate and mobster's girlfriends coming in. At the time I didn't know who they were, but they all talked the "Sopranos"-talk! They were all very nice to us. In fact, they were protective of us. If anybody came along that bothered us, they would say, "Move on. She's a good girl!" These guys dated a lot of the showgirls working in the neighborhood, on Rush Street and on Clark.

All these sweet girls were just being used by these men. I prayed for these girls, but they were just willing victims. I told my minister, "I feel so bad. I do these girls' hair and they go right out and do their business with the men." He said, "Kay, you must do this, because you are one of the few graces in their lives. You treat them like human beings."

These guys were just so clever, giving them money and furs. They gave them their dreams.

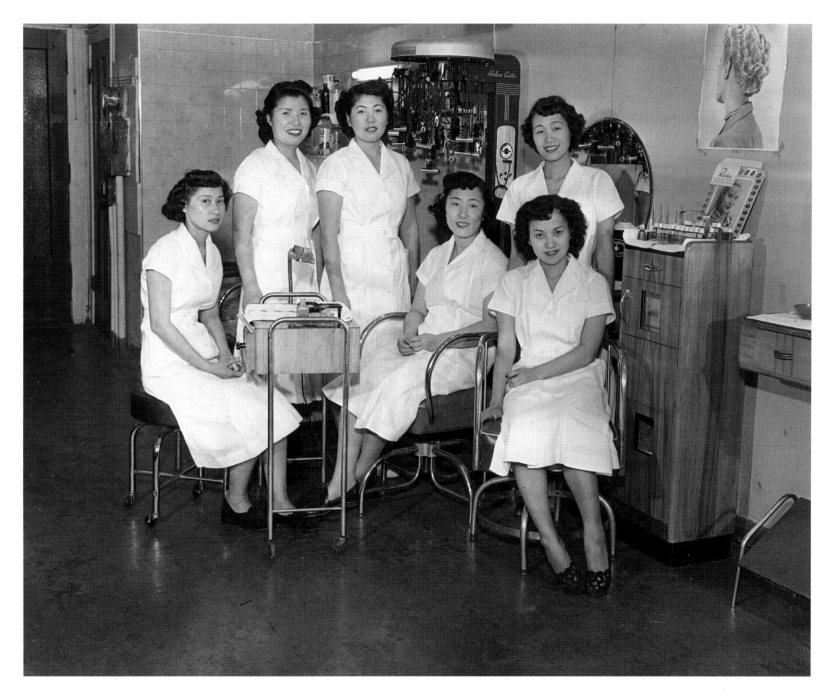

Co-ed Beauty Salon, 1305 E. 53rd, 1949. Hyde Park (Courtesy of the Japanese American Service Committee Legacy Center, Mary and James Numata Collection.)

West Side Historical Society Meeting, 1947. West Garfield Park (Courtesy of Special Collections and Preservation Division, Chicago Public Library.)

Adelaide Gredys Winston
Logan Square

*I*was born in 1919 and moved to Chicago in 1930. We lived in Logan Square in the attic apartment of a bungalow on Richmond near Diversey. I went to Roosevelt High School and graduated in 1936, during the depths of the Depression. I was pretty high in my class and was invited to attend the University of Chicago, but my family couldn't afford to let me go there. So, a girlfriend of mine whose uncle was the head telegrapher at the Chicago & Eastern Illinois Railroad told me about an opening in the telegraph office for a messenger girl. So, I went to work as a messenger girl at the C&EI Railroad. I was always a friendly, outgoing kid, not fresh or anything, but never a shrinking violet. Soon the railroad needed an additional reservation clerk during the winter season. So, I worked two winters in the reservation bureau. It was a different time and world.

The head of the passenger reservations would always walk around and listen to us to see what kind of job we were doing. One day in 1943, I was asked to go to his office. I wasn't worried because I knew I was doing a good job. When I got to his office, he said, "Ms. Gredys, the boys are being drafted too rapidly for us to train another man on the ticket counter. Would you be interested in learning to be a ticket seller?" Well, I was very interested, and that's how I became a ticket seller. And I was paid on the same scale as the men when I was hired. I was moved to the 175 West Jackson Boulevard Consolidated Ticket Office, a lively place during the war. I became Chicago's first female railroad ticket seller when I was hired to sell tickets for the B&O, the Nickel Plate and the Alton Railroad. It's hard for young people today to imagine what railroad travel was at the height of the war. In the days when servicemen were moving from unheard of hometowns to unlikely sounding bases, the job was very stimulating.

One of the trains which I sold tickets for was the Capitol Limited. This line carried many important wartime figures to and from Washington. One such person was Silliman Evans, who was brought from Nashville, Tennessee, by Marshall Field to launch the Chicago Sun. When he returned south after the paper was established, I received what in those days was an unheard-of generous gift — a check for $100 for the help I provided in ticketing his trip. In addition, that Christmas I received a jar of Tennessee Mountain Honey and a crate of Texas citrus with his compliments.

I thoroughly enjoyed my job and I would have been there until the railroad collapsed, but I got sick in 1945. In fact, on April 12, 1945, when Roosevelt died, I was so sick that my mother came downtown in a taxicab and took me home. That was the end of my railroad career.

Speech Class, Mundelein College, ca. 1944. Rogers Park (Courtesy of the Rogers Park/West Ridge Historical Society.)

Wayne Juhlan
Portage Park

In Portage Park the Six Corners shopping area — Irving, Cicero, and Milwaukee — was the big deal. I remember the Sears Department Store, which was the flagship store in the neighborhood, had this giant window they would put displays in. We would all wait with great anticipation for the unveiling of the next big display in the window. During the war they had patriotic stuff in the window, but at Christmas they always had a giant Santa Claus in the window.

Down the street was the Portage Theatre, and going there was a big deal. They had something called the "Fifteen Cartoon Show," where they played all cartoons with no features. Other stores in the area included Klee Brothers and Abraham's Department Store. To get you into the store, Abraham's offered cheap hair cuts, which were popular for mothers who wanted to save a quarter. I remember a delicatessen around there that had this big barrel filled with herring. There were smells in this place that I never smelled before! Big vats of pickles and fish! Then there were the dime stores, like Woolworth's. These stores had a wonderful combination of smells because they sold so many different things. Live fish and turtles would be sold alongside fabric and candy. Oh, the sweet smell of candy!

Not far from there, at Cullom and Montrose, was Rock-Ola Stadium. They had a women's fast-pitch softball league there, and my dad and I would go every night to see them play. The team was called the Rock-Ola Music Maids, sponsored by the jukebox company, and they would play teams like the Queens and the Bloomer Girls. Our ritual was this: my dad would pay for a ticket, and I would crawl through a hole in the fence out in left field! I would crawl through and then meet my dad in the stands. We actually got to know the players pretty well. In fact, I set-up a date for one of the girls. I introduced Josephine Kaybeck to one of the Chicago Cubs who used to come out there. We followed that league for years, and they had some great players. Wilda Mae Turner was the best pitcher. She wasn't a bad looking girl either, real blonde and statuesque. Then, these two massive woman came into the league — Frida and Olympia Savona. A lot of guys thought they were men, because they were so muscular and stocky. They broke all the records! Just shattered them!

After the game we'd walk back home and stop at the hot dog stand. You know, there used to be stands and vendors all over the city before the Board of Health put limitations on them, saying you couldn't serve food without a washroom. And there used to be guys who would come to your door selling all kinds of household items, like needles and thread, and other things that ladies bought. Today, people would be much more nervous about opening their doors. Then, there was the "rags-old-iron-man," the junk man, the knife sharpener, and the ice man. The ice man would deliver ice in a horse-drawn truck. I remember one of the thrills as a kid was to try to run under these big horses without getting kicked!

Radio was a very big deal back then. I knew the daily schedule so well that I would have people test me on the times the shows were on. At night, with my family or alone, I listened. One of my favorites was the "Lux Radio Theater," where they would take a movie and condense it down to a hour-long radio version. On Saturday mornings, they had kid shows like "Let's Pretend," which would have great actors doing fairy tales, and "Grand Central Station," where the actors would come out and announce themselves. Then there were goofy shows like "It Pays to be Ignorant," which asked simple questions and a panel would give unbelievably dumb answers. A question might be, "What Indian tribe weaves Navaho blankets?" Then the panel would give stupid responses like, "Duhh, now dese' blankets you got, are dey thick blankets?"

Another of my favorites was "Steve Wilson of the Illustrated Press." He was a crime-fighting reporter who ended his show the same way every week! It would go like this — he would chase down and corner a criminal with a gun, and then his cab-driving partner would say, "Let me hit him with my noggin-knocking monkey wrench!" "No, that's not necessary," Steve would say, "I'll talk him out of it!" He would then deliver some moral message, and the criminal would always end up saying, "You win Wilson!" Week after week, it would always end the same way!

The 1940s was a special time in Chicago, and this could not happen again. It just couldn't happen again.

Lincoln Park, 1942. Lincoln Park (Courtesy of the Chicago Park District.)

home from a long summer vacation and went over to Lake Street and began walking down the street looking for some work. I didn't find a job until I got to Clinton Street, at a machine tool shop. It was a hard job cleaning up the place, running jigsaws and lathes, and that began my work experience. During those following summers, I worked in a lumberyard, as an electrician's apprentice, at the Chicago Board of Trade, and at the real estate office of Arthur Rubloff and Company."

Street and Alley Vendors

By the end of the 1940s, the era of street and alley vendors was coming to a close. Dating back to the nineteenth century, these enterprising vendors were fixtures in Chicago's neighborhoods providing many valuable services. Knife-sharpeners, junk men, Fuller Brushmen, icemen, fruit and vegetable peddlers and milk men, many in horse drawn wagons, saved customers a trip to their local stores.

Kenwood resident Richard Lukin recalls, "In the '40s, you still had the horse and wagon vendors working in the neighborhoods. Bryman and Wanzer delivered milk every day in a wagon. That was the way customers got their milk. You had a cardboard form stapled to the back of your door and the delivery man would mark off what you ordered. Then, at the end of the month, you would get an invoice. And there were still a few apartments in the '40s that didn't have an electric refrigerator, so they had iceboxes. You would see the iceman trudging up the stairs with a heavy load of ice. In those days, you had to put a delivery card in your back window or door indicating how much weight you wanted — 25, 50, 75 or 100 pounds. The guy could see from the alley what you needed, and he would chop a piece off of a big 300-pound block. It was also very common to see fruit and vegetable peddlers. These guys would get a beat-up old truck or horse and wagon and load it up at the South Water Market, then work the neighborhoods. I remember so many of these vendors in the neighborhoods. By my grandmother's house over on North Avenue there was a guy who sold penny waffles with powdered sugar from a little wagon. When I was in grammar school, there was a guy who parked by the school who sold hot dogs, ice cream, and something I had never seen before — sugar cane — little four or five inch pieces of real live sugar cane."

Peanut Vendor, Sheridan Road, ca. 1948. Rogers Park (Courtesy of the Rogers Park/West Ridge Historical Society.)

Sports and Recreation in the Neighborhood

If you grew up in a Chicago neighborhood in the 1940s you needed to be creative, both in finding places to play and filling up your time. Most children created their own fun, without any adult supervision, in the streets, alleys, courtyards, gangways or one of the many empty lots or "prairies" that dotted the neighborhoods. If they were lucky enough to live near a park, and old enough to cross streets to get there, the parks would be gathering places for activity. Public and parochial school grounds were also used regularly, with baseball and softball played on gravel school yards, and fast-pitch against school yard walls. Other popular neighborhood games including line ball, football, pinners, hide and seek (also known as rolevio), kick the can, street hockey, and red rover. The key element for many children's activities during the 1940s was the almost complete lack of adult supervision — something very different from neighborhood life today.

As children got older, there were many adult-organized activities in the neighborhoods: at parks, beaches and field houses, as well as in public and parochial school yards. In the spring, as the temperature would begin to warm, it was time for playing ball, whether 12- or 16-inch softball or baseball. In the summer, kids would leave home at an early hour and spend the entire day playing sports and games, swimming at the larger parks, and if they could find transportation to Lake Michigan, having fun at the city's beaches. Then, in the fall and winter, the sports changed to football, basketball, ice-skating and hockey.

For kids and adults there were also ample opportunities to attend and participate in the many high school, college, semi-pro, and professional sports in the neighborhoods. Pro games by the Cubs, White Sox, Bears, Cardinals, Stags, and Blackhawks were highly attended, as well as college games by DePaul, Loyola, University of Chicago and the neighboring Northwestern University. High school sports were also significant events in the lives of city residents, and many great public and parochial school teams played in the 1940s. In addition, there were numerous semi-pro leagues, including men and women's hardball and softball leagues, that played at ballparks including Mills, Thillens, Parichy, Shewbridge and Bidwill.

Street and Alley Games

Children of all ethnic, racial and religious groups played street and alley games in the 1940s. Due to limited space in the urban environment, parental admonition against crossing major streets, and the general lack of automobile traffic, streets and alleys were popular locations for boys and girls to play. Invariably, if they played in the alleys, someone would be assigned the task of climbing on top of garages or going into backyards to retrieve the balls. If games were played on the street, manhole covers, street lamps and parked cars became bases and boundaries for baseball and football games. Empty lots or "prairies" that had not been developed for

Opposite: *Lifeguards, Jackson Park, 1940.* Woodlawn
(Courtesy of the Chicago Park District.)

housing or businesses could be found in most Chicago neighborhoods in the '40s. Children, sometimes with their parents, would clear the undeveloped land of bushes, trees, weeds and garbage to transform them into usable places to play. Creativity ruled the day, and children did not have to venture too far from their apartments, bungalows or houses to have fun.

Ian Levin and his friends spent many hours playing in front of their apartment buildings on Estes Avenue, west of Sheridan Road, as well as in the alleys behind the buildings in his Far North Side neighborhood. "During the '40s, there was no Loyola Park on Sheridan Road, so we played on Estes. We used to play pinners, and we liked playing on the street so much that even after the park was finished in the early '50s, we just continued to play our games on the street. The games included field hockey, touch football, bounce the balls off the buildings, and spud. However, the big game for us was pinners. For pinners we used a pink, Spaulding high bounce ball and threw it against a curb or the side of a building. The goal was to make the ball bounce over the opponent's head and land in the area designated for single, double, triple or home run. Pinners was meant to be played in limited spaces. We used a ledge on a building, and we had a batters box by the alley. Interestingly, some of us actually used to slide on the concrete street into second base when we played pinners, but at least I had the sense not to slide head-first. Many times I would come home with torn pants and cuts on my hands and legs. We spent our entire summers playing those games around our apartment buildings."

In Albany Park, Marvin Aspen and his friends also played street and alley games. "As we got older, our recreation included line ball in the alleys and in the streets. Line ball was a variation of baseball and only required two players on each team. The teams would agree on specific fair and foul territories. There would be a pitcher and one fielder on each team and the goal was to hit the ball into safe territory without it being caught. Just like a baseball game there were balls, strikes, and outs. When we got a little bigger space, we played bounce and fly. If you caught the ball either on a bounce or a fly, you were out. We played pinners, and the biggest pinners site was in front of the Albany Park Hebrew Congregation against its facade. The congregation was kitty-corner of the Max Strauss Center, on the southeast corner of Lawndale and Wilson. One of the greatest forms of entertainment was playing in empty lots. It wasn't a prairie to us, it was an empty lot, and our favorite empty lot was one with tall weeds located on Lawrence Avenue, about two or three stores from the southwest corner of Lawndale and Lawrence.

To a kid of three, four, or five years of age, it felt like a forest because the weeds were taller than we were."

A nearby "prairie" became the center of activity for Tom Hynes and his friends in the Gresham neighborhood. "The parks were far away from us, so we basically made our own parks and created a baseball field from a prairie, a vacant block that was actually a half a block wide and a block long. With the assistance of many of the fathers in the neighborhood, we cut down the weeds and small wild saplings and filled-in many of the holes. We had a blast, but it was not exactly up to modern Little League standards. We played mostly 16-inch softball, but we played hardball and 12-inch softball too."

Alderman Edward Burke grew up in Visitation Parish on the Southwest Side. "We played in the streets and the alleys all the time. The games included tag, rolevio, red rover — where you ran to see if you could break through the line — cops and robbers, and of course, cowboys and Indians. We would play touch football, but not baseball in the street. When we wanted to play baseball we would go over to the park."

Ed Brennan grew up in Austin and enjoyed playing softball in the street. "We always played 16-inch softball in the streets, and home plate was in the middle of the street. There wasn't that much traffic back then, although you had to move aside for cars all the time. Living two doors off of Madison Street meant there would always be a certain amount of traffic on the street. But the side streets were a good place to play, and most of the stuff we did was by ourselves."

In Lake View, across from Belmont Harbor, U.S. District Judge James Zagel recalls, "During the 1940s, we played in a vacant lot that someone landscaped nicely — it was our playing field. We used to play softball there, and we would play pitcher's hands out because we usually didn't have enough people. Then, in the winter, we would play football there. I distinctly remember the billboard for Butternut bread that was on the property. The bottom of the picture of the blue-checked loaf was about ten feet above the ground, and it was fairly wide. So, for the first time, we were able to kick field goals. If we place-kicked a field goal and it hit the bread, or went directly above it, we scored three points."

Joseph Lamendella grew up on Lill Avenue near Diversey and Racine. "Lill Avenue was a very homogeneous street that included people of many nationalities. Our play consisted of street games like kick the can, tag, hide and go seek, red rover, and rolevio. In rolevio, there were two teams of children. While one team was hiding around the neighborhood, it was the goal of the other team to find the hidden kids.

The street games were coed, by and large, although some of the hide and seek games were played primarily by boys because they were rougher games. We also played stick ball in the streets, and a game called 'bounce out' where we would take a soft rubber ball and hit it against the steps of an apartment building or a house and depending on where the ball landed, it was a single, double, triple or home run. Other people called this game pinners."

In West Rogers Park, Ron Davis remembers playing football in front of his house. "In the '40s we would play touch football on the street. There weren't many cars in those days, and maybe only one or two would be parked on our street. In the huddle of our touch football game, we would instruct the receiver to go down to the blue car and turn left, and I would pass the ball to him. The games would always be from sewer to sewer and they would become the goal lines. The sewers were 42' apart, and that was how we would play touch football. The cable at the alley became the crossbar to kick extra points and field goals. It was terrific."

Bernie Judge remembers the alley basketball games in his South Shore neighborhood. "Alley basketball was a full-time job during the basketball season. We would play behind Dr. Wall's house. There was a basketball hoop on the garage, and you just showed up. Nolan's Shoe Store was right at the corner of 79th and Bennett, next to the Red Keg, and he used to say that alley basketball was the shoe man's best friend because we wrecked our shoes playing. We played every day. To start a game, you would shoot from the free throw line, and if you sank your shot, you were on the team. The first eight or ten guys who sank their shot, they were on the team. The rule was that you called the fouls — nobody who played alley basketball would last five minutes in a real game. Occasionally fights would break out, but the game was among friends so it didn't last long."

Public and Parochial School Gyms and Playgrounds

In the 1940s, kids and adults often played their favorite sports on gravel school yards and in school gymnasiums. Children used the facilities for activities during the school day, and after school, children and adults used the facilities, playing sports such as softball, line ball, football, and fast-pitch.

Norman Mark remembers playing softball and fast-pitch in his school yard at Dixon Elementary School in Chatham. "The school was only a block and a half from my home. So, I would go over there and we would play 16-inch softball. It was a gravel lot and you were always slipping

Line Ball, 4500 Block of West Congress, ca. 1940. West Garfield Park
(Courtesy of Charles F. Simpson.)

Lifeguard Tests, Washington Park, 1940. Washington Park (Courtesy of the Chicago Park District.)

Tug-of-War, Roosevelt Road Beach, 1947. Near South Side (Courtesy of the Chicago Park District.)

Recreation Demonstration at Portage Park, 1942. Portage Park (Courtesy of the Chicago Park District.)

1st Tee, Jackson Park, 1947. Woodlawn (Courtesy of the Chicago Park District.)

and falling on the gravel. I think that I still have some gravel in my knee! We also had a game that we called 'fast pitch' where you would draw a batter's box on the wall and somebody would throw a tennis ball as fast as he could at the person who was batting. If you hit it over the fence into someone's living room, it was a home run. There was one guy, Jim Mann, who was the best fast-pitch pitcher ever. If they ever created a fast-pitch league, this guy would be incredible!"

Bob Cunniff grew up in Edgewater and recalls neighborhood basketball games inside nearby churches. "We lived right next door to the Church of the Atonement on Ardmore and Kenmore, where we used to play basketball. We had one friend who was an Episcopalian so we could use his resources to play in their gym. We had another friend who was a Presbyterian, and he belonged to the Presbyterian Church on Bryn Mawr and Kenmore. Their gym was a much better gym, and he actually switched from being an Episcopalian to being a Presbyterian in order to use the gym."

Bill Nellis recalls the weekly softball games held at Sullivan High School's gravel field in Rogers Park. "After World War II, around 1946, the big activity after Sunday church services at St. Ignatius was a doubleheader of 16-inch softball. They would use a new Clincher softball for each game. I would describe it as an 'ethnic' or 'religious' game because it was usually between teams of Catholic guys versus Jewish guys. The games would be played on the gravel field at the south end of Sullivan High School and they would usually begin at noon on Sunday. Both teams had some great players ranging in age from nineteen years old at the youngest, to guys in their late 30s, many who were war veterans. They were great games and the teams were a good reflection of the religious makeup of the neighborhood around Loyola University."

Bernie Judge remembers the softball games that used to be played on the gravel school yard at Horace Mann Elementary School in the South Shore neighborhood. "It was very difficult to play hardball at Mann because the ball would take crazy bounces, plus it would ruin the ball. There were big softball money games played there, and sometimes they would have three umpires. They were playing $100-a-man games in the late '40s and early '50s and then a keg of beer afterward. There were also lesser, $10-a-man games every Sunday. There were no leagues, they were all neighborhood games."

The Lake and the Beaches

In the 1940s, many Chicagoans used the beaches that stretched from Juneway Beach on the north to Calumet Beach on the south. Lake Michigan and the waterfront were popular spots for sunbathing and swimming by day, but they also provided important relief from the summer heat at night. In fact, it was not unusual for families to sleep overnight on the beach during summer's hottest nights, mingling with neighbors and enjoying the effects of the cool lake breezes.

Estelle Gordon Baron grew up in South Shore only a few blocks from Lake Michigan. "We lived down the street from Lake Michigan. None of us knew how to swim, so we couldn't go to the lake unless our mothers went with us. We would just splash around in the water. That lake was wonderful, though. In the summer, we would make sand castles on the beach. We went to the lake during the winter, too. I remember how the water would splash up on the boulders and would freeze over until it was smooth. My dad used to bring some cardboard boxes from the grocery store and we would climb up to the top, sit on the boxes, and go down the side of the frozen boulders. So, in the summer we had the lake for fun, and in the winter, when it was snowing and the schools would close down, we had the lake, too."

Irving Park resident Sheila Morris Williams remembers going to the beaches throughout her childhood. "I have many good memories of going to the beach, but most of my neighbors didn't go to the beaches, it was just too far away. In fact, only one family had a car in my neighborhood, and that was quite a novelty. My introduction to Lake Michigan was when my father, an Irish immigrant, threw me into the lake to 'teach me' how to swim. 'This is the way we do it in Ireland!' he screamed. During the last two summers of World War II, I would go to the beach with the wife of a soldier who was away. She was a boarder at my grandmother's house, and she would take me to the beach after she got off work. She was lonely for her husband, and just wanted to talk about him. The evenings were pleasant, but sad for her."

Fr. Gene Smith grew up on the South Side. "Rainbow Beach was important to us. It was a beautiful beach that ran from 75th to 79th Streets. The streetcar went right up 75th Street and made a circle by the beach. I remember that by 11 a.m. on Sunday mornings there were no more parking spots available at Rainbow Beach, and you couldn't see the sand because the people went there in droves."

Touhy Beach was an important part of the Rogers Park neighborhood. Shecky Greene remembers the beach, the field house, and Sam Leone. "When I was a lifeguard at Sam Leone's Touhy Beach in the 1940s, I would spend a lot of time at the lifeguard station with the other guys. During the winter we would ice-skate there, and, in the summer, we would play softball. Many years after I had moved out of Rogers Park, I came

Swimmers at Garfield Park, 1948. East Garfield Park (Courtesy of the Chicago Park District.)

back to honor Sam at a party for him at the American Legion hall on Devon. I was singing to him when I remembered that Sam couldn't hear a thing. He was almost deaf! But I loved being there and seeing everyone and honoring Sam. There was a man who really loved his job, and he loved the kids. I think that if they didn't pay him at all, he still would have done that job."

The Parks

As early as the 1860s, Chicago began to build a comprehensive park system. In 1864, an ordinance was passed to build Lake Park on the North Side. It would be renamed Lincoln Park in honor of the assassinated 16th President of the United States. By 1869, Chicago would begin to develop a city-wide park system that included Humboldt, Garfield, Jackson, South, Washington and Douglas Parks. Each of the parks would have a wide range of facilities available to Chicagoans, including baseball, tennis, boating, swimming, horseback riding, ice-skating, dancing and band concerts. By the 1940s, there were hundreds of large and small parks and play lots across the city.

During World War II, the Park District played an active role in Civil Defense activities, utilizing field houses and other facilities to aid in the home front effort. In addition, many residents planted Victory Gardens in their neighborhood parks, allowing farmers to focus their efforts on growing food for the men and women of the armed services.

To South Shore residents, Jackson Park provided just about every recreational activity one could ask for. Dick Jaffee recalls, "It had been the site of the Columbian Exposition and there were still things left in the park when I was a kid, including the Japanese Gardens. We used to go over there on many summer nights, before air conditioning, and rent a rowboat or fish in the lagoon. I also used to play hooky from Sunday school with my brother, and we would play ball in the park and then tell our mother that we had learned a lot in school that day."

Andrew McKenna's favorite park was also Jackson Park. "Jackson Park was near us, and later on I worked there during the summer when I was in high school and in college. The park was a little bit north of where I grew up, but it was still our park. We could walk down any of the streets we lived on to get there. I lived on Crandon, and it dead-ended at the park. You would just walk through the golf course there. Jackson Park might be the biggest park in the city. It had an 18-hole golf course, a number of different beaches, and a lot of recreational facilities. Jackson Park played a role for all of us growing up in South Shore."

On the Far North Side, Steve Zucker's favorite park was Green Briar. "We would spend every day, from the time we woke up until we went to sleep, at Green Briar Park on Peterson Avenue, between Washtenaw and Talman. I must have started going there when I was seven or eight years old, as soon as I could ride my bike. Ed Kelly, who would later on become Superintendent of the Chicago Park District, was the supervisor at Green Briar and he was always organizing things at the park. There was always something happening at Green Briar, and if they weren't organized games, it would be pick-up games. You usually had 100 guys to choose from, and we would just sit there and wait for our turn to come. It would be one pick-up game after another, and there would be sports questions in-between. My friends would quiz me on sports while we waited for the next game. They didn't have lights at Green Briar, so we played until it was dark and then, unfortunately, we had to stop and go home. In the wintertime, they would freeze part of the park for ice-skating, and we also played basketball inside the field house."

Howard Carl grew up in Albany Park and spent most of his time at Eugene Field Park. "We lived at Ridgeway and Argyle, so we were only a couple of blocks from the park. Every possible day, from the age of eight or nine, I was at the park and on the basketball court. We only played half-court games in those days, and on a Sunday when the place was packed we played three-man team games. If your team lost, you might have to wait as much as 30 minutes to get back on the court. In the winter we played basketball inside the field house at the park. When I attended Volta Elementary School at Argyle and Avers, as soon as school was let out for the day, we would race the seven or eight blocks to get to the park and shoot baskets before the regular park activities would begin. By the time I was twelve or thirteen, I would go to the park and serve as a scorekeeper or timekeeper for the older guys' basketball games. At the end of each quarter, at half-time and in between the games, I would shoot baskets. That way, I could get in more shooting. I was just obsessed with basketball!"

Humboldt Park was the key place for Arnold Scholl when he grew up in the '40s. "We moved to the Humboldt Park neighborhood around 1943. I lived a half block east of the park, between California and Fairfield, and one block south of North Avenue. I did everything at Humboldt Park, including baseball. They had tennis courts, but nobody seemed to play tennis at that time. So, we played baseball on the tennis court since it was on a hard surface and there were no nets on the courts. If we felt like walking, we would go over to the softball field which was a little bit further into the park. At that time, nobody seemed to play hardball, just softball. There was also a lagoon in the park and a boathouse, and in winter, we could ice-skate on the lagoon when it froze. There was also a field house

Chicago Park District Baseball Championships at Wrigley Field, Clark and Addison, 1942. Lakeview   (Courtesy of the Chicago Park District.)

Portage Park Juniors, Champion Baseball Team, Wrigley Field, 1942.   Lakeview   (Courtesy of the Chicago Park District.)

Ed Kelly
Near North Side

I grew up in a neighborhood called, at various times, Smoky Hollow and Hell's Kitchen. It is presently called Cabrini-Green. On Elm Street, there is a park called Seward Park. We were born and raised at Seward. We lived at 340 Elm Street, right across the street from the park, and of course, that was where I played — softball, basketball, and boxing. We did everything over there. It was a great neighborhood, and growing up, we never walked two blocks out of the area.

I went into the Marine Corps during the war, and was in the South Pacific in the Marshall Islands on an island called Majero, where I spent about a year. When the war ended, I went to Tsingtao, China. We were stationed there because of the problems with the Chinese Communists at that time. After I was discharged, I went to DePaul University and I played basketball until I got hurt.

When I returned from the war there was tremendous change in my neighborhood. Many African-Americans had moved into the neighborhood, and a lot of the Italian and Irish families were moving out. This was happening while the war was going on. We had a rapid disbursement of families in the neighborhood. We moved out of the area and into the 47th Ward at 4510 N. Ashland Avenue. The separation from the neighborhood was very drastic. A lot of the people who were born and raised there were moving into different areas of Chicago, including some of the suburban areas.

So, it was difficult to come back and see people you were raised with, your buddies, had moved. We started an American Legion post, and we called it a C.M.C. Post. We started it down at Seward Park and it stayed in the neighborhood. The American Legion post kept us together. I think that is what held us together, along with playing softball and basketball. I went away when I was eighteen years old. When I came back, I was an adult. It was a tough time. The neighborhood was breaking up and people were moving out.

The parks had a key role in holding neighborhoods together, and even though there were changes taking place when I came back, we would still play in the parks. We had our softball games there, and we played basketball, cards and dice. So, basically, the park was what kept us together. And the older guys, who were not playing ball, were over at the American Legion post at the park. That was where you hung out. The park was important because that was where all the different age groups and religious groups could hang out.

where I played basketball when I was older. I was in the park all the time during the summer. If I wasn't in the park, we were playing on the street."

Former Cook County Assessor Tom Hynes grew up in Brainerd, on the borderline with Gresham, and remembers, "The closest big parks to us during the '40s were Brainerd Park at 91st and Racine, and Foster Park at 85th and Loomis. We used to go to both parks, but they did not have the kind of facilities that you see in parks today. They had small field houses, but neither one had a gym, swimming pool, big baseball fields or tennis courts. While they were good parks, they were nothing compared to facilities that existed in later years."

Bill Gleason remembers the popularity of tennis in his Park Manor neighborhood. "When we moved to the neighborhood around 72nd and Normal, near Eggleston, we were near Hamilton Park, and it was an adventure to be there. It was a paradise for me because there were four baseball fields, eight softball fields and action all the time. Hamilton Park was a tremendous producer of tennis players, although I was not one of them. The man who was the supervisor was a tennis enthusiast, and they not only had clay courts but lighted clay courts. This was during the Depression, and for a dime you could turn the lights on. Out of that park came nationally famous tennis players — John Jorgensen won the state tournament two years in a row. These tennis players from the park would get on the streetcars and would travel all around the city — they would beat everybody! I remember a Sunday morning in Hamilton Park when the number one and number two tennis players in the world played an exhibition — Fred Perry and Ellsworth Vines. That's how important this park was. The Rock Island Railroad tracks were the eastern boundary of the park, and the Wabash Railroad tracks were on the western boundary. It was like a little valley between these two embankments. So we sat on the slope coming down from the Rock Island tracks watching these two great players. Looking back on it now, it seems so unlikely."

Softball

When Chicago-style 16-inch softball first developed it was an indoor sport played in gymnasiums with eleven players on a team. By the 1940s, it was primarily an outdoor sport with teams playing in every park, gravel school yard, empty lot and prairie across the city. For kids, it was one of the many sports and activities played throughout the spring and summer. For adults, it could be a passion, with some players competing in as many ten softball games a day, and traveling across the city just to play in another game or two.

James Casey grew up in Beverly and played at Ridge Park. "When I grew up in Beverly, softball was one of the big sports for me. We would play softball in the prairie. There were also a couple of parks in the neighborhood, including Ridge Park at 95th and Longwood Drive, and another one at 91st Street. Softball was totally unorganized, and teams were made up of those kids who just showed up to play. There was no Little League and little, if any, parental involvement. We played 16-inch softball, but no hardball."

Tom Doyle played softball while living in the Back of the Yards neighborhood. "I had my own softball team. Before there was a Clincher, there was the Wilson Top Notch softball, and it was a great softball because it was soft and light. We would play for the ball and a dollar-a-man, and we would play in the empty lots. There was also a ball field at 49th and Troop and we might go over there, or we would play in the park."

Jim O'Connor remembers playing softball in his Gresham neighborhood. "We played 16-inch softball, and Windy City Softball was the main sport. We'd play in the empty lots if they were big enough or in the street and use sewer covers as bases. The closest park was O'Halloran Park at 79th and Wood. That was the neighborhood softball park and left field was south of the alley. There was an apartment building on one side of the park, and only the most athletic people in the neighborhood could hit the ball to that building located a half block away. It was a real distance to hit it there. A guy by the name of Bob Smith from Leo High School could hit the ball that far, and he was a hero in the neighborhood because nobody else could hit the wall."

Charles Bidwill, Jr. grew up in Austin. His father owned the Chicago Cardinals as well as a professional women's softball team. "My father was very active in women's softball, the 12-inch ball thrown underhand. He had a team on the South Side and I used to go to games with him. The team played at Bidwill Stadium on 75th and Euclid. My dad's team was called the Bluebirds. There was also a team from the West Side called the Perishey Bloomer Girls, and a North Side team called the Brachs."

In South Shore, where Jim Dowdle lived in the 1940s, softball was a major sport. "We used to play for some pretty good money and one time we were playing a team from the Southwest Side for $500. While we played the game, there were two guys sitting in a bar with the money. Then, after the game, somebody would call the bar and say, 'The Irish won,' and they would exchange the money. If you brought the money into the neighborhood we were afraid that a fight would break out. So, softball was like a conduit that brought people together."

Bill Jauss grew up in Sauganash on the Northwest Side. During the post-war years, there would be high stakes softball games that could involved large amounts of money. "When the war ended and the veterans would start coming back, there were some pretty serious money games — as much

Tony Reibel
North Center

Softball was a big part of my life when I was young. And it was softball all the time when I lived next to Bell School on the Northwest Side. There were two diamonds there, as was the case in most schoolyards. A softball was very cheap — we kicked in $.10 apiece, bought a ball, and the winning team won the ball. Softball only took a bat and a ball, and with twenty young boys you could go out and play.

Sixteen-inch softball started in Chicago in 1887 at the Farragut Boat Club. George Hancock was the man who came up with the game. The story is this: while watching the results of the Yale-Brown game on ticker tape, attendees took a broom handle and a tied-up old boxing glove and batted it around the gym. That was where it got the name "indoor" softball. It was called that well into the 1940s. They played it in gyms, playgrounds and, obviously, in the parks. One of the big advantages was that you didn't need a lot of space to play the game, like you did with a baseball diamond. I played it at Paul Revere Park where we had an indoor softball league. We played it in the winter before the basketball season would start. They would have eleven players on a side, including two positions that they called "upshort." It was fast pitch and the ball was very soft, not like the Clincher softball that we used later on. The two upshorts were positioned on either side of the pitcher, and they would run at the batter. Sometimes it would be one upshort, sometimes two, sometimes none of them, as the pitch was being thrown at the batter — just to distract him. You played the ball off the wall, and if you caught it off the wall before it hit the floor it was an out. It was a very fast-paced game.

Once spring came, you played softball outside. Softball was being played all summer long, including the grammar school leagues and CYO leagues. Plus, all the parks had their own leagues. During the summer we were using the Clincher, the George Young ball, or the Harwood ball — that ball was like a rock!

The Windy City League began in the '30s. It was very big. Harry Hannin formed the Windy City League — he was Abe Saperstein's right-hand man. Saperstein founded the Harlem Globetrotters. Big crowds watched games played at Parichy Stadium on the South Side, Hilburn Stadium on the North Side, St. Philip Stadium on the West Side, and North Town Stadium on the Far North Side.

The Queens, Welles Park League Softball Champions, ca. 1948. Lincoln Square   (Courtesy of Tony Reibel.)

Ray Meyer with 1944-45 DePaul Blue Demons, 1944. Lincoln Park
(Courtesy of the Chicagoland Sports Hall of Fame.)

Ray Meyer
Austin

I was born on the West Side of Chicago near 13th and Central
Park, right off Douglas Boulevard, in 1913. In the 1940s, I
lived at 925 S. Austin Boulevard, right off Columbus Park, by
the "L" tracks.

At that time, I was working at the LaSalle Hotel in the catering
department and as a room clerk. We had a basketball team there that
I coached, too. All of the players lived at the LaSalle Hotel. When
the hotel was sold, I was out of work.

Jim Kelly was head of Columbus Park, and since I was out of
work, I was refereeing basketball games at the park for $3 a game, or
something like that. Then something odd happened in 1941. I was
scouting for a number of schools — Notre Dame, Illinois, University
of Chicago, Northwestern, Wisconsin and Iowa — and Kelly kept
telling me that I had a good mind for basketball, but I didn't want to
coach. He made an appointment for me anyway to go to Joliet Catholic
High School, but I told him that I didn't want to interview for a job
there. Kelly said that I had to since he had promised that I would be
there. So, I went, and with my wife out in the car, I interviewed for
the job. I was offered the coaching position. They told me that I would
be paid $1,700 a year, but I told them that I couldn't live on that
amount of money since I was married. I needed $1,800 a year. They
wouldn't give me $1,800, so I went home.

That night, I got a call from the president of the University of
Notre Dame. He asked me if I would come to South Bend to coach
the basketball team. Their coach, George Keegan, had just had a
heart attack that afternoon. They asked the Notre Dame players who
they wanted as their coach, and they wanted me. So, on Sunday I
was out of work, and by Monday, I was the coach of Notre Dame! I
was supposed to referee some games on Monday night, and I was
embarrassed about the new situation. So I asked my wife to call and
say that I couldn't make it. Well, she told Jim Kelly that I couldn't
make it and she told him why.

When I went to Notre Dame on Monday, they told me they
would announce it, and that I shouldn't say anything. On Tuesday,
when I was taking the team to play Marquette in Milwaukee, I passed
through Chicago. Irv Kupcinet had a big headline announcing "Ray
Meyer is coaching at Notre Dame." So, when I got back to Notre

Dame, the president called me and asked me why it was announced in the Chicago papers. I said that I didn't know what had happened. I didn't know until I went home about a week later and found out who let the cat out of the bag. Kelly was a friend of Kup, and when my wife, Marge, called Kelly, he told Kup and he had a scoop.

In 1942, I came to coach at DePaul after two years at Notre Dame. Then a big thing happened. I had about 24 players, but then the Selective Service draft came along and all of them were called except George Mikan, who was too tall, and Dick Tripto, who was 4-F. All the rest were gone. They were going to cancel the schedule, so I called Bill Shea, who was coaching at St. Phillips High School. Well, Bill said that he had a lot of 4-F's over there, so we got about four of them and played the schedule. We had about eight players, and when we practiced, the team manager and I played so that we would have ten players. We were successful because we had Mikan.

Actually, it was really tough to deal with the situation at that time. Travel was rough because we had to take the train all night to get to New York to play games there. We had nothing like it is today. We couldn't afford individual compartments on the train, so the players sat up all night or slept in their seats. It was very difficult at that time to even get a schedule of games, especially with Mikan, because the schools didn't want to lose to us.

When George left in 1946, we got Ed Mikan, and he was the second best center I ever had. We didn't know it because every place we went, he was compared to his brother, George. I remember playing in New York City — Ed played there in a tournament — and coaches there asked me, "Where has this guy been all year?" I said that he had been with us, but he was always being compared to George. Ed was about 6'8", a little shorter than George, but he never got the recognition he richly deserved.

All of our kids were from Chicago because I didn't have a recruiting budget. In the late '40s, we started to put kids in rooming houses around the school because we didn't have dormitories. The black players lived at Lawson YMCA. We were recruiting against schools that gave their players tuition, room and board, and books. DePaul only gave them tuition and books. I didn't have a budget at DePaul for 29 years, so I would have to find housing and convince them to play at the college.

At that time, if you had black players on your team, the other teams wouldn't play against you. When we had our first black player and we would play games in the south, we had to call ahead of time and let them know that we had black ballplayers. When we wanted to have dinner, they would tell us that the blacks had to eat in their rooms. I remember in St. Louis, when they brought us our dinner, they said that the black ballplayers couldn't eat with us. Our first black player was in the late 1940s, and we began to get more black ballplayers in the 1950s. Even in the neighborhoods, it was an unfortunate situation for us to play around the city.

When I first started, we played some of the Big Ten schools. We had to play there twice and only once at home. We played our home games at Chicago Stadium because all we had was something that we called "The Barn" that only seated about 2,000 people. So, you couldn't play the big teams there, but you could play the Division II or III teams, and maybe a few lesser teams. So, we played all the big teams at the Chicago Stadium, and the others at DePaul. We played fifteen or sixteen games at Chicago Stadium, and we always played doubleheaders with Northwestern and Loyola. We drew very well at the Stadium.

When we started, the NIT was bigger than the NCAA, so we went to the NIT because we got more money. If you were a conference school, you would share the money with all the other schools. But, being an Independent, all the money came to us. When we were invited to play in the NCAA, I said no, we are going to the NIT. But the NCAA said that we were going to play, and then they put in a ruling saying that the NIT couldn't take teams until the NCAA had chosen all their teams for their tournament. Then the NCAA put in a "crumb" saying that the NIT could have a pre-season tournament, and eventually allowed them to have a post-season tournament. When DePaul played in the NIT, all the games were played in New York at Madison Square Garden. It was great for the kids to go New York, and from 1945-1950, they had the NCAA and the NIT tournaments in New York at Madison Square Garden.

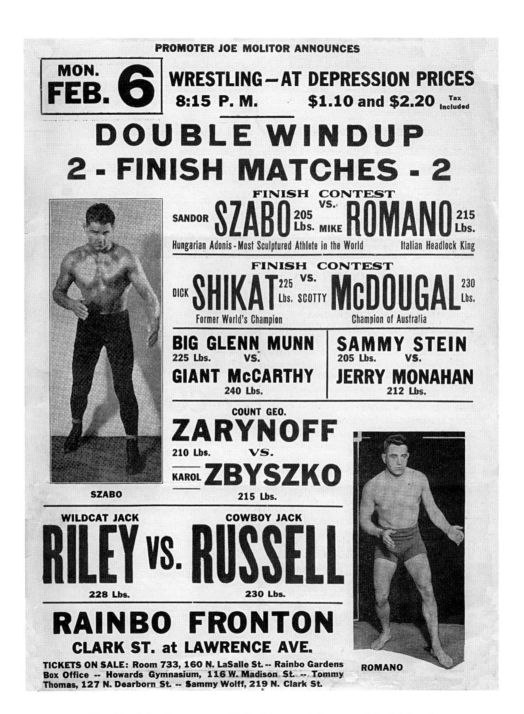

Wrestling Advertisement, ca. 1940. Uptown (Courtesy of Joe Molitor.)

Joe Molitor
Lincoln Square

I was born in 1922 in the Ravenswood Manor neighborhood, and we lived at 4443 North Richmond. My father worked at City National Bank, where he organized special promotions. One that stands out the most was when he set up a wrestling ring in the lobby of the bank. They moved all the tables and desks out of the way and wrestled right there. "Strangler" Lewis and all the big wrestlers were there.

Eventually, my father became a promoter and manager of wrestlers. I would go to a lot of these matches as a kid, always in the best seats that my father would get me. The Chicago Stadium was the big time, but I also went to the Rainbow Fronton at Clark and Lawrence. I used to go up to the edge of the ring and pound on the canvas yelling, "Come on, throw him over here and let me at 'em!" One time the guy did just that! Back then, they used to get a guy over their head and twirl him around. Well, the wrestler threw him right at me — boom! Right in front of me. You have to be in that situation to appreciate it.

Now, these wrestlers would put their opponents into these holds, like the "Boston Crab." If you got stuck in that, you were dead. "Strangler" Lewis had a headlock that was impossible to get out of. He would lock his opponent's head between the big muscles on his arms and then flex so hard they would pass out — that's where the "strangle" comes from. Sometimes, the sport back then could get a little boring — a guy could get trapped in a headlock and head scissors and they would sit there for five minutes or longer. Nothing would happen. "Are you gonna give up?" he'd ask. "Nope!" his opponent would say. So he'd squeeze a little harder. It kills me to watch wrestling today. The wrestlers practice their matches today. Sometimes a guy is supposed to be getting killed and he doesn't even know he's being touched!

My father used to hang out with a lot of athletes. When I was a kid, a lot of these wrestlers used to come over to my house. They would pick me up by the scruff of my pants and lift me up like a barbell. Then, they would pass me around like a football back and forth.

My father also played baseball in the Banker's League. In those days, they had what was called the Industrial Leagues — the Banker's League, the Fireman's League, and the Policeman's League. All these little teams played around the city. A lot of second and third string pro players used to moonlight in these leagues to pick up extra money. Back then, the pros didn't get paid much at all. A lot of former big-leaguers played in the industrials — guys that were just too wore-out, and dumped by the big-leagues. Some of these games could get rough. I remember an Industrial League football game that was played with policemen stationed every ten feet along the field. It wasn't because of the teams fighting, it was because of the fans fighting! The fans could be terrible!

My father used to take me to games all the time. At the Logan Square Ballpark, at Kimball, Addison, and Elston, a lot of kids used to sneak under the grandstands during the game to look for money that had been dropped. If the peanut vendor fumbled the money that had been tossed to him from a four or five rows away there would be kids down there to find it. You'd sift through a few feet of peanut shells to search for change. It was a good ball park, and all the big draws would play there — the House of David team, the guys with the beards, and the Negro Leagues. They tore it down a long time ago.

We'd go to games at Wrigley Field, too. I remember a great triple-header in 1940s — the Major League old-timers played five innings, then the city high school championship was played, and this particular year the Hollywood All-Stars played, with Marilyn Monroe and Ward Bond. Hopalong Cassidy was the umpire and some of the "sweater girls" were cheerleaders.

In 1940, when I was in high school, my father put me to work collecting dues for the Old-Timers Baseball Association dinner. The association was started to commemorate the 50th anniversary of baseball in Chicago, so the old-timers went back to players from the 1800s. Many guests would come, like Mayor Kelly, Fire Chief Bill Hughes, broadcaster Leo Fisher, and Charlie Grimm would play the ukulele. They had a lot of talent in those days, and would sing songs and give toasts. It's a wonder any of them could stand up when it was over because they gave so many toasts, sometimes as many as twenty! This guy would toast to the White Stockings, then somebody would toast to the Cubs, and back and forth.

We didn't have women in the organization back then, so people would get up and tell stories from their playing days. Stories about the long train rides from New York where they'd sneak woman into their bunks, play cards, and drink. The baseball writers would travel with the players, and they could be just as bad! It's not like that anymore, you know.

Dolores "Champ" Mueller Bajda
Belmont Cragin

I grew up around Fullerton and Pulaski on the Far Northwest Side. There were a lot of German, Norwegian, Swedes, and Polish there — a real mix of people. I spent most of my time at Mozart Playground, that's 2200 North Hamlin. We lived at 2148 North Hamlin, so it was just a hop, skip, and a jump to the playground and the school. I lived in that playground from morning until night. I was there everyday. That was it.

One Saturday, when I was about eight years old, I went over to the playground. Before I left, I pinned my father's athletic award medals to my blouse. When I got there a teacher asked, "Are those yours?" I said, "Yes, they are!" She said, "Well, you must be a pretty good athlete. We'll have to call you 'Champ'." That nickname stuck with me the rest of my life.

We played many sports and games there. We had "batball," which we played with a volleyball. It had the same rules as baseball, but you hit the ball with your hand, and the other team threw the ball at you to get you out. We had "fieldball," which was a combination of football and soccer. You couldn't run with the ball, you had to throw it and pass it off, and get it though the goal. That was a tough game, because we played against the boys. We also played softball at Milwaukee and Tripp in the Chicagoland Girls Softball League. We traveled all over the city to play games — at Shewbridge Field at 74th and Aberdeen on the South Side and at 51st and State against the girls there. The games weren't always played on ball fields, but sometimes in big empty lots.

In 1948, when I was seventeen, my gym teacher at Mozart, Mr. Jacobson, started coaching girl's baseball. He asked me if I wanted to play pro baseball. So I went out and bought a glove and he taught me how to pitch over-hand. He'd make me throw about two hours a day! He taught me how to throw the knuckle ball and the curve ball, and that's when I started to play at Thillens Stadium. I played pitcher and third base. This wasn't the All-American Girls League, but it was a farm league with four teams — North Town Co-eds, North Town Debs, Blue Island Stars, and the Blue Island Dianas. The girls on the South Side were good, and there was a lot of competition. If it wasn't for the Thillens family and this league, the girls from Chicago who wanted to play pro ball wouldn't have made it to the All-American Girls League.

Girl's baseball had the same rules as the men's Major Leagues, but the bases and the mound were shorter. We played every night at nine, right after the men played 16-inch softball, and we had good crowds watch us. A season would be about 50 or 60 games, and we got $5.00 a game. Like the All-American Girls, we played in skirts, and each team had their own chaperon. She had to make sure the girls were on time, dressed perfectly for the games, and went right home.

We had fun and played hard. It was great playing under those lights. We girls could hit the ball over the fence, and even beyond the fence into the river. What we did try to do was hit the ball over the center field wall and hit the sign with the armored car. We would aim for that to get the cash prize.

At the end of the season they had a tryout for the All-American Girls League at the field house on Lawndale at 18th Street. We had to practice, play and slide on a wooden floor! All the scouts were there, and they chose from the best girls. I got picked by South Bend to play for the Blue Sox in Indiana, and other girls went to different teams. The league had teams in Peoria, Rockford, Kenosha, Racine, Muskegon, Grand Rapids, Fort Wayne and later, the Chicago Colleens. It was great, and it was the first time I really went someplace. We made good money. When girls first came up they got about $50.00 a game, but some got up to a $100.00 a game. That was a lot of money back then.

When I played home games in South Bend I lived with a private family in town, not at a hotel. When we were on the road we stayed in hotels. We traveled around in those old buses. There were no interstates back then so we took the old country roads. Some girls played cards, some would sing, and some would sleep. It was just like in the movie A League of Their Own.

Even after I was done playing for the All-American Girls I went back and played at the Mozart playground — softball, table tennis, volleyball, horse shoes, or any sport. I loved to play them all.

Dolores "Champ" Mueller Bajda (left) at Thillens Stadium, 1949. West Ridge
(Courtesy of Dolores Mueller Bajda)

as $1,000. It wasn't our money, but it was the backers who would put up the cash. It worked out to $50 a man, a lot of money back then. Those games were played at a park at Crawford (Pulaski) and Touhy. I remember one time we were playing a game and were comfortably ahead with a couple of innings to go, when it started to rain. There was all this money and we had to decide what to do with it while we were waiting through the rain delay. So, it was amicably decided that the fiancees of two of the guys would sit alone in a car and hold the money. So, here were all of these guys on both teams hovering around and wondering if these broads were going to take off with the money. Finally, the umpires decided to call the game and declare that my team had won. We took the money down to Bob Wolf's Village Inn at the corner of Crawford and Devon and dumped it out on the table. I had never seen so much money in my life. As I recall it, there were only one or two $20 bills, maybe a $10 or $5, and the rest were $1 bills."

High School and College Sports

In the 1940s, high school and college sports were very popular across all religious, ethnic and racial lines. Rivalries were played out in both the public and parochial school leagues, drawing large crowds for football, basketball, and a wide range of other sports. For many participants, the games were about more than the final score, as neighborhoods competed against other neighborhoods for bragging rights. DePaul, Loyola, and the University of Chicago often played in front of large crowds in their home gyms and at the Chicago Stadium. In particular, the DePaul Blue Demons saw great success in the 1940s, with Ray Meyer coaching the team to the NIT and NCAA tournaments.

Bruce Bachmann went to Austin High School and remembers great basketball and football teams in the '40s. "The Austin football team was a powerhouse during those years, but not the basketball team because all the great basketball players went to Marshall High School. During the '20s, '30s and most of the '40s, basketball seemed to be a Jewish sport, a ghetto sport. Of course, you didn't need a lot of money to play basketball. When I was growing up, the powerhouses in public high school sports were Von Steuben, Roosevelt and Marshall."

Irv Bemoras was a star basketball player at Marshall High School, the University of Illinois, and in the pros with the St. Louis Hawks. "On the West Side, I grew up around the American Boys Commonwealth (ABC), a Jewish boys club near Lawson grammar school. They had quite a few programs there. They had music, a band, a glee club, and all kinds of sport activities and workshops. There were two important people there:

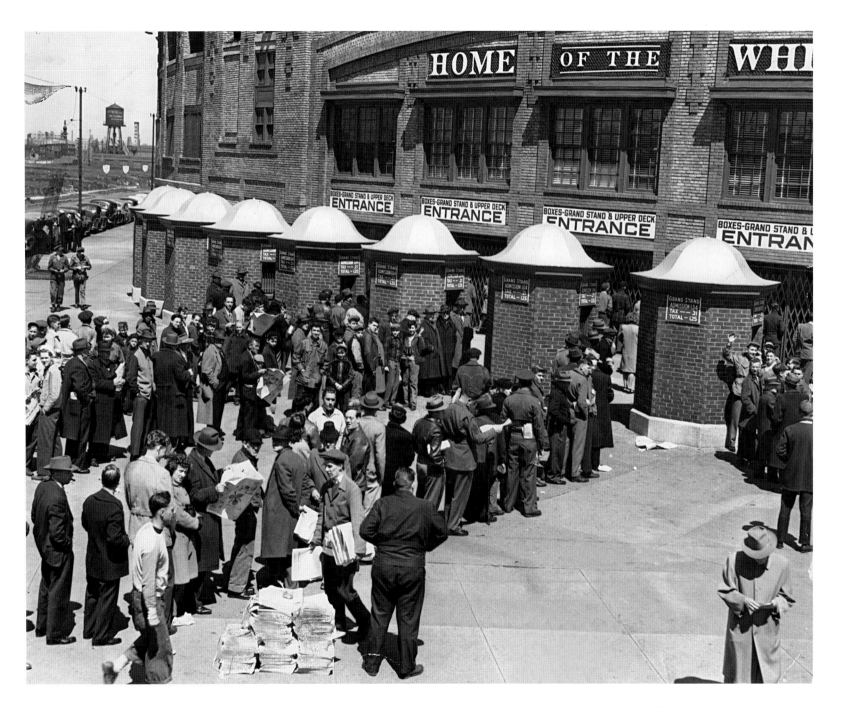

Opening Day at Comiskey Park, 35th and Shields, 1946. Armour Square (Courtesy of the Chicago Sun-Times.)

Ed McElroy
New City

I was born in 1925 on the South Side, at 55th and Morgan, in Visitation Parish. I used to play basketball at Visitation and we won a championship there. Across the street is the church and I used to be in the band and the choir. Visitation Parish was the key to my upbringing.

We used to play football in the middle of Sherman Park, and I probably played baseball there for two million hours, sometimes nine or ten hours a day. I was good at baseball and was batting champ and most valuable player. During the 1940s, at a very young age, I was with the White Sox as the batting practice/bullpen catcher. I was exposed to something that 99.9% of kids were never exposed to. At that time, the ball games were at 3:00PM each day. Don Kolloway, who played second base, would pick up Bob Kennedy, who lived at 9755 Charles, and then they would pick me up at 55th Street. A lot of times we'd stop at a drugstore where they had milkshakes with vanilla wafers for $.15. It was out of this world! Then, we would go down to the ballpark really early.

My name wasn't on the team roster, but I got to meet a lot of people I never would have met otherwise. I was a very young kid, but I was exposed to a lot of things because of this opportunity. It was extremely interesting meeting all these people, most of which I never would have met otherwise. At that time, the clubhouse at Comiskey Park was on the second floor, and you would come down through the runway and dugout and onto the field. So, I'd be coming up and down and people would want my autograph. I felt a little uncomfortable with this, so I went to Mr. Dykes, the manager, one day and said, "Mr. Dykes, I have a question." He said, "Yes, Edward?" He always called me Edward. So, I told him about people wanting my autograph. He said, "Edward, as long as you are in a White Sox uniform, you are somebody." So, from then on, I signed the autographs.

Jackie Friedman, the director, and Bosco Levin, who ran the gym — he was also a gym teacher at Marshall. Those were the days when they had excellent basketball players. That was where I learned all my fundamentals."

Morgan Murphy, Jr. recalls high school sports in the parochial schools. "I remember during my freshman year at Leo High School, Leo won the Catholic League football championship. I played a lot of sports in school, including basketball and football, and my life seemed to be centered around sports at Leo. We used to start our spring practice at the beach when Joe Gleason was our coach. I was the quarterback and captain of the team in my senior year at Leo and I got a football scholarship to Northwestern University where I played for two years."

Jack Hogan also went to Leo High School and remembers intramural basketball in the 1940s. "In 1943, right before I went into the service, even though I lived in St. Sabina Parish, I played basketball with the Leo CYO team. In those days, it was customary for the CYO (Catholic Youth Organization) champs to play the BBYO (B'nai B'rith Youth Organization) champs. The champs that year were Marshall High School's lightweight team. At that point they had won 82 straight games, but we beat them in the game played at Lane Tech on April 1, 1943."

George Mitsos had great success in high school sports. "I was into sports in high school and played basketball for three years at Amundsen. I was also a co-captain of the swimming team. I went to grammar school and high school with Bob Fosse, the dancer and movie producer. He lived on the other side of Montrose, and we were on the swimming team together. In high school, I broke the rules because I swam and played basketball in the same season. But, we had a real good swimming team and they were short on basketball players. Then, my third and fourth years, I ended up playing with two fellows who would lead the Big Ten in scoring for three years. Our high school was the second smallest high school in the city, and Sullivan was the smallest. In my third year, we won North Section in baseball, football, and basketball."

Illinois Secretary of State Jesse White was both a high school and college star athlete, and went on to play in the minor leagues for the Cubs. "At Waller High School, I became an all-city baseball and basketball player. I scored 68 points in a high school game, and then I won a scholarship to Alabama State College in Montgomery. I was a forward and I could jump high. I became an all-conference baseball and basketball player in college. After I graduated from college I signed a contract to play baseball for the Cubs. In March of 1957, I was scheduled to go to spring training, but I was called up for military service. After I was formally discharged from

Bob Kennedy
Washington Heights

I was born and raised on the South Side of Chicago, and baptized at Visitation Church at 55th and Halsted. We lived in the parish until I was about seven years old, and then we moved out to 7146 S. Morgan. The next move was to 9722 S. Loomis, then 10220 Charles, 10041 Charles, and 9755 Charles. Can you imagine? I haven't thought about those street addresses in years! I went to St. Margaret's grammar school, and then to De La Salle High School.

I signed my first baseball contract on June 22, 1937, at Comiskey Park, the same place I sold Blue Valley popcorn for the Louis-Braddock fight when Joe Louis won the title. The boxing ring was at second base for that fight. I went away to play ball the next day.

The White Sox didn't have a minor league system, but they had a couple of players planted here and there. I went to Dallas for a while and then went to Vicksburg, Mississippi, and then back to Dallas and finished the season. A funny thing happened in 1938 when I went to spring training in Dallas. We were playing an exhibition game — I was just seventeen years old — and I'm warming up before the ball game. I threw the ball and Lou Gehrig walked right between us and I almost hit him in the head. I hollered to him and he ducked and the ball just missed him. I apologized and he said, "Don't worry about it kid, don't worry about it." That was when he was starting to get sick.

So, I went to the plate, and Bill Dickey is catching and "Bump" Hadley is pitching. Dickey looked at me and could see that I hadn't begun to shave yet. He said, "Can you hit the fast ball?" "Yeah," I said. He threw a fast ball. Strike one. He said, "You didn't believe me, did you?" I said, "No, I didn't." He replied, "Okay, be ready, here's another fast ball." And, I hit a line drive base hit. The next time up, he said, "Can you hit the curve ball?" I said, "Yes, sir." So, Bump Hadley, who had a real good curve ball, threw the curve and I hit a line drive base hit. He looked at me like, " What the hell was going on!" The next time I came up there were a couple of men on base, and Bill says, "Okay, kid, you're on your own."

I got to the majors on September 1, 1939, with the White Sox. I came up for the month of September to finish the season, and I was paid $235. I was a third baseman, mostly, then I moved to the outfield. When I was with the Sox I lived at home in Chicago at 95th and Ashland Avenue. I would travel to the games by streetcar because my dad wouldn't let me have a car. I did the same thing when I went to high school, and took the same streetcar to get there. When I got off at 35th Street, instead of taking the 35th Street streetcar east, I would get off and walk from the corner where Bob's Tavern was located at 35th and Wentworth. It was tough getting home after we lost because there wouldn't be any seats on the streetcar, and you'd be standing there holding onto one of the straps and the guys who were sitting in front of you would say, "Why the hell did they get that third baseman? That guy can't play ball!" I would have to listen to that jazz all the way home.

A trivia question — what team played nine innings in the big leagues and no averages changed? The Sox were the only team in history where that happened. Bob Feller no-hit the White Sox to begin the season on Opening Day of 1940. We started with zero and we ended with zero. That was the only no-hitter ever pitched on Opening Day.

In 1940, I played 154 games for the White Sox, and, in fact, I batted more than 600 times as lead-off hitter. I was paid $400 a month. That year, the White Sox had a pretty good season. Of course, the war was coming and everybody thought about that. I was in the military from 1942 to 1945, and was stationed in the Pacific toward the end of the war. I was a fighter instructor in Pensacola, Florida. In fact, I was one of Ted Williams' first instructors down there. We became great friends.

When I returned from the war, I immediately came back to the White Sox. In 1946, everyone was damn glad that we were back. Those were tough times. Owners were trying to get organized and get back to the way baseball had been before the war.

I went to Cleveland in 1948, then Baltimore, and I finished my playing career with Brooklyn in 1957. I came back to Chicago to manage the Cubs in 1963, 1964 and 1965, and I became general manager of the Cubs on November 1, 1976. I was with the Cubs organization until the Wrigleys sold the club to the Chicago Tribune in 1981.

I don't have a squawk in the world about anything. I had just about the most wonderful life that a man can have.

Children Cheer for the Cubs Victory over Harry "The Cat" Brecheen 3-1, 1948. Lakeview (Courtesy of the Chicago Sun-Times.)

Andy Pafko
Kelvyn Park

I was born in 1921 and grew up in a little town by the name of Boyceville, Wisconsin, about 25 miles out of Eau Claire. I didn't get to Chicago until the tail end of the Pacific Coast League season of 1943. When our season was over, the Cubs had about thirteen games left, so they brought four of us up from the club. Of course, I had never been to Chicago before and I had never seen Wrigley Field. That was quite a thrill for me, and I'll never forget my first time at bat. I had an extra base hit and drove in a couple of runs. The next time up I got another hit and drove in a couple of more runs. I broke in kind of good, and it was a great feeling. I will never forget the feeling of walking into Wrigley Field for the first time. I opened the clubhouse door, and the first guy I ran into was Stan Hack, the Cub's third baseman. He said, "Andy Pafko, welcome to the big leagues. Welcome to Chicago!" That was the greatest moment of my life. I mean, just getting into a big league clubhouse, and then playing in Chicago for as long as I did. The Cubs radio announcer, Bert Wilson, used to call me "the kid from Boyceville."

I played outfield, and primarily I was a center fielder. I also played right and left field, and eventually I even played third base for the Cubs, when Stan Hack retired. They had no third baseman at the time, so I filled in and had a good year. I made the all-star team as a third baseman.

When I first came to the Cubs, I didn't move to Chicago. I always lived back home, but after I played with the Cubs for a couple of years I met a girl in Chicago and we got married. Then, of course, I made my home here in Chicago. We lived on the Northwest Side, at Grand Avenue and Camerling. We later moved to the Kelvyn Park neighborhood, and I lived there for about 20 years, until we moved to Mt. Prospect.

When I was living in Chicago, I used to drive to the baseball games at Wrigley Field. I drove my car the same route everyday, but if I had a bad day, I would skip a couple of streets in order to change my luck. I was kind of superstitious, and I don't know if it helped. I think that a lot of ballplayers have their own pet superstitions. When I drove from Kelvyn Park, it was Diversey to Southport, then Southport up to Addison, and then right to the ballpark where I would park my car. They had a special place for the ballplayers to park their cars, along the railroad tracks just south of the fire station.

Wrigley Field was a beautiful place to play baseball. A lot of players complained about the wind blowing in — of course it blows in. People said it was a pitcher's park, but it's a fair park, and the distances are fair for the pitcher and hitter. If you hit a home run at Wrigley Field, you deserve it. It was not like a lot of other ballparks where I played, like the old Polo Grounds. It was so close, you could drop kick the ball over the left field fence there. It was only about 280' down the line. So, Wrigley Field was a fair park for both pitchers and hitters.

The year the Cubs were in the World Series was a great year. In 1945, we were battling the Cardinals for the championship and I drove in the winning run to clinch it for the Cubs. I hit a fly ball into right field and that put us in the World Series. Of course, playing in the series was a tremendous, tremendous feeling. There is nothing else like it. Ultimately, when you get to the big leagues, your number one thing is to get into the World Series. I was very fortunate in my career, because I played on three different clubs and they all went to the World Series. I'll never forget the first one in 1945 — that was thrilling.

I used to room with Bob Rush, a great pitcher, and when I was traded to the Dodgers, I roomed with Johnny Schmidt, a former Wisconsin resident. But, with the Cubs, Bob Rush was my roommate most of the time. I was with the Cubs until 1951, just about the time Hank Sauer came to the Cubs. Do you know how the trade happened? We were playing the Dodgers in a three-game series in the middle of the 1951 season at Wrigley Field. I came out on the field before the second game of the series, and we were standing around the batting cage during batting practice. Big Don Newcombe came out of the Dodger dugout and he yells to me, "Hey, Pafko, you're going to be a Dodger tomorrow!" My God, did my ears perk up. I hadn't heard any rumors around Chicago about me being traded, but I guess the Dodgers were looking for a left fielder. So, we played that second game and I showered, went home and my wife made dinner. The phone rang, and it was the Cub's front office calling to tell me that the Cubs had just made an eight-player trade, four Dodgers for four Cubs. I was one of the eight. My poor wife started to cry because I had to go out to the ballpark the next day and pack my bags because the Dodgers were leaving for St. Louis. So, I went to the ballpark and into the Cub clubhouse to get all my personal gear. After I got my stuff together, I walked across the infield and went into the Dodger clubhouse on the first base side — I was a Cub one day and a Dodger the next. It was a strange feeling. In those days you got traded, so you didn't mind that issue, but the way it happened right in the middle of the season. If you get traded in the off-season, you have time to adjust. But, *here I'm a Cub one day and I'm a Dodger the next day. The trade was very unpopular among Cub fans. I had many good seasons with the Cubs, and I appreciated that the fans of Chicago were loyal to me. But no matter what, I always gave it 100%.*

Now, that was the same year that Bobby Thompson hit the "shot heard around the world." I was the left fielder in that game and the ball went over my head. Everybody knows that Ralph Branca threw the pitch and that Bobby Thompson hit the homer, but very few people know that I was the left fielder who watched the ball go over his head. Yours truly.

People tell me now, "Andy, don't you wish you were playing today with all the big money?" I always say, "No." And I have no regrets. I played during the greatest era of all, the '40s and the '50s. I played against Joe Dimaggio, Ted Williams, Bob Feller and all those guys. You can't replace those guys. It was a great, great era.

To me, it was just a thrill to be in the big leagues. I played with the Dodgers and the Milwaukee Braves, but I think that the greatest fans are here in Chicago. They have to be — they've been so loyal all these years. It's been since 1945 that the Cubs were in their last World Series. It's hard to believe that they haven't won one since 1908, or been in the World Series since 1945. I think that the Cub fans are the best fans in the country.

Andy Pafko at Wrigley Field, ca. 1948. Lakeview
Photograph by George Brace.

Billy Pierce at Comiskey Park, 1949. Armour Square
Photograph by George Brace.

Billy Pierce
Hyde Park

I was born in 1927 in Detroit, Michigan. During my playing days I lived in Detroit in the off-season, but when I played in Chicago, I lived in an apartment hotel in Hyde Park. I stayed at the Flamingo, the Piccadilly, the Shoreland — they all had furnished apartments and I would bring my family along.

I got into professional baseball when I signed my first contract in the fall of 1944 with Detroit. My first season was 1945, and I was with the Detroit Tigers about 3/5 of the year, while the other 2/5 of the year was spent at Buffalo. I was eligible for the World Series against the Cubs. I didn't pitch in the games, except for during batting practice. It was a tremendous thrill to be in the World Series. The year before I was still in high school, and here I was a year later in the World Series. It was quite a thrill, I tell you. I don't think that a young person really realizes what is going on, but it was a tremendous thrill. There is no doubt that the World Series is the top thing of all. The Tigers played in Briggs Stadium, and it changed to Tiger Stadium after that. Wrigley Field was the same that it is now, and it hasn't changed much over the years. We were playing in the fall, so the vines weren't very green. I had never been in a National League ballpark before, and it was very exciting. The ballpark was jammed, and there was bunting all over. The Tigers won the series 4-3.

In fall of 1948, I was traded to the White Sox. So, from 1949 to 1961, I was in Chicago with the Sox. I had 211 victories in baseball, 186 with the White Sox. I was traded for Aaron Robinson, who was a catcher, and with the short porch in right field, Detroit wanted to get a catcher to hit that porch out there. They had Trout, Newhouser, Trucks, and a big group of young pitchers. I was so bad that they threw $10,000 into the deal. As for salaries around that time, I was fortunate. I received a bonus when I signed my original contract, but I was signed to a major league contract at minimum salary of $600 a month for seven months. It was a little different than it is now. Back then, for a young fellow only eighteen years old, that wasn't bad.

My first full season with the Sox was in 1949 and my record was 7-15. At that time Frank Lane was making trade after trade because in 1948 they had lost a hundred or so games. They were getting rid of all the older veterans on the ball club and going with *youth. We had trades with every team in the American League, and probably with the National League. Teams were changing all the time, and things didn't really develop in Chicago until 1951. Attendance wasn't too strong at Comiskey Park when I got here, but we would draw a little better when we played the Yankees. In later years, we drew fantastic crowds when they came to town.*

One of the worst things about the White Sox in the 1940s — and it changed after a while — was the aroma from the Stock Yards during the night games. When I was with Detroit, I made up my mind that there were two towns I hoped that I would never go to — one was Philadelphia, and the other was Chicago — just because of the aroma from the Stock Yards. But, after a while, maybe the winds changed and slowly the odor started dwindling. We would get the breezes at Comiskey Park first, and then the odor would move toward downtown Chicago.

When I got to the Sox, I had a good opportunity to pitch. Jack Onslow was our manager and we had a lot of young fellows on the 1949 team. One of the key things that year was that we had veteran Luke Appling, and we had a young man by the name of Gus Zernial, who was just starting out and hitting home runs for us. But then he dove for a ball and broke his collarbone, and that hurt us. Later, Gus went to Philadelphia.

If I remember correctly, in spring training in 1949 we had seven left-handed pitchers who were trying out for the club. The Sox were thinking about signing kids for bonuses or making trades. In those days, there were two different trade deadlines — May 15 and June 15. You never knew who was going to be traded. We went out for a picnic one time to our pitching coach Ray Berry's cottage. When we got back, two of the fellows had been traded. We were always thinking that it could happen.

Comiskey Park changed from when I first arrived there. It was 440' feet to center field and the wind blew in most of the time. I remember once when Vern Stephens, a pretty good hitter, hit a ball off me. I turned around and saw the outfielder go out a couple of steps, but then he came in a couple of steps and caught it. It was a big park for pitchers. But soon they moved center field in, and actually after my first three or four years there Comiskey was not what you would call a "pitcher's ballpark" anymore, because the balls carried and more balls were hit out of the park. In fact, one year they put in a temporary fence about 10'-15' feet closer to the plate. There were about fifteen home runs hit, and the Sox hit two of them. So, they took the fence down. It was 352' feet down the right and left field lines, and that was a pretty fair distance. Now all the ballparks are smaller, meaning more home runs.

Things began to change for the Sox by the early 1950s. In 1950, Nellie Fox came to Chicago and that helped. Slowly, he became a different kind of a hitter and he began using a bottle bat and spraying the ball around. He became a very tough hitter to get out. In 1951, Minnie Minoso came to the Sox, and we had Chico Carrasquel at shortstop, who came over from the Dodger organization. Even in 1950, we had a pretty good defensive ball club. By 1951, the team really started developing. In fact, we were in first place at the All-Star Game. But, we were all young fellows and although some of the guys were hitting .330 by mid-year, they ended up dropping off to .290 in the second half of the season. Then, by 1952, we had much of the team that would be successful in the 1950s, including Jim Rivera, Minoso, Fox, Sherman Lollar, and me. That team stayed around a long time. Minnie, Nellie, Sherman and myself were each with the White Sox for ten years or longer.

The White Sox fans were tremendous and they were rooting for us all the time. Whenever we went into the local taverns after a game, the fans were always good to us and they enjoyed the game and the players. In those years, we had fan clubs. Nellie had one, I had one, Rivera had one, Lollar had one, and Minnie had one. They were little clubs with boys and girls and we were invited over to their houses with their parents and, one time, even had dinner with them. In fact, when we had our first child in 1953, they brought my mother over so they could have a shower for my wife. It was a very close-knit situation here on the South Side. Fans were very dedicated and loyal. It is always remarkable to me how many families are split on their loyalties — one is a Cub fan, one a Sox fan. But, it is a good thing because it gives them something to argue about.

the military in March of 1959, I began my baseball career. I went to Mesa, Arizona, and then, after spring training, they shipped me off to Carlsbad, New Mexico. That was class D Ball, the lowest classification. I led the team in hitting and stolen bases, and I played center field."

College basketball was of interest to Otho Kortz when he was growing up on the South Side. "In the 1940s, I went down to the old Chicago Stadium where they had great college basketball doubleheaders. I could take my little brother to the Stadium and it only cost $.07 for me on the streetcar and $.03 for him. We would watch great basketball games, as well as hockey games with the Blackhawks. I would even go down there to see prizefights with some of the big names in boxing. I loved going there."

Professional Sports

Chicago had some very successful professional teams throughout the 1940s. The Cubs won their last National League pennant in 1945, only to lose in seven games to the Detroit Tigers in the World Series that year. The White Sox, while popular on the South Side, continued to rebuild their franchise during the '40s and struggled to attract fans to Comiskey Park. Despite this, they did finish as high as 3rd place in the American League standings in 1941.

Like professional baseball, Chicago also had two professional football teams — the Bears and the Cardinals. The Bears were champions of the National Football League in 1940, 1941, 1943 and 1946, and after going 11-0 during the 1942 season, lost the championship to the Washington Redskins. Their cross-town rivals, the Chicago Cardinals, won the title in 1947 and lost the championship in 1948 to the Philadelphia Eagles.

The Blackhawks also did well during the '40s, competing in the Stanley Cup finals in 1944, but losing to the Montreal Canadiens. The National Basketball Association had its first year in 1947, and the Chicago Stags lost the championship series 4-1 to the Philadelphia Warriors.

Growing up in Chicago has always meant choosing a favorite team. You were either a Cubs or Sox fan. Although neighborhood location often influenced choice of teams, many South and West Siders became Cub fans during the '40s because the Cubs had more success during the decade. Bill Jauss became a big Cub fan in the 1940s. "I would get on the Peterson bus in Sauganash, take it to Clark Street and then take the Clark Street trolley to Wrigley Field. I went to Cub games with my dad the first few times, and then he said that since I knew how to transfer buses, I could go with my friends. I would get by with $1.00 to pay for admission, food and drink, but I was at least twelve or thirteen years old before I started drinking beer at the games! My reaction when I went to my first Cub game was,

'Oh my gosh!' Wrigley Field was like a cathedral. Although I usually sat in the bleachers, I really loved to sit in the grandstands because the seats were so close to the field. In those days, the Cubs were all over the radio band on five or six stations — WGN Radio didn't have exclusive rights. I can remember announcers like Charlie Grimm, Hal Totten, and Harry Creighton."

Harriet Wilson Ellis was a Cub fan when she grew up in the '40s. "We could almost walk to Wrigley Field, and I went there a lot. My mother would let my brother take me when he was ten or eleven years old and I was just seven. He would drop me off in the bleachers and then he would go sit in the grandstands. There was a fabulous vendor there called 'Gravel Gertie,' a man with a gravely-sounding voice, and he would kind of look out for me. Then, after the game, my brother would pick me up and we would go back home. I first started going to Wrigley Field in 1944 or 1945. My father only had two tickets for the 1945 World Series, so he took my brother. We grew up idolizing Phil Cavaretta, Andy Pafko, and Charlie Grimm."

Joseph Lamendella remembers going to Wrigley Field in the '40s. "I started going to the Cub games at Wrigley Field when I was around ten years old, and I would sit in the bleachers. I brought my lunch one day and it fell onto the center field warning track, and Andy Pafko, the Cub center fielder, picked up my lunch and threw it back up to me. I probably still have the bag somewhere. I can remember going to the Cub games during the war when Dominic Delassandro and Bill Nicholson played for the Cubs. I enjoyed being out there in the open with the guys."

Albany Park resident Joel Weisman has gone to Cub games since childhood. "My mother would take us. We would get on the Montrose bus and take it to Clark, then take the Clark streetcar to Addison. We would just walk up to the window and buy tickets. I went to my first game with the Cub Scouts. My father used to take me on Sundays because he had to work all week, and I always would talk him into going to doubleheaders. It was quite a long day. I was a big fan and I really liked baseball. By the time we moved to West Rogers Park, I would come home from school and turn the sound off the television and announce the game myself. I actually was allowed to go to some of those Cub games by myself — sometimes for free — if you collected the cushions from the seats after the game, you would get a free pass to another game. I later worked at Wrigley Field and Comiskey Park as a vendor."

Dan Rostenkowski remembers getting into the games for free as well. "If you cleaned up the place a little — wiped off the seats — you could come back and watch the next game for nothing. They would give you a little ticket to return the next day. The games started at 3 p.m. each day, and sometimes the nuns would let us out of school at 2:30 p.m. if we had a ticket to the game. I remember being at the park with my dad the day in 1938 when the Cubs played the Pittsburgh Pirates and Gabby Hartnett hit the 'homer in the gloaming.' They were going to call the game because it was dark and foggy, but they continued playing and Gabby hit the decisive home run. I was ten years old and my dad put me on his shoulders, turned me around and said, 'Danny, look at all these people. You'll never see happier people in your life.'"

West Sider Mike Perlow has similar memories of the Cubs in the 1940s. "I used to go to Wrigley Field a lot. When I was eight or nine years old, I'd go with my friends. After the game, we would clean up the park and they would give us free tickets for the next game. About 40 or 50 of us kids would clean up the ballpark and pick up the seat cushions. I went to 30-40 games in 1945, but not the World Series. I remember Andy Pafko, Hank Sauer, Stan Hack, Hank Borowy, and Lenny Murillo. I happened to have been there when Andy Pafko lost the ball in the vines and someone got an inside-the-park home run. Very rarely did I go to White Sox games. It was much easier to get to Wrigley Field. I would take the Madison streetcar to Clark Street and then the Clark streetcar or the "L" to Wrigley Field."

During the 1940s, many of the Cub and Sox ballplayers lived in Chicago's neighborhoods. Marvin Aspen recalls, "Bill Nicholson of the Cubs lived in our Albany Park neighborhood. They used to call him 'Swoosh.' He hit a lot of home runs, but he also struck out a lot — that's why he got the name 'Swoosh.' He was an outfielder who had some great years during the war, but when the 'real' ballplayers came home, he wasn't as good. One of the things the kids in the neighborhood would do, and these were innocent kids, believe me, was after school they would ring the doorbell and ask for Mr. Nicholson's autograph. The only reason they did that was to get Mrs. Nicholson to answer the door. She stayed at home in the afternoon, and she always answered the door wearing a slip. That, of course, in terms of dress today, means absolutely nothing. But to some young pre-teens, that was the big thrill!"

Ed Brennan also grew up on the West Side and became a Cub fan. "We were mostly Cub fans out there in Austin, but there were some kids who were White Sox fans. Since there were all kinds of taverns near us and we could get a deposit if we brought beer bottles back, I would fill my wagon up and take it down Madison Street and get the money to go to Cub games. We would get on the Madison streetcar and go to Central, then take the Central bus to Addison and the Addison bus to Wrigley

Field. I went to Wrigley Field in 1945 when they won the pennant, and I knew all the players. I remember that some of my friends were White Sox fans because they liked to listen to Bob Elson when he announced the games by reading it off the ticker tape."

As Bill Gleason remembers it, "I became a White Sox fan at birth. My grandfather, who came from Tipperary, Ireland, was the family's first Sox fan. Then came my dad who saw his first game at the old White Sox Park at 39th and Wentworth in 1904. Now, me and my sons and grandsons are Sox fans. For variety, one of my sisters is an ardent Cub fan, and my dad says that's worse than if she left the church."

Fr. Gene Smith was also a White Sox fan. "I saw my first White Sox game when I was ten years old — a Labor Day double header against the Detroit Tigers. When I was a little older my mom would make a couple of sandwiches for me, and a couple of the other kids would do the same thing, and we would take the Green Hornet down Wentworth Avenue to Comiskey Park. We would spend Sunday there, right after mass. We would get autographs and talk to the players."

Jim Dowdle has been a Sox fan since growing up in South Shore. "I grew up on the South Side and have always been a die-hard White Sox fan. My first job was as an Andy Frain turnstile operator at Comiskey for a dollar a game. I wouldn't be caught dead at Wrigley Field! Ironically, in 1981, I made the presentation to the *Chicago Tribune* board and convinced them to buy the Chicago Cubs. One of the members of the board said to me, 'Well, you've got to be proud of this deal.' And, I responded, 'Well, I am. But there is a tombstone in Calvary Cemetery that has just moved — my father would be very upset with me for what I just did. He was a die-hard White Sox fan.'"

Sandy Bank grew up in Hyde Park/Kenwood. "My father was a grain broker at the Chicago Board of Trade. After the Board of Trade would close at 1:15 p.m., my father would leave work, get on the streetcar, and during baseball season, he would often go to White Sox games, since they started in those days at 3:00 p.m. Occasionally, when there was no school or I got out of school early, I would meet him at Comiskey Park. During the summer, I would go to the White Sox games quite a bit, and I remember one year I saw 75 games."

The 1940s were a great decade for Chicago football. Both the Bears and Cardinals were champions during the era, but after 1959, there was only one football team remaining here. Charles Bidwill's father owned the Chicago Cardinals, and he has strong memories about professional football during the war years. "At the time of Pearl Harbor, my father owned the Chicago Cardinals. He had bought the team in 1932, and they played all

Neighborhood Kids at the Home of Phil Cavaretta, ca. 1940. Photograph by George Brace.

their games at Comiskey Park. The impact of the war on the Cardinals was great. I remember that in 1944 the team merged with the Pittsburgh Steelers and became the Pitt-Cards for one year because they couldn't get enough players and my father and Mr. Rooney couldn't afford the payrolls at that time. I remember my dad talking about how hard it was to keep the team going. Attendance was light during those years, and the situation didn't change until the war was over."

Don Stonesifer was raised in Logan Square in the '40s and became an All-American football player at Northwestern University and a star for the Chicago Cardinals. "I started high school in 1941, graduated in 1945, and then I went into the service from 1945 to 1946. I came back from Germany in 1946, and 1947 was my first year at Northwestern. That helped me with football because I was two years older and forty pounds heavier. Otherwise, I would probably not have made the football team. My dad was a big Bears fan, and when George Halas told me that he was going to draft me in the upcoming NFL draft, my father was very happy about that. But instead, the Chicago Cardinals drafted me because they were higher in the draft. My father said to me, 'I hope that you play well, but I will always pull for the Bears.' I played six years with the Cardinals, from 1951 to 1956. I signed my first contract for $7,000, with a $500 bonus. When the Cardinals decided to move to St. Louis, I chose to stay in Chicago."

Entertainment in the Neighborhood

In the 1940s, residents of Chicago's neighborhoods had a wide variety of entertainment options to choose from. In addition to first- and second-run movie theaters in each neighborhood, residents could also listen to music at jazz and night clubs, dance in one of the many ballrooms or dance halls, and thrill to the rides at Riverview Amusement Park.

Of course, radio was in its heyday, and Chicagoans listened to the many popular entertainment programs, news broadcasts and soap operas that filled the airwaves. Listeners were devoted to their favorite radio programs and the stars that performed in them: "The Jack Benny Show," "The Lone Ranger," "Fibber McGee and Molly," and "Jack Armstrong, All-American Boy" — as well as the music programs that featured big bands and popular orchestras.

Many special events would take place at one of the city's two main arenas. The International Amphitheater, at 42nd and Halsted, would host trade and farming shows, the circus and special exhibits, and the Chicago Stadium, at Madison and Wood, would have boxing and wrestling matches, bicycle races, roller derbies and concerts.

During the war, socializing and morale-boosting were critical elements of the home front effort. In addition to the USO Centers downtown, servicemen and women, war workers, and residents alike found a release from the stresses of daily life in the many neighborhood-based entertainment venues. It was during this time of global conflict that many residents made the most of their nights, uncertain of what the future might hold.

In this last decade before the automobile would draw residents further away from the city, Chicago residents didn't need to travel far to have fun. It was all there in their own community — close to home.

Movie Theaters

Movie theaters provided the least expensive and most accessible form of entertainment in the neighborhoods. Residents could spend hours "at the show," viewing full-length films, shorts, serial adventures, cartoons and newsreels. Some of the neighborhood movie palaces were as lavish as the big shows downtown, especially those operated by the Balaban and Katz movie chain. Moreover, the ornate theaters could be attractions in themselves, capturing the imagination of the public with their elaborate furnishings and exotic motifs. Somehow, life was more bearable during the '40s because of the availability of neighborhood movie theaters and the opportunity to escape, even if briefly, from the concerns about the war.

One of the most beautiful movie palaces on the South Side was the Avalon Theater. The Persian-inspired theater still exists today as the New Regal Theater. Dick Jaffee grew up in South Shore and recalls the Avalon experience. "We went to movies at the Avalon Theater on 79th Street, just a block east of Stony Island Avenue. The movie routine was something we did every Saturday at the Avalon. We would walk to the movie and my first memory was that it was $.11 to get in, and a nickel for the candy. My

Opposite: Century Theater, Clark and Diversey, ca. 1940. Lakeview (Courtesy of the CTA.)

friend's mother would make us take his younger brother with us. Because he was little, we would sneak him in and then we used his admission and candy money to buy more candy. We would go there on a Saturday morning for a double feature and we would come out hours later. Our eyes would be so sensitive to the daylight! We first became aware of the war in the newsreels we saw at the movies. The war seemed unreal because it was so far away, but real because we could see pictures of it. Once in a while, we would go down to South Chicago to the Cheltenham Theater at 92nd and Commercial because they had triple features for about a dime. When we went to South Chicago, we rode the bus or streetcar. When we left the movie we would go across the street to 91st and Commercial, where our friend's dad was a dentist in an old walkup. We would sit there and wait until he was done and he would drive us home."

Sheldon Rosing was also from the South Shore neighborhood. "In addition to the Avalon, we also went to the Shore Theater at 75th and Essex and the Ray Theater at 75th and Exchange, where they had triple features. My allowance was $.11 and we went to the movies every weekend. If I went to the Ray Theater at 1 p.m., the three movies were over at 5 p.m. I would stay for a second round and my mother would pull me out at around 7:30 p.m. Two other popular theaters in the neighborhood were the Hamilton Theater and the Jeffrey Theater and they were both located near 71st and Jeffrey."

Raised in nearby Chatham, Norman Mark recalls the rich history of movie theaters in his neighborhood. "First, there was the Rhodes Theater — it had a miniature Graumann's Chinese Theater in the lobby. There were about two-dozen footprints and hand prints of movie stars on display. The Rhodes was located at 79th and Rhodes and they would have cartoon Saturdays. You would show up at 10 a.m. and you would stagger out of there at 5 p.m. in the afternoon having seen a million cartoons. In the middle of the cartoons, if you remembered to hold your ticket, they would have a drawing. I remember that I won a Bugs Bunny sweatshirt. It was the only thing that I won as a kid and I was very proud of it. Another movie theater for us was the Avalon Theater. When you walked into the Avalon, on the left was a blank wall, and it was odd because everything was decorated except for this wall. But when the theater first opened, it had air-cooling, and that wall was really a window. So, if you were waiting in the lobby, you could see technicians dressed in white and wearing gloves, and they were keeping the air-cooling system going.

"Occasionally, we would go to the Capitol Theater, another B&K theater. It was famous because it had a capitol dome on it. A neighbor complained that the dome was 18 inches onto her property line and that she was going to sue them. Late one night, they got about 50 guys and jacked up the dome and moved it back a foot and a half. That solved the problem! When you were inside the Capitol Theater, it was like you were at the nation's capitol. They had a portico, and inside the portico there were columns — that was where the movie screen was located. They were so involved in building the theater that they didn't install a projection booth, so they had to take out 300 seats in order to put in the booth. It was the only theater with a main floor projection booth."

Raised on the South Side, Sandy Bank remembers the theaters in the Hyde Park neighborhood. "When I grew up in Hyde Park in the '40s we were always going to movies. The Piccadilly Theater, at 51st between Dorchester and Blackstone, was a major theater. We also went to the Harper Theater on Harper, between 52nd and 53rd, and the Hyde Park Theater on Lake Park, between 53rd and 54th. Those were the three main movie theaters in the neighborhood. There was also one on 55th between Maryland and Ingleside called the Frolic Theater. The Frolic was a minor movie house except for one amazing thing: the auditorium was the reverse of what you normally expect. When you entered the auditorium you didn't face the screen, you faced the back of the theater. There was another theater at 47th and Kenwood called the Ken Theater, and one on 47th between Drexel and Cottage Grove called the Pix Theater. The Pix was located on the borderline between the black and the white areas."

On the Southwest Side, Tom Hynes recalls the theaters in the Auburn Gresham neighborhood. "We would go to the Capitol Theater at 79th and Halsted. It was a big fancy theater, and across the street was the Cosmo Theater. The Capitol would have double features, while the Cosmo would frequently have triple features, plus cartoons. We often went there because we got to see three movies instead of two. The Cosmo didn't get the first-run movies, but the Capitol did. So, we kind of alternated, but that was our major source of entertainment. In fact, we would go to the show once a week. There was also another theater, the Beverly, at 95th and Ashland, that was about a mile and a half away. They had single features there and we could never understand why anybody would pay admission to only see one movie."

On the West Side, movie-goers had many beautiful theaters to choose from, including the 4,000 seat Marbro Theater and 3,600 seat Paradise Theater. Ed Brennan recalls his favorite movie theaters while living in Austin. "The primary one for us was the State Theater, located between Austin and Central. It was a very big movie theater, although not as big as the Marbro Theater on Crawford — that was a Balaban and Katz theater. There was also a small theater on the south side of the street, called the Austin Theater. In addition, we went to the Byrd Theater located near Larrabee, and the Paradise Theater on Cicero. Movie theaters were really

Regal Theater, 47th and South Parkway, ca. 1940. Grand Boulevard (Courtesy of the CTA.)

Ambassador Theater, Division and Waller, ca. 1935. Austin (Courtesy of the CTA.)

Southtown Theater, 63rd and Lowe, ca. 1935. Englewood (Courtesy of the CTA.)

Kedzie Theater Bike Contest Winners, ca. 1948. East Garfield Park (Courtesy of Special Collections and Preservation Division, Chicago Public Library.)

the social centers for the neighborhood, and during World War II Hollywood was turning out movies like crazy. There were double features that changed twice a week. They also had serials and cartoons, as well as newsreels about the war."

In North Lawndale, Irv Bemoras remembers movie theaters clustered along Roosevelt Road. "The Central Park Theater was the main one, between St. Louis and Central Park, on Roosevelt Road. Across the street was the 20th Century, and then further east, the Independence Theater. You could also go up to Madison, where they had the Marboro and the Paradise. Next to the Central Park Theater was Ye Olde Chocolate Shoppe, famous for their hot fudge sundaes, and a very popular place. In those days, we didn't eat out much, but when we did, we went to Fluky's — that was about three or four doors down from the Central Park Theater."

In the '40s, many movie-goers bought their candy and popcorn before they entered the theater. Dan Rostenkowski, who lived on the Northwest Side on Noble Street near Division, recalls, "I remember that if you took popcorn in a theater, you bought it at a confectionery next door. And you better not dirty up the theater! That was always the argument against selling food inside the theater. Of course, in those days, they would give you a plate at the movies on Fridays. In 52 weeks, you would have a set of dishes. Every once in a while a plate would fall and break and everybody would stand up and applaud. As for movie houses, there were tons of them. At the corner of Milwaukee, Ashland and Division, was the Chopin Theater. Across the street on Division Street, on the west side of Ashland Avenue, was the Crown Theater. Down Blackhawk Street, on Paulina near Milwaukee Avenue, was the Paulina Theater. Then, up Milwaukee Avenue, were the Banner Theater, the Royal Theater, and the Wicker Park Theater. The biggest theaters in the area were the Congress Theater and the Harding Theater.

"I remember when I was a kid there was something called 'late checks.' For example, if you went to the Crown Theater, you didn't have to wait for the movie to begin. You just went in during the middle of the picture. They would give you a blue check, and then you would sit down. I remember that there were often two of us in a seat, and it might be a kid you didn't even know. At the end of the movie, the house lights would go up and they would come around and collect the 'late checks.' If you had a 'late check' you could stay for the next movie, but if you didn't have one you had to leave. That was the way they handled all the kids. At that time, the movies cost about a nickel or $.06."

Howard Rosen recalls that movie theater give-aways and promotions could be just as important as the films he was seeing. "Movies were an important part of everyone's social life in my neighborhood. As a kid, one of my best memories was the time my family went to the Crystal Theater in Humboldt Park. On certain nights, the Crystal used to have a game called 'Screen-O.' When you bought a ticket you were given a card, and if they called the number on your card you went on the stage and chose a number. If you picked the winning number, you won the prize that was under the number. One time, my mother had the winning number and she won $10. In those days, that was a very big deal. I also recall that when we lived in Albany Park, there were two movie theaters that dominated our life. One was the Terminal and the other was the Metro. They were both on Lawrence Avenue, and every Saturday we spent our entire day at either one of those two shows. The Metro had triple features, and in order to get the kids to leave, they would give us comic books. Otherwise, we would stay there all day!"

Albany Park was also Marvin Aspen's neighborhood. "Our movie theaters included the Terminal Theater, a little bit east of Kimball, and across the street was the Metro Theater. The Terminal Theater had second- and third-run movies. The movie would play downtown first, then it would be at the Uptown or Gateway, and then it would be at the Terminal. At the Metro Theater, they had the old movies that had been everywhere else before. The Metro Theater was especially interesting because you walked in backwards. At the Terminal Theater, you walked in like you do at most theaters — the screen is in front of you. But at the Metro Theater, the screen was in front, so you would walk in past the screen. The Terminal Theater was special because it had a balcony, and on Friday nights you would go there to have a rendezvous with a young lady. You would find your place in the balcony and do 'your thing', which in those days was kissing and holding hands, or putting your arm around her and hoping it didn't fall asleep. The wonderful thing about both theaters was that they showed double features as well as cartoons, serials, short subjects, and documentaries. It meant that you could go into the theater on a Saturday afternoon and spend six hours, or if you wanted to see something again, even longer!"

Ed Kelly grew up on the Near North Side in the Cabrini neighborhood. "On Saturdays or Sundays, we would go to the movies. There was a show called the LaSalle Theater. One guy would pay and the rest of us would sneak in through the back door. We weren't too smart because we used to sit in the same seats every time, and the manager would just come and get us and throw us back out. The theater was on Division Street, between La Salle and Wells. When we wanted to go to a higher-class show, we would go to the Windsor Theater, over on Clark Street, north of Division. A famous movie theater that was open when I was really small was the Sittners Theater on Sedgwick and Division. I remember going there when I was very small.

The singer Frankie Laine came from that neighborhood, although his original name was Frankie Lavechio."

Chuck Schaden grew up in Norridge, just west of the city limits. Since Norridge had no theaters at the time, residents needed to travel to the Northwest Side of Chicago for entertainment. "There were many movie theaters that we went to in the '40s. One of them was the Patio Theater at Irving Park and Austin Avenue. No one ever called it the Patio — they called it the 'Pay-Show.' We used to think they called it the Pay-Show because you had to pay to go to the show. At Milwaukee, north of Irving Park, was the B&K Portage Theater. If you went further north on Milwaukee, to Lawrence, you were just a few steps away from three theaters: the Gateway Theater, the Times Theater, and a little storefront theater in Jefferson Park called the Jeff Theater. That was the theater where they would say that they were going to raffle a bicycle every Saturday for the matinee. You would go in there and they would supposedly have a drawing from the ticket stubs. So, you would hold onto your own half of the ticket to see if you were a winner. Well, they would come out with a bicycle on stage just before the movie started. They'd get everybody to be moderately quiet, because the kids were making a lot of noise, and then they'd read the number — once. As you were trying to read your ticket, the lights would go out — nobody ever had a chance to win the bike! They repeated this procedure every week, and I don't think that the bike was ever raffled off. There were second- and third-run features at the Jeff, while the Gateway had first-run features. The Times was always showing triple features, but never anything first-run. They would show three comedy shorts, such as Laurel and Hardy, Abbott and Costello, or Olsen and Johnson, and other cartoons and shorts. Occasionally, they would have an all-Western day or all-mystery or all-ghost story show."

The North Side was home to many of the city's best movie palaces. Bob Cunniff remembers that admission was sometimes optional at a few of these grand theaters. "When I was growing up in Rogers Park, we went to the 400 Theater, on Sheridan Road near Columbia, and when we moved to Edgewater, we went to the Bryn Mawr Theater at the "L," the Devon at Broadway and Granville, the Granada Theater on Sheridan and Devon, the Nortown Theater on Western and Devon, and the Uptown and the Riviera Theaters at Lawrence and Broadway. You could sneak in the Granada Theater by going up the marble steps on the side of the building. The ushers really didn't give a damn, although sometimes they had to pretend that they cared. One time, an usher grabbed my friend Tom O'Malley and me and told us they were going to call our school. He really scared us, so I went home and told my father, who told me to forget about it. At the Devon Theater, you could always sneak in through the bathroom window."

Lawrence Pucci
Uptown

I grew up on Sheridan Road in the shadow of the old Edgewater Beach Hotel. At that time the hotel was famous internationally, with guests coming from all over the country and the world. Remember, this was before the Outer Drive was built. The hotel had a boardwalk, restaurants, and shows. The boardwalk was on the threshold of the beach, and at night, the boats would float in to listen to the music. People would walk along the boardwalk, like a promenade, with lighted Chinese lanterns glowing.

The Meriel Abbott Dancers were one of the big acts there, and all the big orchestras played there — Wayne King, Len Gray, Jimmy Dorsey, and the Ted Weems Orchestra with Perry Como. Perry Como played in the band at the time, before he turned into a star. In the hotel, they had the Marine Dining Room and a very famous bar called the Captain's Quarters. As you came into the bar you had to cross a rolling gang-plank that felt like the sea, which, as you left, seemed to be rolling even more! They had a number of dining rooms, including one that was famous for its pancakes and waffles.

Many movie stars who came to town stayed at the hotel. I remember Cary Grant and Katherine Hepburn being there. There were these long corridors leading to the different rooms, like the Empire Room, and on the walls they had pictures of the actors and actresses who had stayed there.

The hotel had a quality, a feeling about it. It wasn't like the modern age, they had the traditions of the past. The service was magnificent, with the old-time waiters. At that time, men always dressed in a suit, or a sport coat and tie, and the women always dressed well. People don't understand today, but back then, if you had a position, you had to dress like you had a position. If you were a doctor, than you looked like a doctor. If you were a lawyer, than you looked like a lawyer. Today, you can't tell a doctor from an orderly! People don't have the pride they once had.

A good example of how things have changed were the Easter Parades. In the 40s, people would get dressed-up, go to church and have what they called an Easter Parade — and they would promenade. Then, they might go downtown to Michigan Avenue, all dressed-up, some even in top hats. You don't see Easter Parades like that anymore. There was an elegance to the past.

Edgewater Beach Hotel, Sheridan and Balmoral, ca. 1946. Uptown (Courtesy of the CTA.)

For many North Side residents, Rogers Park's Granada Theater had no equal. From 1942 through early 1945, John James was a head usher at the Granada Theater at Sheridan and Devon. "My job at the Granada was Chief of Service, or head usher. I told a fib about my age and got the job when I was a little younger than fifteen years old, instead of the required age of sixteen. The usher force consisted of some eighteen young men attending Sullivan, Senn, and Amundsen High Schools. I also had the additional assignment of preparing the payroll at the theater. As head usher, I made $.03 an hour more than the other ushers, which brought my hourly rate up to $.37 an hour. I remember that on the back door of the old usher supply room, near the elevator on the third floor, was a hand-written list of all the ushers who went into military service in World War II, including those who had been killed in action. I maintained this crude list on the closet door until I entered the Marine Corps in April 1945."

West Ridge resident Burt Sherman remembers the overall experience of going to the movies in the 1940s. "When you talk about the '40s, movies were the top form of entertainment for kids. From the earliest time I can remember, we used to go to theaters like the Nortown, the Granada, or the Adelphi. Most of the kids loved Abbott and Costello movies. They were very funny and we had a terrific time when we saw them. I don't think that it cost even a dime for a kid to get in to the movies. There were always double features, and, in addition, you often saw a half dozen cartoons, serials and newsreels. They really gave you your money's worth in those days. When you got to the theater, you went in even if it was the middle of the movie because it didn't seem to make any difference. You didn't check the time beforehand, you just went there. If the movie was already in progress, or almost half over, you just sat and saw it all over again."

Community Theater

During the 1940s, religion played a big part in the stability and unity of each Chicago neighborhood. Religious education provided a foundation for young men and women, and the religious institutions they attended also served as centers for social interaction and events. Community theaters, many housed in church basements and auditoriums, brought neighbors together and offered the chance to perform on stage.

On the Far North Side, many people remember the importance of the Loyola Community Theater at St. Ignatius Church. Former Lt. Governor Neil Hartigan grew up in the Rogers Park parish and his mother, Coletta Hogan Hartigan, was very active in the Loyola Community Theater. "The participants were called the 'Green Room Players' and they were part of a six or seven element program that was held annually at St. Ignatius Church's

Dorothy Ash
Near North Side

*I*n the early 1940s, I was living in apartment 1703 of the Seneca Hotel. The Seneca is on Chestnut about a block east of Michigan. It was truly elegant, and magic. It had the magic that some places just had. The Seneca was the hotel where all the entertainment stars stayed, like Sophie Tucker. After ten months of living there I gave birth, and our one-bedroom unit was no longer big enough. So, we opened a wall between apartments to make more room.

I remember that during the war our children's nurse, Grace, couldn't wait for Sundays. She would get dressed-up in her nurse's outfit and make herself pretty, and take the kids to Seneca Park to see all the servicemen. You see, the armory was right next to the park and would be filled with hundreds of navy boys in full uniform. They looked gorgeous! She had more dates — I'm telling you! And she married one of them!

Before I got married I worked as a dancer. I started in high school. During the summer we would do state fairs all across the country — vaudeville-type shows at race tracks and fairgrounds. I got my start performing at Navy Pier in the Children's Civic Theater. We lived at 3330 North Bell at the time, and I had to take three streetcars to get there — Roscoe, Damen, and then down to the pier. During the summer the theater ran from morning until night. And it was free — sponsored by the Chicago Drama League. We had dancing training for two hours, music for two hours, and then it was drama. We then performed twice a week. Thousands of people came to see us. It really was a training ground for kids in the arts. Some children went into radio, some into music and a lot of the girls went into dancing, and that's what I wanted to do.

I went on to be a dancer in two different lines — I was a Winnie Hoover girl and a Betty Coletts girl. We danced in Chicago at the Oriental Theater and at Harry's New Yorker, as well as big theaters all over the country. I was in a show called the Circus de Paris, and they had lions. One of the numbers had a girl dancing in a cage with the lions, about ten of them. The girl would go in and flick her veil at the lions. Well, the audience at one of the shows thought that the lions weren't scary enough, so the girl tried to agitate them a little. She put a bolt at the end of her veil so when she flicked it they would really roar. Well, one day, at a matinee, a lion came down and mauled her — and killed her. It was really terrible. They closed the show because of her death.

Loyola Community Theater, St. Ignatius Auditorium, ca. 1948. Rogers Park   (Courtesy of the Rogers Park/West Ridge Historical Society.)

Jim DeLisa
South Shore

When my dad, Jim, came from Italy he first stopped in New York to visit relatives and friends. My uncle Mike was a tailor there, and my uncle Louis was a shoemaker. My dad came to Chicago and became a carpenter. After he got here he called my uncles and said, "You gotta come to Chicago because there are bushels of money being made here." This was in the 1920s, and it was moonshine that was making the money. So, they came and opened five places on the South Side — five stills. Then, when Prohibition ended, they opened up the Club DeLisa at 55th and State in 1933. When it first opened, they would give free pretzels and popcorn to draw the crowds. They kept getting bigger and bigger, but then the club burned down due to an electrical fire. So, they decided to open a bigger Club DeLisa. People said they wouldn't be able to open up another club quickly. Well, my dad said that you could put your finger through the plaster, but he was going to open it up, and they did, about a year later. The new one sat 1,000-1,500 people, and it had a stage with sets under the floor. First, you would hear "Red" Saunders beating on the drums, then the stage would rise, and there would be Red with Louis Armstrong or whoever was performing there. There wasn't a bad seat in the house with that raised stage.

At the old club, John Barrymore would arrive from the Blackstone Hotel wearing his robe, and he would be eating salami, drinking and admiring the women. The Blackstone would always call and ask if my dad was stealing John Barrymore. He would say, "You can ask Mr. Barrymore yourself." Bob Hope would come and stop in, as well as John Wayne, who wasn't too good of a tipper. All of the top jazz people came to Club DeLisa, and Monday was the breakfast show at 6 o'clock in the morning. Everybody who was appearing in Chicago would come to the club and do their thing on stage and then watch the other performers. The Kirby's, the Eckstine's, Joe Williams, La Verne Baker, and Moms Mabley all started there. Even Sammy Davis Jr. appeared, along with his dad, when they came through Chicago. My dad and his brothers fed them because they didn't have enough money to eat. Sammy acknowledged that later in his career.

"Blind" John Davis at the Boulevard Hotel, California and Warren, 1944. East Garfield Park (Courtesy of Special Collections and Preservation Division, Chicago Public Library.)

Patrons, Ritz Lounge, Oakwood and South Parkway, 1943. Grand Boulevard (Courtesy of Special Collections and Preservation Division, Chicago Public Library.)

Joe Levinson
Hyde Park

There were many places to hear jazz across Chicago from the late 1930s to the early 1950s. On the South Side, there was Jump Town at 47th and Western Avenue. This joint always had stars playing there, including Louis Jordan's Tympany Five. In those days, they cordially welcomed the white listener and you could have a great time. There was also the famous Regal Theater on South Parkway around 47th Street. It was a large, well-appointed theater that featured movies followed by a stage show. I saw Pearl Bailey's stage show there, and whites and blacks always were at that theater. The Sutherland Lounge, located at Drexel Parkway and 47th Street, was near the Regal. That lounge was high-style and they had some of the greatest black jazz artists of the day, like Ahmad Jamal and Nat King Cole. You needed to have money to go there. On 63rd Street was the Crown Propeller Lounge, where I heard some fine local talent along with many traveling jazz artists.

One of the most famous nightclubs in Chicago was the Club DeLisa at 55th and State. That was the legendary black-and-tan club that was famous for running late, late shows known as "The Milkman's Matinee" beginning around 2 a.m. and ending after 6 o'clock in the morning, always with huge crowds. Everybody who was anybody got their start at the Club DeLisa, and all the movie celebrities made it a point to hit the club during their stays in Chicago. Many local musicians played long stretches there and developed their styles at the club. It wasn't a cheap place to go.

Also on the South Side was Robert's Show Lounge at 65th and South Parkway. It was a big hangout for black musicians and white audiences in the 1940s and was a very famous spot. A few other South Side places that I remember were the Emerald Lounge, where musicians would sit in with the bands; Gussie's Kentucky Lounge at 67th and South Ashland Avenue, where Ira Sullivan and Tommy Ponce worked; the famous Cotton Club at 63rd and Cottage Grove; the Bee Hive on 55th Street near Lake Park Avenue, where I heard Charlie Parker, Gene Ammons and Miles Davis; and Chimaqua's at 14th and Pulaski that featured Latin Jazz when it first emerged on the scene in the late '40s and early 50s, and where the late, great pianist Gene Esposito got his early training.

A big place for top name dance bands was the Trianon Ballroom on the South Side. It was jammed during the war years with people who came to listen and dance to the popular music of the day.

When you went downtown, there were several great jazz clubs. One was called the Downbeat, located in the basement of the Garrick Theater. It featured Henry "Red" Allen's band with J.C. Higginbotham on trombone and Cozy Cole on drums. Allen was a Dixieland trumpeter and he was a great entertainer and showman. Then, there was the Blue Note, often called Frank Holzfiend's Blue Note. It was a world famous place that began as a joint on the second level of a building on Madison, west of State Street. I saw many groups there including Dizzy Gillespie's and Duke Ellington's bands, as well as the giant Sauter-Finnegan Band. Even though I was a teenager of seventeen or eighteen, I could still get into the Blue Note to hear great jazz. There wasn't a famous jazz group that didn't play at that club in the 1940s.

Another popular location in the Loop for great music was the Panther Room, located in the College Inn of the Sherman Hotel. The Panther Room was elegant and featured most of the big traveling jazz and dance bands that were working during the 1940s. I saw Woody Herman's great First Herd there, although I was too young to do more than stand by the doorway and watch and listen as people went in and out. It was the place to take an important date if you were a college man and had money.

You can't talk about the scene in Chicago during those exciting days without recalling the city's most sophisticated Dixieland jazz nightclub, Jazz Ltd. It was located at the corner of Grand and State, right by the subway entrance. The club was owned and managed by Ruth and Bill Rheinhardt. It was long and narrow and could only seat about fifty patrons, with a tiny bar for a few more. On weekends, there always was a line outside waiting to get in and hear the band. Ruth ran the club with an iron hand while Bill played clarinet and led the band. The band was always a five-piece outfit — piano, drums, clarinet, trombone and trumpet. For many of the club's years the players besides Bill were Dave Remington, trombone; Norm Murphy, trumpet; Eddie Higgins, piano; and Bob Cousins, drums. Freddie Kohlman, a wonderful New Orleans drummer, worked there too for a long time, as did Waldron "Frog" Joseph, a trombonist also from New Orleans. Famed jazz pianist Art Hodes worked there often. Ralph Hutchinson, the best jazz trombonist in town in those years, often played there. Freddie Williamson played trumpet there, as did Sidney Bechet, the great soprano sax virtuoso. Doc Evans on cornet was there, too, as was Max Hook on piano and Fred Greenleaf on cornet, from Detroit. Trombonist Miff Mole played there a lot — he was a jazz legend. Often I would show up at the club around 1 a.m. with my bass, after I played at a society party in the Loop. Bill Reinhardt would ask me to sit in, because they had no bass player in the band. I'd close the joint with the rest of the guys early in the morning. It was a fine place to learn the Dixieland repertoire, and the guys were wonderful characters to hang out with.

When you reminisce about those days you have to describe the London House at Wacker and Michigan Boulevard. This was a world famous nightclub owned by George and Oscar Marienthall. The world's most famous jazz and pop artists performed there: George Shearing, Oscar Peterson, Lionel Hampton, Woody Herman, Errol Garner — a list that goes on and on! For a while, I worked there on Sunday and Monday nights with the Eddie Higgins Trio and I got to see and hear and meet many of the "name" artists who worked there. It was an advanced education in jazz performance and I absorbed it like a sponge. One Sunday night I was there, taking a break in a booth at the back of the room with Eddie Higgins and Jack Noren, our drummer, when Bob Hope came by and sat next to me in the booth. He just wanted to "chew the fat" with musicians, and had us in fits telling one-liners, none of which I can repeat here. It was that kind of room: movie stars, politicos, athletes, radio and TV entertainers all came to the London House. And the steaks and chops were divine. We had a rule of thumb: never get on the bandstand to play with an empty stomach! The waiters came by carrying those trays filled with stupendous dinners, and the odors wafted up to us as we were playing. It could drive you mad.

One of the most popular music venues in downtown Chicago was the Blackhawk on Wabash Avenue. It was a famous restaurant, featuring the "spinning salad bowl," and they had the top pop and jazz groups performing there. It was where my parents took me to hear my first live jazz performed by Fats Waller and his quintet. He was a sensational pianist, the king of the stride piano, and a fantastic entertainer and composer. His works include "Ain't Misbehavin'," "Your Feets Too Big," and "Honeysuckle Rose." Big name bands worked at the Blackhawk and they also aired radio broadcasts of the music around the country from the bandstand at the restaurant. Bob Crosby's band was often featured there.

At State and Van Buren was the Rialto Theater. Before World War II it was a burlesque house, but during the war years it changed formats to a movie and stage show venue. I heard Cab Calloway and Duke Ellington's bands there, as well as Andy Kirk and his 12 Clouds of Joy, a wonderful dance band that swung harder than any others. There also was the Cloister Inn at the Maryland Hotel on Rush Street. The lounge in the lower level of the hotel was where you could hear black vocalist Lurlean Hunter backed by pianist Dick Marx and bassist/violinist Johnny Frigo. It was a piano bar and you could sit close to the performers. Nearby was the Back Room on Rush Street, and you could only find it by walking down a tiny, narrow alley. A lot of jazz piano players worked there. There was also the Preview on Randolph, a second floor joint that featured Louis Prima, The Dukes of

Dixieland, Al Cohn, Zoot Sims and other well-known entertainers and jazz men.

Another downtown club was the Capitol Lounge, located one door south of the Chicago Theater and featuring small jazz groups in a loud, raucous and garish environment. Finally, I remember Lipp's Lower Level near South Water Street below Michigan Avenue. It was a small, inexpensive club that featured Roy Eldredge during the '40s.

On the North Side, the Aragon Ballroom on Lawrence next to the "L" stop, like the Trianon on the South Side, was a popular place for big band music. As a teenager, I went to the Aragon to hear Jimmy Dorsey's band with Helen O'Connell and Bob Eberle as the vocalists. I was part of the crowd that always gathered right in the front of the bandstand to get a close-up view.

Then, there were a group of small clubs on the North Side — Abstract Lounge on Fullerton Avenue which featured many local jazz players; the Key of C on Broadway near Wellington, a small and dark club; the Warm Friends in the Wilson Hotel in Uptown where jazz musicians used to jam; the Lei Aloha at Windsor and Sheridan where Johnny Frigo and Dick Marx made their reputations; and the Spotlight Lounge at 3113 N. Broadway where local jazz artists played.

I also remember dives like Mario's Lounge on North Milwaukee Avenue. On weekends, Mario featured a quintet that included trombonist Eddie Avis. I used to play some bass there on weekends in the late '40s when I was young and tough and smoked cigarettes. A jazz place still in operation is the Green Mill at Lawrence and Broadway. All the great jazz players eventually wound up at the Mill, either playing on the tiny stage or egging on the musicians who were performing. There was the Holiday Ballroom at Milwaukee and Lawrence, owned by Dan Bellock. Many big bands played there. I played there many times with the Bill Scott Orchestra which featured great sidemen like Joe Daley, Bill Porter, Eddie Avis and Tom Hilliard. Finally, there was the 1111 Club at Bryn Mawr and the "L" stop. This was a popular Dixieland jazz joint that, for many years, featured the band headed by George Brunies, the famous tailgate trombonist. The bar was very long and the legendary drummer "Hey Hey" Humphries played there. Hey Hey got married in the club. He and his bride walked down the length of the bar to the preacher who read the service. This has to be one of the world's most bizarre marriage ceremonies ever.

Jazz and big band music dominated the scene in the late '30s and throughout the 1940s, and this music had a tremendous influence on the development of my career.

1,000-seat theater. They had shows with all sorts of national acts involved, and in later years it was also the site of teenage shows that involved hundreds of kids and their parents." Bill Nellis, who also attended St. Ignatius, recalls the professionalism of the program. "The Loyola Community Theater was a big thing in the parish. When we attended St. Ignatius you were lucky if you were selected to participate in the show, which was done in a Broadway style. Professionals put the show together each year, and it was a real show with song and dance numbers. One year we did *South Pacific* and it was a really great show. It helped to reinforce the sense of community in the parish."

Ball Rooms, Jazz Clubs and Night Spots

Throughout Chicago's neighborhoods, there were numerous music halls, jazz clubs and night spots. Some were just tiny dives down an alley, while others were nationally-known clubs that were able to showcase the top musical talent of the decade. For dancing, many Chicagoans frequented the ballrooms around the city, including the Trianon Ballroom, at 62nd and Cottage Grove, and the Aragon Ballroom, at Lawrence and Broadway. Built by the Karzas brothers in the '20s, these grand ballrooms and the dance bands and orchestras that played in them were extremely popular during the '40s, particularly by the many servicemen and women stationed in the Chicago area.

For many young Chicagoans, a love of music began in high school during band practice and music classes. Hank Mitchell grew up on the West Side and became a musician in the '40s. "I didn't start playing a musical instrument until I got into high school. My parents decided that I should learn to play a musical instrument to keep me out of trouble. It was 1944 and I liked the trumpet because Harry James was popular at that time. So we went downtown to Wurlitzer on Wabash Avenue and we bought what we thought was a trumpet. It turned out to be a coronet. My parents bought it for me, on time, with lessons, and that was how I got into music. At Harrison High School, I got into the beginners band and studied with Captain Joseph Ewald who was a strict technician for classical music. He wasn't too hep to bebop music, but we convinced him that he should have a swing band. The war was going on and the big band thing was very popular. The big bands playing jazz included Cab Calloway, Duke Ellington, Count Basie and Harry James."

Bob Cunniff's love of jazz began at Senn High School in Edgewater. "Students would stay at school during lunch and dance to records on the auditorium stage. It was a fun thing to do. Tommy Dorsey and Glenn Miller were very popular during those years. Several friends and I were big jazz fans, and we would go to the Regal Theater at 35th and South Parkway — we saw Lionel Hampton and Duke Ellington there. I remember when we saw Duke Ellington — the curtain came up and there he was in a white suit, and I realized that I had seen my Zen master. He just owned us. I also went to the famous Club DeLisa during those years at 55th and State. There was also the Blue Note on Randolph Street, just west of State Street, where they claimed that the "World's Greatest Trombone Player" played — J.C. Higginbotham. On Argyle, there was the Tail Spin, and on Broadway there was the Green Mill, where Charlie Parker and Lester Young would sometimes play. On Bryn Mawr by the "L" there was the 1111 Club. We also went up to Howard Street after the war, and Art Tatum was performing at the Club Silhouette to an empty room. So, I got my own personal 'audience' with Art Tatum."

On the northern border of Rogers Park, there were several music and jazz clubs on Howard Street. Many servicemen, tourists, and suburbanites would fill these clubs, particularly those from neighboring Evanston and the North Shore. Comedian Shecky Greene got his start in entertainment on Howard Street during the '40s. "I remember Howard Street because I really started my career as a comedian at the Club Silhouette. I was going to college at the time, and I stopped by the club on amateur night. Sarah Vaughn was on the bill at the time. So, I got up and performed and won the amateur contest. Years later when I became friendly with Sarah I told her the story about my appearance, but she didn't remember it. I also remember places like the Club Detour and the Bar-O on Howard during those years."

Auburn Gresham resident Jack Hogan traveled all across the city to hear music. "The '40s were a very, very important part of my life because of the music. The Aragon Ballroom and the Trianon Ballroom were the places to go. Even though I was a South Sider, I didn't really frequent the Trianon as much as I did the Aragon, probably because of my desire to hear the Dick Jergen Orchestra. They would bring in different bands like Kay Kyser, Glenn Miller and Eddy Duchin. Another place for music was the Panther Room, down at the Hotel Sherman (also known as the College Inn). That was a great place for kids to go. The Walnut Room at the Bismarck Hotel, on Randolph near Wells, was also very popular. Back in those days, there was music everywhere, including the Blue Note, Helsing's Lounge, and many other places downtown. The '40s were just a great time for music.

"In 1942, there was a place that was going to open at Clark and Montrose, geared for young people. There wasn't going to be any hard liquor, just Cokes, sandwiches and ice cream. The night that it was supposed to open, it was going to feature the Charlie Spivak Orchestra and Dinah Shore. We went opening night, and everybody was mingling around waiting for it to open, but they never opened because they didn't have the proper licenses. We ended up over at the Aragon Ballroom, not too far away. It was customary in those days, if it was a big name band, to hang around the bandstand and

Johnny Frigo
Roseland

I was born in 1916. I grew up in Roseland on 116th Street at Kensington Avenue, just east of Michigan Avenue, across from St. Anthony's Church. We lived in a house when I was growing up, and at one point my mother had fourteen boarders who she cooked and washed for.

My musical career really started when I began playing violin with the son of the ragman to whom I sold junk. I used to do this when I was young after school: I would collect junk, and when the ragman would come by on Saturdays with his horse and wagon to collect rags and iron, and I would sell him my weekly collection and get a quarter. I can remember when copper was five cents a pound and it was like finding gold! He eventually talked my mother into having me take violin lessons with his son, Nathan Oberman. So, I started taking lessons when I was seven years old.

During my last year at Fenger High School, I was playing and singing at Club Citro on Taylor and Halsted. It was broadcast on WKYW radio. We weren't there for too long, maybe a month or so. When someone asked me for a request, they would give me a tip and put the money right into my bass. At the end of the night, I had to lift up my bass and shake it to get the money out. One time, a guy came up and dropped some money into my bass. I remember seeing a bill going in, and the next night someone told me that it was Al Capone. He had put in $5.00 or $10.00.

One night there my voice cracked on a high note, and the bouncer said, "Don't sing no more!" I thought he meant not to sing that song anymore. He meant don't sing at all. So, the next night I was singing and he rushed up on the stage and grabbed me by the back of my collar while I was on the radio. He dragged me off the bandstand and onto the dance floor on the back of my heels. All the kids wondered what had happened to me!

I started playing jazz because I didn't have enough formal training to be a concert violinist. So, I just started playing, and in 1940, I began playing bass with a group called the Four Californians. We played at the Morrison Hotel and at the Drake Hotel. I played bass because Curtis Junior High School on 115th didn't have an orchestra, they only had a band, and the only instrument that nobody wanted to play was a tuba. So, I got stuck with the tuba. When I got into high school, the obvious thing to play was the string bass. I made 95% of my living playing string bass for the 50 years because of that situation. If they had an orchestra, I would have probably stuck with the violin.

I remember playing in many clubs in Chicago's neighborhoods. There was Giovanni's on 111th and Michigan, and I used to play on the "National Barn Dance" on WLS-AM. After we finished with our broadcast at midnight I would rush over to Giovanni's and play there until 3:00 o'clock in the morning. I also played at the Embassy Club at 119th and Michigan, and Jay Berkhart played there, too. I played at a lot of clubs on 63rd Street. Mostly, I played bass at the Trianon Ballroom with Wayne King and at the Aragon Ballroom with Dick Jergen.

On the South Side, I would sit-in at the black jazz clubs after my gigs. I would park my car in an alley on a Saturday night at 2 a.m. and take my violin into some jazz club like Club DeLisa. On Monday mornings they had what was called a "Milkman's Matinee." They had eight dancing girls there — the sun was already up — and they had Albert Ammons and his band, the son of the great tenor player, Gene Ammons. They would let me sit-in. When you sit-in, you play one or two sets and then let somebody else play. I was so ignorant — once I kept playing the entire time. When I finished, the announcer said, "OK, Johnny, let Teddy Wilson play on piano."

In 1942, I played with Chico Marx at the Blackhawk Restaurant. They would broadcast live every night. Mel Torme would sing, and we had the quartet. He was from the Hyde Park area, and had just gotten out of high school. It was during the time with him that I signed up for World War II. I picked the Coast Guard because I thought I would be on some stormy shore looking for German submarines, but they heard that I played violin, so they sent me to Ellis Island. I played bass with the band, and I played tuba and trumpet with the military band from 1942 to 1945. I did concerts at Walter Reed Hospital and radio programs.

After I got out of the service in 1945, I came back to Chicago and began traveling with Chico Marx. I joined Chico at Tower Theater in Kansas City, and we did theaters all over the country. When he saw that I played violin, he asked me to bring it on stage one day — we sort of fell into a comedy routine. He had an Italian accent, and we would do stupid stuff and improvise routines like, "You noodle on the fiddle, and I'll spaghetti on the piano."

Roller skaters, Savoy Ballroom, 47th and South Parkway, 1941. Grand Boulevard   Photograph by Russell Lee. (Library of Congress)

Dancers, Rhumboogie Nightclub, 343 E. Garfield, 1941. Washington Park Photograph by Russell Lee. (Library of Congress)

"Red" Saunders and Band, Club DeLisa, 55th and State, 1941. Washington Park   Photograph by Russell Lee.   (Library of Congress)

Ramsey Lewis
Near North Side

I was born on the South Side of Chicago in 1935. We lived there for only a few years, then we moved to the North Side when I was five. We lived in a number of places — on Scott Street, and then we moved to the Cabrini Homes, a series of low rises. We didn't live there for a long time because you had to make a certain amount of money, both minimum and maximum. Once my dad passed the maximum, he didn't qualify any more, so we moved to 1142 N. Orleans Street. I went to Schiller and Edward Jenner grammar schools, and to Wells High School.

As for the neighborhood, life focused around the immediate blocks where I lived. There were about five of us — Tommy and Claude Kennard, Leroy Austin, Buddy Boyd, and a couple white guys who were a part of our group. We hung out together and played baseball, touch football, basketball or stood on the corner. We didn't do a lot of standing on the corner that I recall, unless we were planning how we were going to raise money to go to the movies. Until a certain age, you earned your money. In those days, you could collect pop bottles, loose paper, as well as old iron, and sell it at the junkyard. Of course, we couldn't go to the movies unless we had gotten all our housework done, practiced piano and done our homework.

During the years when I was five to fifteen, that would be 1940 to 1950, I had a regimented schedule. It was a pretty tight schedule although I didn't realize it at the time. I was taking piano lessons from the time I was four years old, and practicing, going to school, and going to church. This pretty much filled up my life. My parents were very religious, so they were conservative in nature. There were certain records we couldn't play at home because they were too racy, and certain movies we couldn't see. I started playing for our church when I was nine years old, so not only was I going to church regularly, I was playing at the church, and there were church choir rehearsals and concerts after church, and piano lessons.

When I was fifteen, one of our church musicians needed a piano player. He was a little older than me, and played on weekends for fashion shows or whatever was available. They asked me at church one Sunday, and my parents had a long talk with him about seeing that I got home and other stuff. So, I started playing with the Clefs. Wallace Burton was the leader, and had it not been for Wallace teaching me the ways of jazz music, I wouldn't have played jazz. He thought that I could play jazz because he heard me play gospel on Sunday mornings.

We didn't even rehearse that first night at this dance where we were playing. They just thought that I could play, and he said, "Let's play a Charlie Parker piece based on the blues in a medium tempo. Ramsey, you start." All I knew about the blues was from some records that my dad had brought home when I was eleven or twelve years old, and it was the boogie-woogie. So, that's what I started playing, but it didn't quite fit. So, he said, "Let's play a couple of standards. What do you know?" I didn't know any. So, he told me to sit out the rest of the night. I figured it was over, but he said I should come to his house the next day, and Wallace Burton took the time to introduce me to jazz music.

As for life in the '40s, I don't really have any other recollections about those years. If you can picture me getting up in the morning and going to school, coming home and doing homework and practicing the piano, that was my life. Dad was very, very strict on practicing, and when he would come home from work, the first thing he would ask my mother was, "Did Sonny practice?" As I got older, I had a job working after school, in addition to practicing and homework and going to church. That was pretty much it. I thank my lucky stars and I thank my parents for being conservative.

My father was a janitor and maintenance man at W. Hall Printing Company. He raised three kids and put all three of us through college. It was wonderful, and my structured life was good for me. It probably helped me with my jazz, too. The life that we lived taught us responsibility, sharing, to be sensitive to other people's needs, and commitment and follow-through. When my sisters and I are together, we often relate to each other how mom and dad were very, very tough, but we thank God that they were.

Bartender and Tavern Owner, South Side, 1941.
Photograph by Russell Lee. (Library of Congress)

Richard Lukin
Kenwood

I grew up in Kenwood, at 822 East 46th Street. It was a middle-class neighborhood. On my street, and really in that area, almost everybody lived in apartment buildings. There were some homes around 47th and 48th and Woodlawn, but almost everybody lived in apartments. I wouldn't say there was any particular ethnic group living there. It was a real mixture, we had everything. In fact, on my way to school, I passed a synagogue, St. James Episcopal Church, Woodlawn Community Church, St. Ambrose Church, and the Swedenborgian Church. So, we had a real mixture, and everybody was friendly with one another. We were just people. We never made any differentiation in those days. We were just people. It never occurred to me that anybody was different.

My dad owned a restaurant at 28th and Wabash called the Wabash Tavern and Grill. It was blue collar, and it catered to the local people. It was a "shot-and-a-beer" joint with good food. There were a lot of industries in the area so workmen would come in for their breakfast in the morning, lunch at noon and a shot and a beer in the afternoon. This kind of place was common, and it provided a couple of families a life. They're still around, like the Anchor Bar downtown, and Gianardo's on Taylor Street. These are shot-and-a-beer joints, and they serve good food in the back, too.

There were some interesting places around back in the 1940s. At 79th Street there was a liquor store called Twin Liquors. It was a regular store like you see today, with shelves and so forth, but in the back, behind a swinging door, it was set-up like a living room, with couches, cushioned chairs, tables, and a small service bar. They were Swedish, and they had a table with free pickled herring and cheese and crackers. You could sit there and talk to your neighbors. In those days a lot of guys would go suck on a beer for a few hours after work. Life back then was work, work, work.

We didn't go out much back then, but on Sundays we would occasionally eat out. If somebody you knew had a car, you could go to what we called "destination" restaurants. You know, let's get in a car and go there! Places like the Terminal Tap in Blue Island for Polish sausage. Of course, the big South Side restaurant was Phil Smidt's, at 1205 Calumet Avenue in Hammond, and it's still there today. They had lake perch and chicken, with big baskets of rolls, butter, cottage cheese, beets, and potato salad served family style.

The Morton family, of Arnie Morton's Steak House, had a place run by Arnie's father at 54th and Lake Park, and that was always a nice dining place. They moved to 56th and the lake after the city tore up Lake Park Avenue in the late 1940s.

One of the major hamburger chains in the city, and this was years before McDonald's, was Wimpy's at 51st Street and Dorchestor. They started in Chicago and eventually expanded. They even went to England.

Cafeterias were very big in the 1940s, and one of the best was Pixley-Ehlers. Like Krispy Kreme, they had a bakery with the oven in the window. They had great sweet rolls and raisin rolls. Another great cafeteria, which is still around today, is Valois on 53rd Street. Valois is an icon for American food. What a lot of people don't know is that Berghoff used to have a cafeteria line in the lower level until 1956. They always had brats, corned beef hash, roast beef, turkey wings and a daily special. You would get a choice of entree, mashed potatoes, and vegetable for $.45. I think the best restaurant in Chicago is Berghoff. I started eating there when I was four years old, and have been going ever since.

The first Mexican Restaurant I ever saw was at 95th and Ewing. This was back in the late 1940s. The steel mills at that time were among the first to hire Mexican laborers, who used to congregate on the east side around 95th Street.

For hot dogs on the South Side, everybody went to Carl's. It was in an old, dumpy garage converted into a hot dog stand. That's what a hot dog stand should be! It should be in a shack! Carl's was in a typical old Chicago wooden garage, with a window cut out, on the corner of 83rd and Jeffrey. I remember he would always buy his potatoes from the Jiffy Potato Spud Company, but he only bought the left-over chips. As you know, the potato is round, and after it goes through a square cutter there are these little chips left over — that's what Carl used. He would give you a tremendous handful of those and a hot dog for a quarter. People would go there and order ten or fifteen of those things.

And there were a lot of great barbecue places on the South Side, including the Tropical Hut. The Tropical Hut, for anyone living around Hyde Park, was the place to eat in the 1940s. It was by the University of Chicago. They had an unusual cooking device, a vertical medium, and the roast beef would twirl around on a chain in the window as you were waiting to come in. They had wonderful barbecue!

There were many destination spots — Rainbow Cone at 95th and Western, where you could get nineteen flavors on one cone; Horvath, for Bohemian style food on Harlem Avenue; Russell's Barbecue, at Thatcher and North; Gianetti's, the big Italian Restaurant on Roosevelt Road west of Harlem; or any of the Czech restaurants on West 22nd Street.

Now, if my mother wanted to cook a certain ethnic dish, we had to go to that particular neighborhood to shop. For instance, we would take the "L" over to the West Side to California and North Avenue to the Swedish neighborhood. We'd buy herring, pickled fish, sauerkraut, potato sausage, and cheeses and breads there because these things were never carried at the major grocery stores. It was the same with Italian food. If you needed Italian you would go to Taylor and Halsted — sausage, ham, pasta, or Italian cheeses — you had to go there to buy these. So much of this food is impossible to get today, like finan haddie, nobody eats this stuff today. It's smoked haddock — I love it. And blind robins, a north Atlantic herring that's been hard smoked like a beef jerky. These used to be sold in bulk to bars which would sell them for a dime. Now you can't find them or buy them! You don't see pickled eggs anymore or pickled pig's knuckles — absolutely delicious!

Everyday shopping was done in the neighborhood, at the smaller corner shops and at the independent stores. I can remember two different bakeries and three different butcher markets in my neighborhood, in addition to the larger Jewel. For sweets, there were many small Greek-owned confectionery stores. Cunag's, at 53rd and Ellis, was one my favorites. Generally, next to every movie theater was a Greek-owned candy store that offered popcorn, candy, ice cream, and all the confections. We would shop much more often than we do now — everyday or every other day. We did have electric refrigerators, but there were no freezers, so if you went to Walgreens to get ice cream, you only got a pint. As the population changed, and the older people died off, the independent places just melded in, and everybody became an American. You went to Jewel, National, Kroger, or A&P.

Now, if we really wanted to do something that was cheap, there was smelt fishing. People still do that now, but not to the extent that they did in the 1940s. Back then, the rocks along the lake at 31st Street, all the way to the point at 55th Street, would be packed with people. It was a rite of the season. To get a good spot you would get out there before it turned dark and set-up your line, but you couldn't put your net in before sunset, which was the state law. What you would do is this — you would throw out your line as far as you could, anchor it, attach your net to series of rollers that move up and down the line, and the smelt would get stuck in the net as they swam through. Between drinking cans of beer, you'd pull it in. It was cold, icy, usually around thirty-one degrees, but it was free, and it was a good source of protein. Sometimes you could get thirty, forty, or fifty pounds of smelt out there. The first of April everybody would be out there smelt fishing. You would freeze, but smelts are good. A smelt is a derivative of a freshwater herring, about eight or nine inches long. You whack the head off, dress them, and fry them up.

listen to the music and watch the musicians, as opposed to dancing. That's what I was doing that particular night, when Dick Jergen's Orchestra was playing. All of a sudden, the band vocalist, Harry Cool, came down off the bandstand and tried to make out with my date! I remember that so well! As for the Trianon Ballroom, when I came out of the military, I used to go to the Trianon quite a bit. Lawrence Welk played there, and he was one of the resident bands there. The entire time I went to listen to Lawrence Welk, I never knew he had an accent. He never talked, and if he did it was very brief. I didn't know he had an accent until I saw him on television."

Ted Saunders father, "Red," was the lead drummer at Club DeLisa beginning in 1936. " I was born in 1935, and we lived behind a famous place called the Rhumboogie Club at 343 E. Garfield Boulevard, but the most famous club in Chicago was Club DeLisa at 55th and State. It was the first place where blacks and whites could go in and mix and sit down and watch shows together. There were white acts and black acts in the show—they called them 'black and tan' shows. All the famous people came to Club DeLisa, including John Barrymore and Bob Hope.

"My dad's full name was Theodore Dudley 'Red' Saunders. He was a light-skinned black man and they called him 'Red.' After I was born, my parents went on the road with a show called 'Harlem Scandals' and my dad was the drummer in the show. When my dad was performing at Club DeLisa, I used to be there all the time. In fact, when I was four years old, they made me a miniature set of drums and I would play them at the club. My father came up to Chicago from Memphis, Tennessee, around 1917. Lil Armstrong, Louis' wife, had just come up from Memphis around that time. She and my auntie had gone to school together and they lived together in Chicago. Chicago was the key place for entertainment from the 1920s on, and the hottest recorders were the Red Hot Five and the Red Hot Seven. Lil Armstrong was the piano player for the group and also the one who wrote the music. Lil was a wonderful woman and that was how my dad got interested in music."

Phil Holdman was a musician and record salesman in the Chicago area during the '40s. From calling on juke box operators to playing in bands, he acquired a special knowledge of the Chicago music scene. "I remember going to Jump Town at 63rd and Western with a bunch of my friends from the West Side. One of the guys was able to get his father's car and take a load of us to hear good music. They featured Anita O'Day, as well as many of the great jazz singers and trios. It was a very hot spot. I went downtown to the Panther Room at the Sherman Hotel many times. I took my girl, Alberta, there and she later became my wife. There was no cover charge at the Panther Room and a beer was $.50 a bottle. We didn't drink, so we just sipped it like we were drinking beer, and most of the time we would go up on the

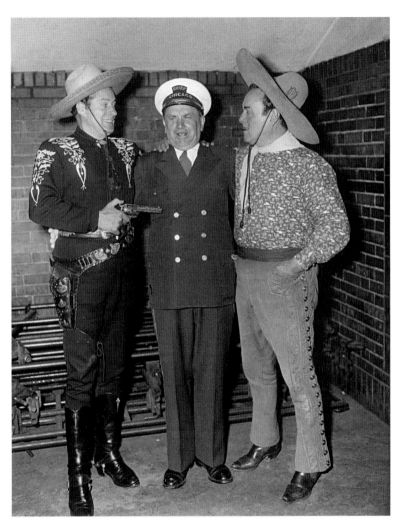

Joe "40,000" Murphy with Cisco Kid and Pancho, Chicago Stadium, 1949. Near West Side (Courtesy of Bill Swislow.)

Joe "40,000" Murphy was an Andy Frain usher who lived in Bridgeport. His passion was to be photographed with the famous people he met on the job — Frank Sinatra, Bob Hope, Milton Berle, Jimmy Durante, and Louis Armstrong — the list goes on and on. After he died, he left behind hundreds of photographs in his three-flat on 34th Street documenting his colorful career.

Joe "40,000" Murphy with Marilyn Monroe, Comiskey Park, 1949. Armour Square (Courtesy of Bill Swislow.)

Raymond DeGroote
West Ridge

We always went to Riverview on the Western Avenue streetcar. It was perfect for us, we rode right down Western Avenue. My mother knew the secretary to the owner there, so we got free passes and reduced rate tickets all the time. We would usually go on a Saturday after lunch and stay until about five o'clock, leaving enough time to get home for dinner.

We would go as a group of four or five kids, starting when I was eight or nine years old. There was no concern about harm coming to us back then, unless we did it to ourselves! There was just no thought about kidnappings or stuff like that.

We went there for the rides. We weren't really interested in the sideshows. We wanted the exciting stuff! You see, we didn't have that much money, so we saved our money for the rides. Most rides were $.05 or $.10, which in those days could be a lot. But they did have $.02 days, where everything was $.02, except for the more exotic rides, which might have been $.05. We would not eat much at Riverview, though there were plenty of places to eat, especially things like cotton candy. But these things cost money! We only had a certain amount we could spend — a couple of bucks. When it was gone it was gone.

The entrance was on Western, at the corner of Western and Roscoe. When we entered we would always follow the same circuit— go west, and head for the Greyhound. There were about five roller coasters at Riverview, the Bobs being the steepest, fastest, and most exciting. The initial drop was a really big fall, and then you came right up again. You could really feel that pull of gravity! I didn't get on the Bobs at first because it was too much for a youngster. I was confined to the Greyhound or the Silver Streak. They were tamer and had covered cars. They were not quite as fast, but thrilling enough for a ten- or eleven-year-old. The Silver Streak was a basic roller coaster covered with a streamlined shell, sort of an Art Deco design.

Aladdin's Castle was a fun house, where you could walk over rolling barrels, go through a house of mirrors, or watch the jets of wind blowing up the girl's dresses. Of course, there were dark passageways you could walk through where monsters would jump in front of you and then disappear. It was a $.02 ride, so everybody would go there. There would always be a tremendous crowd.

The Shoot the Chutes ride started in a big pond where you would board a large flat-bottomed boat, probably fitting almost twenty or so people.

Soon the boat floated to the back of a big tower where an elevator lifted you to the top and shwoosh — you came down at a twenty-five degree angle into the pond where, of course, everyone would scream. It was great on a hot summer day with the cool water spraying on you. I guess it seems kind of corny by today's entertainment standards.

The Caterpillar was a round, circular-shaped ride with small cars that were all connected together. It would roll around a track with small hills and gradually a covering would come over you, like a convertible car top. Eventually this shell totally covered the car and it looked like a caterpillar. Finally, it would slow down and the top would come off, and it was over. It was a pretty good ride. It was fun, and smelly, from all the grease, and made lots of noise from the clattering gears.

Then there was the Mill and the Floss, which was a ride through water on a slow moving boat, sort of like a love boat. These were long boats that weren't just for one or two people. It was a more relaxing ride through slow moving waters that you could go on with your parents or a date.

We always finished the circuit at the Pair-O-Chutes ride. Generally, by the time we got there it was getting late in the day, and we had probably spent most of our money. The Pair-O-Chutes was on a big, tall tower with arms that stuck out of the sides. There were two to a seat, and you'd get hauled up very slowly to the top of the tower. When you hit the top — bang! It was automatic — it would open up the chute and you'd come flying down really fast. It was a gorgeous ride, because on a clear day you could see all over the city, for miles and miles around. I wish I would have taken my camera with me, because it was a magnificent view. That was the thrill of the day, and it was the last ride of the day for us.

Riverview Scout, Riverview Amusement Park, 1948. North Center

dance floor. Charlie Barnet played and we would sway while we listened to the band. We had a great time! The entire night cost me a dollar, and then Alberta took me home in her mother's 1938 black Ford. It was a great date, a great time, and it was cheap!

"The Aragon and the Trianon were the most beautiful ballrooms in the city. I went to the Aragon more than the Trianon, which was on 62nd and Cottage Grove. The Aragon was on the North Side, at Lawrence and Broadway, and was closer to us. We liked Dick Jergen and he was featured a lot there with Eddie Howard. I think that the place opened in 1923, and the Paul Whiteman Orchestra was the first to perform there. At that time, only society people went there, sometimes in carriages drawn by horses. Another beautiful place was the Rialto Theater, at State and Van Buren. It was one of the most popular burlesque shows in Chicago, and for a while, the only one outside of New York. They had big name acts and some great comedians started at the Rialto, including Ada Leonard who led an all-girl orchestra. She was one of my favorites. We also saw famous strippers there, and they would have hawkers during intermission, including some who would walk down the aisles selling Cracker Jack. There were also smaller burlesque shows in that area, including the Gym — that only cost a dime to get in. It was a very sleazy place and they didn't have any good headliners. A lot of bums would go in there to sleep since it was so cheap to get in."

Riverview Park

By the 1940s, Riverview Amusement Park was the only one of its kind in Chicago. White City on the South Side burned down in the '30s, and except for the neighborhood carnivals and amusement fairs, Riverview was the only place to go for rides and attractions. Originally built as a gun club in 1904, the owners began adding rides and amusements to quiet the complaints of the shooters' wives and children. Eventually, it grew to include over 30 rides, a midway, and even the Riverview Ballroom, a popular spot for dancing during the war years. It was truly a memorable experience to go to Riverview.

Howard Rosen remembers going to Riverview to celebrate graduation from grammar school. "Riverview was a major part of the lives of kids growing up in my era. My father could afford to take us there because they used to have 'two cents day.' You could go on just about any ride for $.02. I remember that the big deal was the Bobs and the Blue Streak, but the Bobs was the favorite. I remember on the night of my graduation in '43, I did something that my father would never allow me to do — go on the parachute ride. You would sit down and get harnessed in, then it would go way up in the air until it hit a release — then you were free-falling. Apparently it was a very safe ride."

Sam Carl
Albany Park

I started working at Riverview Park in 1946 when I was fifteen years old. I started working there as an extra, and that meant that you would wait in front of the park and a guy would call out your name and then you would be assigned to a different ride each day. As an extra, you would get a uniform that you would put on over your street clothes. At the end of the week, you would go and collect your little envelope that had cash in it. I worked on various rides, and eventually worked on almost every ride in the park. I worked on the roller coasters, and would take tickets and help people off the rides. Some days there was no work. We would stay by the corner with a bunch of guys, and they would call out names and if you weren't called, you would go home.

Mondays, Wednesdays and Fridays at Riverview were two-cent days. So you could get into the park for $.02, and many of the rides cost $.02 during the daytime, and they were $.05 or $.10 at night. Tuesdays and Thursdays were nickel days. It was always a very busy place with big crowds.

One summer, when I was in high school, I worked there as a boatman and would take the boats down the Shoot the Chutes. I would steer the boats from the back by controlling the rudder, and leaned with my weight. The water would splash when the boat hit the water at the bottom of the ride. It was a great ride! On Thursdays, we used to test the rides for an hour, so they would give us $.50 extra. I did that for a whole summer.

I always liked basketball and I always played whenever I could. So, on my breaks, I would go over to the basketball concession and shoot baskets. I became very friendly with the guys who operated that concession. The following year, after working at the park for about three years on the rides, I worked the basketball concession and, eventually, in the early 1950s, I took over the concession. I didn't own it, but managed it. I went on to the University of Iowa for one year on a basketball scholarship, but I broke my foot, and then I came back to Chicago and went to Wright Junior College.

Riverview Chutes, Riverview Amusement Park, 1948.   North Center

Joel Weisman grew up in Albany Park and remembers going to Riverview Park a lot. "My sister had tuberculosis and my mother used to take us on the streetcar to a public health clinic, and we had to take the Western Avenue streetcar. So, every time we would come back from the clinic, we would go to Riverview at Western and Belmont. I knew every single ride, including the roller coasters, the Bobs, the Silver Flash, the Blue Flash, the Greyhound, and the Comet. I remember the Shoot The Chutes, Aladdin's Castle, the Freak Show, the Caterpillar, the Whip, and the Tunnel of Love, as well as the Merry-Go-Round. I loved going there when I was growing up."

Joseph Lamendella lived in Ravenswood in the 1940s. "I started going to Riverview as a child. I went there on penny nights, free nights and nickel nights. I probably went to Riverview from the time I was eight until I was a teenager, when I would cut classes at Lane Tech to ogle the girls who were part of the "come-on" in the Freak Show. I never went into the Freak Show, I just looked at the pretty girls outside. Being a coward, and knowing the kid who was killed on the Bobs by standing up at the top, I rode the Greyhound, which was kind of the sissy roller coaster. Once, perhaps, in bravery, I think I rode the Silver Streak. I do remember that next to Aladdin's Castle, which was a popular place, there was a mentalist named Lady Nina. I would stand there and watch her very carefully with the audience. I was convinced that she had to be given some clues. I thought that her assistant might approach people before hand and to get clues. I would stand for hours trying to figure out the angle, but I was never successful."

The Arrival of Television

Although television did not have its spectacular growth until the 1950s, there were some Chicagoans who owned televisions in the late 1940s. The new medium would have a tremendous impact on the daily lives and overall entertainment habits of neighborhood residents. Most importantly, television altered the way Chicagoans spent their evenings, causing a drastic reduction in attendance at movie theaters, restaurants and clubs, and reducing interactions among neighbors since they remained indoors.

When television sets were first arriving in the neighborhoods many residents were unsure if there would be long-term health risks. Norman Mark remembers the rules his parents established in the house when they bought their first television. "My parents didn't want television because they were sure that it was going to ruin our eyes. But, finally, they decided to get one because we had neighbors who had one. However, the deal was that you had to sit back one foot for every inch of the screen. I recall that we bought a 12" or 14" television, so according to the rules I was supposed to sit 12' to 14' away from the set. Of course, since we had a 12' living room I would have

had to almost sit in another room."

Albany Park resident Marvin Aspen recalls the beginning of the television era in his neighborhood. "I remember that 1948 was a very important year because that was when television became available. My first memory of television was going to the home of Bobbi Terry, a girl in my class whose father owned the Terry Cigar Store on Kedzie, just south of Lawrence. Her father had done very well in the cigar business and they had the first television set in the neighborhood. It was a DuMont television with a small, round screen inside a big console. It looked like a window in a washing machine. A group of about twenty of us kids would go over to her house to watch television that, of course, was only black and white in those days. In the late 1940s, I recall watching Dave Garroway doing a program from the roof of the Merchandise Mart before he went to New York. I only remember seeing local programs back then. Television was a major change in our lives."

Finally, Tom Hynes recalls how the availability of television changed life in his Gresham neighborhood in the late 1940s. "There are so many conveniences that people now take for granted that didn't exist prior to 1945. Even if they had been invented, everything went to the war effort. After 1945, there was a boom in the production of consumer goods, including air conditioners and televisions. I remember the first television set that appeared on our block was a small DuMont with a 7" screen and a rabbit ears antenna that sat on top of the set. My buddy's parents bought it because they were the wealthiest people on the block, and it got to the point where everybody would be over there watching shows and old movies that they would never have gone to the theater to see. They would also watch Friday night wrestling with people like Chief Don Eagle and Gorgeous George. They would turn out all the lights because the screen was so small that it was the only way to see the picture. Everyone would sit there and watch those programs and appear to be enthralled by what was on television. Of course, within a few years, we got our own television set and soon watching television became the number one thing for everyone to do. Television totally became the center of family entertainment by the end of the 1940s. I think it was probably the worst thing that happened to the intellectual growth of America."

Index

Opposite: *Patron, Chicago Public Library, Legler Branch, ca. 1944.* West Garfield Park (Courtesy of Special Collections and Preservation Division, Chicago Public Library.)

Photograph Index

Interviewee Index

Page 208: *Pushball Contestants, Loyola University, 1946.* Rogers Park (Courtesy of the Rogers Park/West Ridge Historical Society.)

Poster Contest, 1945. South Chicago (Courtesy of Special Collections and Preservation Division, Chicago Public Library.)